UNRIGGED

ALSO BY DAVID DALEY

Ratf**ked: Why Your Vote Doesn't Count

UNRIGGED

HOW AMERICANS ARE BATTLING BACK TO SAVE DEMOCRACY

David Daley

LIVERIGHT PUBLISHING CORPORATION

A DIVISION OF W. W. NORTON & CO.

INDEPENDENT PUBLISHERS SINCE 1923

For information about permission to reproduce selections from this book,
write to Permissions, Liveright Publishing Corporation, a division of
W. W. Norton & Company, Inc., 500 Fifth Avenue, New York, NY 10110

For information about special discounts for bulk purchases, please contact
W. W. Norton Special Sales at specialsales@wwnorton.com or 800-233-4830

Manufacturing by LSC Communications, Harrisonburg
Book design by Daniel Lagin
Production manager: Lauren Abbate

ISBN 978-1-63149-575-5

Liveright Publishing Corporation, 500 Fifth Avenue, New York, N.Y. 10110
www.wwnorton.com

W. W. Norton & Company Ltd., 15 Carlisle Street, London W1D 3BS

1 2 3 4 5 6 7 8 9 0

For my wife, Jennifer Smedes, for everything

The right to vote freely for the candidate of one's choice is of the essence of a democratic society, and any restrictions on that right strike at the heart of representative government. And the right of suffrage can be denied by a debasement or dilution of the weight of a citizen's vote just as effectively as by wholly prohibiting the free exercise of the franchise.

—*Reynolds v. Sims* (1964),
Chief Justice Earl Warren, for the majority

Power concedes nothing without a demand.

—Frederick Douglass

The people have the power.

—Patti Smith

 # CONTENTS

● *INTRODUCTION*

Despite months of pre-electoral hype and civic optimism, election night 2018 did not bring the much-hoped for clarity to the nation's deep divisions. On one hand, Democrats claimed the U.S. House for the first time in a decade, netted more governorships than in any election since 1982, and also flipped control of six state legislative chambers and some 325 state house and senate seats nationwide. Across the aisle, Republicans expanded their majority in the U.S. Senate, knocking off incumbent Democrats in Indiana, North Dakota, Florida and Missouri. Ted Cruz extinguished liberal heartthrob Beto O'Rourke in Texas's U.S. Senate race, and hopes that Georgia and Florida might elect their first black governors came to a bitter end, as well, with the defeats of Stacey Abrams and Andrew Gillum. On cable news, the nation's top political analysts debated the key midterm takeaways and shrugged.

It is, of course, only natural to measure our politics in wins and losses, by blue waves and red firewalls—especially on election night. It's even possible for fair-minded pundits to examine the same results and view them as disheartening through one set of eyes and historic through another. But those usual frames of red versus blue failed to capture something far more important, even transformative: a nationwide awakening of small-d democratic fervor. For, this election night, America's soul would not be discovered in O'Rourke's impassioned concession speech in El Paso; nor would it be found while watching the blue lights climb ever upward along Rockefeller Center, as NBC projected the real-time battle for Congress against the seventy-story art deco beauty. In this moment of civic crisis, democracy itself was on the ballot. While Americans devoured ominously-titled best-sellers about the impending death of government by and for the people, the biggest story was actually something far more optimistic: how determined ordinary citizens were to fix the nation.

It was a David and Goliath story for the twenty-first century. The barriers these citizens faced—gerrymandering, draconian voter ID bills, racially motivated purges of voting rolls—were massive and only grew more imposing. In 2017 alone, thirty-one state legislatures considered ninety-nine different bills that would make it harder for citizens to cast their votes.[1] In the first three months of 2018 alone, according to the Brennan Center for Justice, twenty-four states introduced another seventy proposals to make voting more difficult. And even after these legislatures adjourned and balloting itself neared, roadblocks continued to be constructed. In many Southern and GOP-controlled states, running for office in 2018 was like competing on the hit TV show *American Ninja Warrior*: the obstacle course became more difficult to conquer the closer one came to the finish line. In Georgia, for example, Stacey Abrams needed to surmount the massive Warped Wall put in place by Brian Kemp, Georgia's secretary of state and, not coincidentally, her Republican opponent. Just weeks ahead of the election, Kemp suspended the registration of 53,000 Georgians, predominantly minorities, using an "exact match" system that struck names from the rolls as fraudulent for something as common—and finicky—as a missing hyphen.[2]

But while one side deployed the electoral equivalent of Swinging Spikes between American voters and their democracy, citizens stood up and fought back. They took on the deepest structural inequities, the hardest battles that experts said could not be won. They pushed back against gerrymandering in Michigan, Utah, Colorado and Missouri, some of the most tilted and conservative states in the nation—and won. They fought to restore voting rights to millions of former felons across the South who had served their time and paid their debt—and won. In zinfandel-red Idaho, Utah and Nebraska, where legislatures refused to expand Medicaid under the Affordable Care Act, young people organized petition drives and pushed ballot initiatives—and won. Nationwide, voters considered sixteen different initiatives and constitutional amendments that would make elections more open and fair. Fifteen of them—94 percent—passed.

The winners on election night were all of us. Americans want their democracy back, and they're doing something about it. This is their story.

In 2016, my book *Ratf**ked: Why Your Vote Doesn't Count* broke the story of how Republicans weaponized gerrymandering, the oldest political trick in the book, into a precise yet blunt-force tool that entrenched GOP power in state legislatures and congressional delegations nationwide, even when the party earned far fewer votes. It revealed a national Republican strategy called REDMAP—short for the Redistricting Majority Project—keyed around dozens of small-town legislative races during the 2010 election. The key to REDMAP's success in 2010 would be found in the U.S. Constitution, which requires that every state legislative and congressional district in the nation be redrawn every ten years, after the census, to account for population shifts. In three-quarters of all states, local legislatures draw those lines. Savvy Republicans, led by Chris Jankowski of the Republican State Leadership Committee, had a "eureka" moment not long after Barack Obama's 2008 victory, as they confronted the reality of America's changing demographics (a nationwide transformation toward a voter profile that was historically more sympathetic to the Democratic Party) and tried to plot a path back to power. Conveniently for Jankowski and his colleagues, the census was coming. This would be their breakthrough: what if Republicans targeted inexpensive down-ballot state legislative races in closely contested states like Pennsylvania, North Carolina, Michigan, Ohio and Wisconsin, with the goal of claiming every seat at the redistricting table and drawing themselves a *decade-long* advantage? It worked more effectively than Republicans could have dreamed, in part because Democrats, still celebrating 2008, snoozed while the GOP schemed, even after Karl Rove revealed the entire playbook in March 2010 on the op-ed page of the *Wall Street Journal*.[3] Republicans won their wave, and with it the ability to design a decade of domination. They took full advantage.

The availability and easy manipulation of big data by powerful computers armed with sophisticated mapping software made it possible for Republicans to etch themselves a long-lasting edge. In those five swing-state targets alone, Republicans held 49 of 69 congressional seats by 2016, and Democrats had not flipped a single one all decade. They also held all ten legislative chambers in those states, some of them with veto-proof supermajorities, even surviving years when Democrats won more votes, including the 2018 wave.

After Donald Trump's surprising victory in 2016, I was often asked to explain how Republicans could hold the White House and both branches of Congress even in years when they received a minority of all votes, and also how, in a closely divided nation, Republicans could control nearly 70 percent of all state legislative chambers and a modern record of governors' offices. The toxic combination of gerrymandering and voter suppression laws passed by newly unaccountable legislatures tied our democracy into a profoundly depressing double-knot of unfairness, and established nearly unbeatable minority rule in otherwise competitive states. It was not easy to see a path out of this antidemocratic crisis that contributed so dramatically to the extremism, polarization and hopelessness that plague our politics.

Then, later that November, I saw a Facebook post by a young Michigan woman named Katie Fahey.

Fahey doesn't look like a revolutionary, with her dark jeans, gray blazer and comfortable shoes. But don't let her broad, easy smile fool you: she is the Che Guevara of the gerrymander. The ballot initiative in Michigan—

which will bring an independent redistricting commission to one of the most gerrymandered states in the nation—started with this Millennial's social media post. Maybe it resonated so widely because of the smiley-face emoji that Fahey added at the end, or perhaps because gerrymandering in Michigan had severed the connection between the ballot box and the people's will. But that single call to action, written by a twenty-seven-year-old woman who worked as a program manager for a recycling nonprofit, pioneered a winning redistricting revolution that marshaled over 4,000 volunteers, collected more than 400,000 signatures and raised almost $15 million.

Later that winter, I met Desmond Meade, who launched the Florida rights restoration effort. Meade still has the barrel chest and commanding demeanor of the Miami celebrity bodyguard he once was, before it all went wrong.[4] He got kicked out of the army for stealing liquor in Hawaii. Then the death of his mom and a detour into drug addiction resulted in the foreclosure of his home, a deep depression and, ultimately, a fifteen-year sentence for felony weapon possession. One afternoon after his release, homeless and still struggling with drugs, Meade stood before the railway tracks just outside Miami and steeled himself to jump before the next train. He walked across the tracks instead, as if guided by a higher power, and found himself outside a rehab clinic. Meade checked himself in and, before long, turned his life around: returned to college and even earned a law degree. The one thing he could never win back in Florida, however, along with 1.4 million other former felons (including more than 20 percent of the state's black citizens), was his right to vote. Meade began volunteering with the Florida Rights Restoration Coalition, and quickly became its president and executive director, galvanizing a victorious statewide movement that the *New York Times* called the most important civil rights triumph since the Voting Rights Act.[5]

Inspired by these stories, and maddened by the culture-wide sense of political despair, I set out during the summer and fall of election year 2018 to join these quiet revolutionaries who were reinvigorating our civic fabric at the very time it was most needed. This book is the result. I spent much of 2018 meeting with, and learning from, these democracy heroes nationwide, watching from a front-row seat as regular people demolished barriers that experts had long deemed too high, too stout, too imposing. I joined the Voters Not Politicians canvassers as they knocked on tens of thousands of doors across Michigan; and I journeyed south to Orlando to watch Meade and his team train hundreds of former felons as activists for the vote—transforming individual lives as well as their state. In Alabama, where the legislature finally reinstated voting rights that were unfairly denied to tens of thousands of citizens released from prison, but refused to allocate a dime to actually register them, I went door to door, from bus station to barbershop, with concerned citizens who wanted to help restore their neighbors to the voting rolls. On the other side of the country, across the red rock desert of San Juan County, Utah, and the hardscrabble tribal lands of North Dakota, I watched Native Americans organize desperate, heroic efforts to preserve their voice against surgically focused voter ID bills, intricate precinct closures and gerrymandered chicanery.

At a time when American politics seemed weighed down by a profound sense of despair, when the news cycle fed never-ending exhaustion, when we picked up our phones every morning and wondered what fresh presidential hell was tweeted out during that morning's "executive time," it was rejuvenating to ride alongside those who turned off cable news, logged off Twitter and got to work. I spent several days in July 2018 riding across Idaho aboard the Medicaid Express—a rickety, kelly green RV that teetered dangerously when it approached the 80-mile-an-hour speed limit on the state's highways, but, as the mobile HQ for Idaho's Medicaid for All initiative, swiftly changed the state's politics nevertheless.

These efforts were not led by politicians or parties. They began with regular people, and their stories and successes are as diverse as they are inspiring. While the political media occasionally ventured beyond their coastal bubbles by camping outside Midwestern diners in search of Trump voters and heartland white-male wisdom, a new national activism emerged elsewhere, concentrated around women, focused locally, nearly all of it operating well outside traditional structures. Nationwide, everyday citizens asked how they could contribute. They quickly found answers to some of our most troubling political riddles, right in their hometowns. In these pages, you'll meet the genius mathematician in Pittsburgh who realized his work might also apply to gerrymandering and became a crucial expert witness who convinced the state Supreme Court to invalidate a congressional map that locked in a 13–5 Republican advantage in this Democratic-leaning state. You'll come face to face with college students from New Hampshire, Texas, Florida and Iowa who noticed voting inequities designed to mute their voices and fought back in legislatures and the courts.

Four self-described "bad-ass grandmas" in North Dakota turned their weekly coffee-and-kvetch gatherings into a winning push for a statewide constitutional amendment that created a state ethics board, banned foreign money from campaigns and closed the revolving door of elected officials serving as lobbyists.[6] In Maine, home to a rich tradition of independent candidates, citizens demanded a voting system that allowed them to rank all their choices and avoid a plurality winner whom most people opposed. Both parties obfuscated and stood in the way, so determined Mainers braved long winter petition drives not once but twice—and won. Women from Ohio who had never taken part in a protest before met on a bus to the Women's March in Washington, DC, and came home determined to take on gerrymandering. "Nothing structural changed on November 8, 2016, but a new set of people woke up to what was wrong," Indivisible cofounder Ezra Levin told me. The resistance guide Levin and his wife, Leah Greenwood, first shared as a Google document provided a roadmap and galvanized activism nationwide. "That kind of engagement changed what was politically possible. Just the act of showing up in your community and saying, 'I disagree,' was powerful."

No book can tell every story. This one focuses on citizens repairing democracy, and not on equally inspiring stories of action and activism, such as teens battling gun violence, for example, or teachers striking for better schools, or the drumbeat demanding urgent action on climate change. What all of these movements have in common is the determination of everyday citizens to push our government back onto the rails of normalcy. "When democracy is working, citizens can go about their daily lives," says Sam Sandmire, a college gymnastics coach and the Ada County co-chair for the activist organization Reclaim Idaho, over coffee in her Boise kitchen. "But with today's real threats to our democracy, we cannot sit back. We must do everything we can to defend our democracy and protect the rule of law. Failure is not an option."

These battles were not easy. Many of these initiatives were challenged in court. Activists needed to overcome picayune legal claims, multimillion-dollar negative ad campaigns funded by dark money entities with ties to the DeVos family and Koch beneficiaries, and powerful special interests equally determined to defend their status and influence. And while not all of them won, a crucial battle was engaged. The stakes were serious and real. The hydra-headed threats to our political insitutions weren't coming merely from Russia or Facebook. In horror movie parlance, the call was coming from inside the house. We the people answered and responded, citizens who never imagined themselves as activists suddenly finding the hope we longed for inside collective efforts that hardly seemed possible. We began the long process of unrigging our politics.

Americans had little choice other than to fight back and safeguard democracy themselves. No one else was riding to its rescue. Certainly not the U.S. Supreme Court, which continued to step away from creative solutions to systemic problems. In 2013's *Shelby County v. Holder*, the court ruled that anti-discriminatory provisions of the Voting Rights Act targeting states that had historically disenfranchised voters were no longer necessary. Five years later, the court's decision in *Husted v. A. Philip Randolph Institute* gave the green light to Ohio's policies of purging voters from the rolls if they had not participated in three federal elections (and not responded to a postcard mailed to their homes).[7]

That same month, the Supreme Court—on narrow, technical grounds—punted on two crucial partisan gerrymandering cases, one from Wisconsin and another from Maryland, which had provided an opportunity to rein in this toxic, destructive practice that has accelerated the extremism and polarization in our politics. One year later, in June 2019, a Court pushed rightward by the departure of Justice Anthony Kennedy declared partisan gerrymandering nonjusticiable—a political issue beyond the Court's power to decide—and slammed the federal courts closed to future lawsuits. Both decisions proved crushing defeats for voting rights.

In 2018, polls found that upward of 70 percent of Americans hoped that the high court would help defend American democracy by reining in partisan gerrymandering.[8] It hardly seemed like wishful thinking to imagine Kennedy as the decisive voice when two cases came before the court, one a Republican gerrymander of Wisconsin's state assembly map (*Gill v. Whitford*), the other a Democratic gerrymander of a single congressional seat in Maryland (*Benisek v. Lamone*). Both closely followed the tantalizing breadcrumbs the longtime swing justice had laid out in a concurrence in a 2004 partisan gerrymandering case from Pennsylvania. In that case, *Vieth v. Jubelirer*, Kennedy had expressed his grave concern about gerrymandering's pernicious effects on the First Amendment's freedom of association, as well as harms under the Fourteenth Amendment's guarantee of equal protection, when one political party draws lines that intentionally dilute the voting power of the other side. He suggested he could be persuaded by a "clear, manageable and politically neutral standard" that defined excessively partisan redistricting, and seemed encouraged by fresh, ambitious approaches. "New technologies may produce new methods of analysis that make more evident the precise nature of the burdens gerrymanders impose on the representational rights of voters and parties," he wrote.[9]

Kennedy, the court's ever-equivocating Justice Hamlet, proved impossible to satisfy. The Supreme Court returned the Wisconsin case back to the lower courts on standing, determining that individual voters from a single district did not have the right to allege harm by a statewide map. (Imagine calling 911 to report a fire, and the dispatcher responding that they'd only send a fire truck if the owner of the house placed the call.) This dodge, of course, also fails to grapple with the new challenge presented by the GOP's surgical 2010 gerrymanders: entrenched one-party, minority rule that implements policies a majority disagrees with but has little recourse to alter at the ballot box, a hijacked democracy that ignores bipartisan wishes and hands supermajority powers to a superminority of voters. The fallacy behind the court's thinking was on full display in 2018, when Wisconsin voters ousted every statewide Republican incumbent and preferred Democratic assembly candidates by 190,000 votes, but only managed to flip a single assembly seat and nudge the GOP's ill-gotten edge down to 63–36.

Several Supreme Court insiders and high-ranking Washington officials in a position to be familiar with Kennedy's thinking suggested to me that Chief Justice Roberts—a consistent opponent of adjudicating the fairness of legislative maps in federal court—had played a savvy long game. The Chief Justice knew that Kennedy had a long-standing interest in finding a solution to partisan gerrymandering. He also knew that this was likely to be Kennedy's last term on the Supreme Court before retirement. Roberts simply needed to prevent Kennedy from siding with the four liberals one last time, and then await the arrival of a more conservative justice the following year, when another set of partisan gerrymandering cases would appear before the Court.

As draft opinions circulated, Kennedy, multiple sources said, faced determined arguments from court conservatives eager to make partisan gerrymandering nonjusticiable. Roberts targeted the eighty-one-year-old justice with an argument that these new academic standards were too complicated or confusing to ever be clearly managed and applied by lower courts or accepted by the public. They were "sociological gobbledygook" that the man on the street would interpret as mere politics. While an agonized Kennedy wanted to act, Roberts focused on the complicated math and successfully dissuaded him from joining forces with justices Kagan and Breyer, both of whom believed the court could find a manageable First Amendment rationale for getting involved. Finally, after one of the ten longest deliberations in modern Supreme Court history, all sides signed onto a unanimous Roberts decision that kicked the can down the road. Kennedy, exhausted, threw his hands up in defeat. He retired days later and would be succeeded by a much more conservative justice, Brett Kavanaugh, dimming hopes that the Court would save the day. Indeed, in June 2019, when *Benisek* returned along with the North Carolina case, *Common Cause v. Rucho*, Roberts got his way: a 5–4 court, divided along ideological lines, slammed the federal courts shut forever just as lower-court judges nationwide, appointees of both Democratic and Republican presidents alike, in cases from Ohio, Michigan and Wisconsin as well as North Carolina and Maryland, agreed that it was necessary for the judiciary to curb egregious gerrymanders and that clear tools existed to do so.[10]

While the court dithered and ultimately abdicated its responsibility, the people did not wait for judicial superheroes or democracy-saving silver bullets. They became the protectors of democracy that they hoped the courts might be. Indeed, after the 2016 election, eagle-eyed citizens became much more attuned to voting issues, even in the smallest towns, and even where local governments worked to conceal them.

Voters weren't the only people paying more attention to gerrymandering and voter suppression issues. They infused mainstream culture and became such a big issue that even late-night talk show hosts took notice and turned twisted district lines into hilarious punch lines. Samantha Bee did multiple episodes on gerrymandering, including one not long after North Carolina Republicans used a 2016 lame-duck session, before a new Democratic governor took office, to gut his power and increase their own. "While Democrats are busy signing petitions and frantically googling the word 'emoluments,' savvy Republicans get elected to the state house, shut the door and go hog-wild, until one day you wake up and wonder, 'Hey,

where'd the Planned Parenthood go?' and 'Why is my tap water so thick?'"
she ranted. "So if you're looking for a place to put your energies, stop trying to overturn a national election and start working on a local election.
They matter."

Gerrymandering even became the stuff of valentine cards featuring
monstrous-shaped districts as hearts, along with quips like "Who needs
representative democracy when I've got you?"[11] A former A-list Hollywood
stylist created "gerrymander jewelry"—gold pendants in the shape of hor-
ribly contorted districts—that started at $195, with all proceeds going
to elect Democratic governors with veto power over twisted Republican
maps. In super-vegan Asheville, North Carolina, cracked down the middle by Republican legislators and represented by two of the most conservative members of Congress, I joined the local League of Women Voters
and others who filled the streets for an ankle-splitting, twenty-eight-turn
5K run along the district's borders, nicknamed the gerrymander meander.
The word "gerrymander" became so integral to the pop-culture lexicon
that *Sports Illustrated* baseball writer Tom Verducci could praise the adept
bullpen management by the Milwaukee Brewers' Craig Counsell by noting that "In the history of postseason baseball, no manager had ever gerrymandered three shutouts with at least five pitchers each time."[12] The comic
strip *Doonesbury* introduced a character named Gerry Mander. In Austin,
Texas, high schooler Josh LaFair and his siblings turned gerrymandering
into a board game and funded it with a Kickstarter promoted by gerrymandering terminator Arnold Schwarzenegger. They reached their goal in six
hours, and ultimately closed with 1,400 backers and more than $67,000 in
sales. Gerrymandering, LaFair told NBC, "has all the right mechanics of a
board game—scheming, strategizing, backstabbing."[13]

Scheming, strategizing, backstabbing—how could politicians not take
notice? In Washington, Nancy Pelosi and House Democrats observed the
citizen focus on democracy issues and finally turned that message into

action. Now, less than twenty-four hours after capturing the gavel, flanked by giddy colleagues on a symbolically yet unseasonably springlike January morning in Washington, Pelosi introduced her day-old majority's top political priority.

House Bill 1 was not a hot-button topic, such as health care or immigration. Nor was it a pocketbook-pleaser such as college loan forgiveness, or rocket fuel for the base in the form of immediate impeachment hearings. H.B.1 did not tackle long-standing Democratic concerns about climate change or gun control. Instead, Pelosi put forth the ambitious, 600-page For The People Act—5 pounds and 10 ounces of nonpartisan electoral reforms that would end partisan gerrymandering, restore the full protections of the Voting Rights Act, automatically register Americans to vote, create multiple days of early voting and establish election day as a national holiday, among other good-government fixes. "Our agenda is restoring the people's faith in government," Pelosi said. "No American should face hours-long lines, broken voting machines or rules rigged to keep their vote from being counted in our election."[14]

Pelosi outlined an imaginative and intelligent package designed to head off ongoing threats to our democracy, threats that had existed ahead of the 2016 election but which seemed all the more critical, if not existential, after Donald Trump assumed the presidency amidst questions over foreign interference. One by one, leading Democrats expressed their support, including the iconic Georgia congressman John Lewis, who had been beaten and bloodied on the Pettus Bridge in Selma over half a century earlier, demanding his right to vote. "The vote is the most powerful nonviolent instrument of transformation we have in our democracy," he proclaimed. "It must be strengthened and preserved. There are forces trying to make it harder and more difficult for people to participate, and we must drown out these voices."

Maryland congressman John Sarbanes, who led the task force that wrote the bill, called these nonpartisan fixes the crucial first step that a dysfunctional government must tackle before any other concern. Just like that, nerdy process reforms were suddenly popular *and* cool. It was as if "I'm

Just a Bill," the animated civics lesson from the 1970s Saturday morning cartoon *Schoolhouse Rock*, had not only been covered by Beyoncé but also topped the pop charts. "We heard loud and clear from the American people that they feel left out and locked out too often from their own democracy," Sarbanes said.

Politicians love to invoke of the voice of the people—but in this case, it was true. House Bill 1 represented a political sea change inside a Congress long convinced that structural reform issues made voters' eyes glaze over or, even worse, made it sound like politicians were blaming the rules for their inability to get anything done. Oftentimes, of course, politicians liked those rules just fine, particularly when they protected their side, their seat or their ability to raise gobs of money. "Before you would have encountered a lot of people who would sort of say, 'Yeah, it's a terrible system,' then smugly add, 'But I kind of know how to play this game,'" Sarbanes tells me. "Now they're saying, 'God, we can't go on like this.'" This attitude shift includes leaders from all sides. Nancy Pelosi, after all, didn't just oppose the 2008 and 2010 California independent redistricting initiatives that became a model for the national commission embodied by the For The People Act; she bankrolled the fight against it. As they introduced H.B.1, however, Pelosi and other members praised an honor roll of past and present lawmakers who had tried to play the role of Paul Revere on the antidemocratic horrors of gerrymandering—only to have their urgent warnings ignored, their bills quashed, by this same leadership. Citizen energy transformed practitioners of politics as usual into champions of change.

"It's the people leading the members," Sarbanes says. He describes members of Congress telling one another about a palpable disbelief in the room when they talked to constituents and vowed to clean up the environment, raise the minimum wage or make Wall Street pay its fair share. Why? Not because voters didn't want to see those things done. They simply knew that none of it could happen in a rigged, gerrymandered system. "Astute candidates started to throw into the mix this idea that we're going to try to fix the system so that it actually works for you. What they discovered was that message caffeinated all the other messages. The audience was saying, 'Now you're talking. A minute ago, we were all pretending that we could do these things without fixing the underlying system. Now you've told me you get it.'"

In a government where control of the legislative branch is split between two parties, any attempts to fix the system will need to survive staunch opposition. This was the case, predictably, for H.B.1, which met with fierce resistance from a Republican-controlled Senate and their spokesman, Mitch McConnell. "That's not going anywhere," the Majority Leader told the *Wall Street Journal* as Pelosi readied H.B.1. He then authored a *Washington Post* op-ed that labeled the bill "a partisan power grab," suggested it be renamed the "Democrat Politicians Protection Act" and charged that it would make it easier for Democrats to commit voter fraud.[15] There's something discomfiting about McConnell's willingness to make voting rights and democracy issues just another partisan food fight; after all, we'd have a healthier process if both major political parties were pro-democracy and pro-voting. But this also felt like an example of a party's leadership which has become disconnected from its constituents. After all, voters of all ideologies understand that the system has become rigged; it's the one word that backers of Donald Trump and Bernie Sanders might agree on. Redistricting reform in Missouri and Utah—let alone the 64 percent victory for felon re-enfranchisement in Florida—didn't happen without the support of fair-minded red state Republicans every bit as eager to unrig the system as Democrats and independents.

When I mention McConnell's words to Sarbanes, his long sigh whistles through the wires. "I think what's happened is the Republican Party has gotten more comfortable taking shortcuts around our democratic institutions. Getting power and holding power becomes the rationale for the means you use," he says; "not a great place to be. People are angry and disillusioned. But they still care enough to be frustrated. They haven't walked away completely. They're hanging by a thread in many instances."

Voting rights reforms could walk our entire democracy back from this precarious ledge. Either we find constructive political responses that unrig our politics and address the anger and powerlessness so many citizens of all persuasions feel, or some will reach—as they did in the 2016 presidential election—for impulsive and destructive solutions instead.

•

Not all of the stories in this book end in victories—and not all of the victories end the stories. That's to be expected: Many of these struggles are as old as our nation, and, sadly, they go on. Our frayed democracy, far more fragile than we imagined, will not be healed with a single election. Progress must not be measured by any individual win, but by the number of battles and people engaged. Success does not mean the end of a fight, not in Michigan or Florida, not in Pennsylvania, Idaho or Maine. Defeat and long odds are no reason to cede the field. Keeping a democracy, it turns out, requires lots of work. Far too many of us halted this labor after 2008, assuming that the historic election of our first black president meant that many long American struggles had ended, that our voices must only be raised every four years in presidential elections, that the arc of the moral universe would bend toward justice on its own. Turns out, it only bends when we pull.

What all these stories show is that when regular citizens unite and fight for the kind of democracy they want, there's isn't a structural barrier that won't buckle. These battles on behalf of what's right—led by Millennials, by former felons, by suburban women, by Americans of all ages and races who refuse to believe that creating change is beyond them—are the proof. A mighty unrigging is underway. May these tireless and inspiring efforts leave you with the same rebirth of optimism that they did for me.

UNRIGGED

CHAPTER 1

Second Chances and Rights Restored

"I will be a lifelong voter."

The night that Hailey* lost her voting rights forever began like any other teenage evening in late nineties' rural Alabama. A group of high school friends piled into a classmate's ride. A drive-through run. Dinner on the hood of a car. Someone passed around a joint. Then the sound of a police car rolling over loose gravel, and two white officers emerge, wondering what that herbal odor might be. Plenty of cops might have looked the other way or let the kids off with a warning. In more affluent suburbs that evening, no doubt, the exact same encounter ended differently. But Hailey's evening ended with drug possession charges for everyone. In the eyes of the state, Hailey and her friends were no longer just high school seniors: they were felons. And in Alabama, felons guilty of a crime involving "moral turpitude"—such as this minor possession charge, an offense so small it would not even be a crime in many states—forfeit their right to vote. Forever. Hailey was seventeen, and had yet to vote in an election. After that night, she never would—her most important right as a citizen erased before she'd even had the opportunity to exercise it. "I had no idea," she tells me almost two decades later. "We weren't thinking about voting at all."

---

* I've changed her name to protect her privacy.

How is this possible? Well, the framers of Alabama's 1901 state constitution certainly had voting on their minds. The convention's goal,
announced presiding attorney John Knox, was "within the limits imposed
by the Federal Constitution, to establish white supremacy in the State."[1]
When the convention adjourned that September, delegates had effectively
disenfranchised black voters in the state through a combination of poll
taxes, literacy tests—"When you pay $1.50 for a poll tax, in Dallas County,
I believe you disenfranchise ten Negroes," pledged Henry Fontaine Reese,
a delegate from Selma—and by labeling minor crimes likely to be committed by the desperate and poor acts of "moral turpitude." Those citizens
could then be deleted, permanently, from the voting rolls. Erased. These
vicious techniques had the intended effect. As Ari Berman reports in his
masterful *Give Us the Ballot*, the number of registered black voters in Alabama quickly dwindled from 182,000 all the way to 4,000. Almost a century
later, those very laws, hardly consigned to history, would ensnare Hailey.

What is moral turpitude? Alabama left that up to local county election
officials to define and enforce. They, in turn, used the vagueness of the law
to compound its racial inequity for decades, customarily striking the voting rights of blacks but reinstating them for whites convicted of the same
crime. "Purposeful racial discrimination," U.S. Supreme Court Justice
William Rehnquist called it in 1985.[2] Still, like so many vestiges of the Jim
Crow South, it never really disappeared. Alabama's state legislature quickly
reinstated the moral turpitude clause, tiptoeing to just the right side of the
legal line without changing the reality for blacks in Alabama. Minor drug
or petty theft convictions entailed moral turpitude; white-collar crime did
not. So when Alabama's Speaker of the House, Mike Hubbard, was convicted of public corruption, defrauding taxpayers and making millions off
his service, he retained his voting rights.[3] When Hailey was charged with
drug possession, her right to vote was permanently taken away.

Finally, in spring 2017, with additional litigation underway, Alabama's legislature ended "moral turpitude" for all but the most serious
crimes: murder, rape, treason. Still, it wasn't perfect. Arbitrary fees, often

amounting to tens of thousands of dollars and applied disproportionately by judges to black defendants, would still need to be paid before voting rights were reinstated. But this was a historic moment: more than fifty years after Selma, one of Alabama's most efficient tools of voter suppression had been put to rest. Trouble is, the state was determined to keep news of this correction as quiet as possible.[4]

Alabama's secretary of state, John Merrill, declared that there was no need for a public education campaign or any effort to reach out to these newly enfranchised voters. He wouldn't even update registration forms to make it clear that 70,000 former felons were now eligible to vote in Alabama.[5] Forget about instructing parole officers to help as they guided former inmates through reentry. Citizens would need to learn about getting their right to vote back from news accounts, and puzzle through eligibility requirements on their own. (Many, no doubt, wouldn't risk negotiating the process alone. In Texas and North Carolina, more than a dozen people on probation or parole for felonies were arrested, even jailed, for accidentally voting illegally in 2016.)[6] A public opinion poll found that 72 percent of Alabama residents with a felony conviction had no idea their rights had been restored.[7] "If you change the law and don't tell anybody, effectively it's like you didn't change the law at all," says activist and organizer Blair Bowie, "especially if the law has been intentionally confusing for a hundred years." If the secretary of state wouldn't work to register these voters, Bowie would.

Bowie, a whip-smart young attorney with a law degree from the University of Pennsylvania and a background in environmental politics, launched the Alabama Voting Rights Project, an ambitious tag-team effort with the Southern Poverty Law Center and the Campaign Legal Center, to undertake the public education and outreach work that the state so blithely refused to do. Volunteers go door to door searching for these newly eligible voters. They fill out the labyrinthine paperwork themselves. They have built easy-to-navigate websites to tell people whether their rights have been restored. They set up tables outside barbershops, unemployment offices, the mall and bus stations, and make the necessary forms available. I joined them for three days as they made their way across Birmingham and Montgomery and they trained me as a canvasser. "The laws are so complicated that it seems like just being able to talk to someone who knows how the law works will help so many people," says Bowie. "When we encounter someone who has a conviction, we help them figure out what paperwork they need, help them fill it out, then keep track of them and make certain they're registered."

I hear Hailey's story outside the Birmingham bus station just after 6 a.m. one summer morning, as she waits for a ride to the hair salon where she works. When I approach her and ask if she is registered to vote, she waves me away, embarrassed and unwilling to respond. Bowie trained me for exactly this response; no one wants to admit a felony conviction to a stranger. So I simply tell her that we're out informing people about a change in the law, and that a felony conviction no longer costs people their right to vote permanently. Hailey's eyes grow wide. "I can't vote. I have a conviction," she tells me cautiously, quietly. I hand Hailey the clipboard with the list of serious crimes and tell her that if hers isn't one of those, we can likely sign her up to vote that moment. "No, no," she says, "nothing like this. Just possession, we were stupid, seventeen. I can vote?" I hand her the registration form and walk her through it. It takes only a couple of minutes of paperwork to give Hailey back her civic voice, and by the end of it, we're both crying. "I've never voted," she says. "I was seventeen and thought I never, ever would. All I wanted to do was vote for Obama once"—at this her voice cracks—"but I wasn't allowed to do it. This is, this is, unbelievable."

Felon disenfranchisement is civic death. Once freed, former felons tend to stay quiet about their conviction, making it that much easier to construct barriers between them and public life. Now those walls are coming down, having collided with another long-lasting American notion: fairness. The story of how it happened—across Alabama, Florida and many other states—is one of the most inspiring and surprising political stories of our time. An ancient set of laws grounded in racism is being torn down, and though obstacles remain, a new civil rights movement has grown around a simple yet profound phrase: *When a debt is paid, it's paid.*

When Desmond Meade stood ready to hurl himself before the next oncoming train on that August afternoon, he imagined the agony and wondered how long it would last before he never felt anything again. "I was a broken man," he says now. "Even the thought of the pain associated with getting run over by a train did not make me move." When no train arrived, his life changed course. The drug treatment center led to a homeless shelter. He went back to school to become a paralegal, then earned a bachelor's in public safety, summa cum laude, then finally his law degree in 2014.

Meade's dramatic triumph, however, couldn't overcome one hurdle: Florida doesn't allow anyone with a felony record to vote. The Florida Bar won't admit anyone who can't vote. Even home ownership is impossible in most Florida communities without that basic civil right. By 2018, more than 1.68 million Floridians, according to the nonpartisan Sentencing Project—more than in any other state in America—faced a lifetime ban from voting, permanent except under extraordinarily rare circumstances, long after they'd completed their sentence and paid their debt in full.[8]

Under these conditions, Meade couldn't practice law. He couldn't even cast a ballot for his wife, Sheena, when she ran for state representative in 2016. "In spite of the many obstacles I've been able to overcome, in spite of a lifelong commitment to giving back to my community, to making my world a better place," he says, with a shake of his head, "I still couldn't vote. It was a knife being twisted in an old wound, reminding me I'm not a full citizen."

Meade built that pain into a movement. As president and founder of the Florida Rights Restoration Coalition, launched in the early 2010s after nearly a decade of organizing work by the Florida ACLU, the Brennan Center and the Sentencing Project around restoring voting rights to former felons they prefer to call "returning citizens," Meade led one of the most impressive grassroots petition drives in state history. He inspired an all-volunteer army that collected 799,000 signatures statewide, enough to force a 2018 ballot initiative that would amend Florida's constitution and end this insidious vestige of the Jim Crow South. In order to accomplish this seemingly insurmountable task, Meade assembled perhaps the oddest political coalition in modern memory—starting with his political director, Neil Volz.[9] Volz, a longtime Republican, became a powerful congressional aide to U.S. Representative Bob Ney after Republicans took the House in 1994 and a chief of staff by age twenty-seven, only to lose everything after slipping into Washington's dark side.[10] In early 2002, Volz turned his access to the GOP into a job with super-lobbyist Jack Abramoff—the man at the heart of one of the most explosive lobbying scandals in recent memory—and landed amidst one of the capital's shadiest influence-peddling shops. By the time the federal investigation ended in 2006, Volz had pled guilty to conspiring to corrupt public officials and cooperated with the investigation that sent Ney to prison. As he moved to Florida, found custodial work and began to put his life back together, volunteering at his church, helping neighbors recover from opioid addictions and even rising to chairman of the local homeless coalition, it seemed even more unfair that Volz could be so involved, yet still so voiceless. He heard Meade speak at a Florida university in 2015 and realized that his initial fear that felon voting rights was some "liberal thing"[11] was completely wrong. It affected him, too—and here was a second chance to do something worthy with his political skills. Together, Meade and Volz united former felons and second-chance-believing churchgoers, tattooed Trump-voting "deplorables" and radical criminal justice reformers, black and white, into a mighty moral coalition funded by both the ACLU and the Koch brothers.

Now, on another swampy August morning, thirteen years after Meade believes God's grace lifted him across those train tracks and toward rehab, he takes the stage at the FRRC's summer convening to the sound of raucous whoops and Eminem's "Lose Yourself," trying to will this unlikely political force across one more finish line. Meade thrusts his right fist in the air and sings along: "Look, if you had one shot, or one opportunity / . . . Would you capture it, or just let it slip?"

As in Alabama, as long as African Americans have had the right to vote, the state of Florida has used felony disenfranchisement to weaponize the law and keep black citizens from the polls. These efforts swept across the old Confederacy in the years after the Civil War, beginning with Florida, Georgia, South Carolina, Georgia and Mississippi in 1868, and moving on to Texas (1869), Tennessee (1871) and North Carolina (1871), as Jeff Manza and Christopher Uggen detail in the groundbreaking book *Locked Out: Felon Disenfranchisement and American Democracy.* The timing is not a coincidence. The U.S. Congress required that states ratify the Thirteenth, Fourteenth and Fifteenth Amendments to the Constitution—ending slavery, creating equal protection under the law, and guaranteeing black men the right to vote—as a condition of reentering the Union. Congress also insisted that black men be included as delegates to these state constitutional conventions.[12]

This created a dilemma for the white political elites that stood against Reconstruction. If African Americans were given the vote in a state like Florida, their voices would create a significant shift in the political landscape, given that they already outnumbered eligible whites. At first, the former Confederates dug in their heels. Florida governor David Shelby Walker insisted in 1865 that the state, "of course, could never accede to the demand for Negro suffrage." Furthermore, if the state somehow managed to reenter the Union without ratifying the Fourteenth Amendment, its smaller population count compared to other states which counted African Americans as citizens would result in fewer seats in Congress. The state legislature declared resentfully that Florida "must be shorn of our representation or give the inferior and unintelligent race the supremacy in state government."[13]

Florida's anti-Reconstructionist forces hit upon the solution during a deeply divided constitutional convention in 1868 that included a dramatic walkout, followed by a triumphant power grab upon the white power bloc's return. They would ratify the federal amendments, yes, but write felony disenfranchisement into the state constitution, guaranteeing that actual equality would be an illusion. Blacks would be enfranchised legally, just not in reality. They would be allowed to vote but it would not be easy, and the legislature and other offices would design the laws to ensure they wouldn't have a shot at actual power.

Whereas Florida had previously disenfranchised those convicted of "bribery, perjury and other infamous crimes," Section 4 of the new state constitution added larceny—previously a low-level civil matter—to the list.[14] That allowed the state to permanently disenfranchise someone like Cuffie Washington of Ocala for the theft of three oranges in 1880, as Pippa Holloway detailed in her book *Living In Infamy*. The legislature then enacted the Black Codes—new laws on vagrancy, petty theft and other crimes they believed most likely to be committed by blacks—and elevated those crimes to felony status. Senator W. J. Putnam happily declared that the new laws "kept Florida from becoming niggerized."[15] Forced prison work camps took the place of slavery. Between 1869 and 1888, blacks represented some 77–88 percent of the prison population in Florida; more than half of those people had been jailed for larceny or petty theft convictions.

Cuffie Washington wasn't the only black citizen unfairly stripped of his right to vote. These late nineteenth-century measures proved extraordinarily effective at suppressing voter turnout for decades to come. Black turnout in Florida tumbled from 67 percent during the early 1880s to just 11 percent by 1892.[16] Even by the mid-twentieth century, it had not improved. According to the *Miami Herald*, only 6 percent of all blacks in Florida were registered to vote in 1940.[17] In 1960, majority-black Gadsden County—nestled in the Florida panhandle just a few miles from the state capital, Tallahassee—had a population of almost 13,000 people but only seven registered black voters.[18]

The passage of the Voting Rights Act and a series of landmark U.S. Supreme Court cases in the 1960s and 1970s began the long, bumpy road back to fairness in Florida and across much of the South. Much of that intermittent progress, however, was tragically interrupted in the 1980s by the "war on drugs" and its mandatory sentencing requirements, all of which disproportionately targeted communities of color. Blacks were significantly more likely to be arrested and jailed for drug offenses than whites, despite the fact that they were no more likely to use drugs. The statistics are stark: In 1976, 1.17 million Americans were unable to vote because of a felony conviction. By 2016, that number soared to 6.1 million, according to the Sentencing Project.[19] Nearly half—48 percent—of disenfranchised felons who have finished their sentence and paid their debt in full live in Florida.[20] More than 10 percent of Florida's adult population can't vote; almost a quarter of the state's African American population are kept away from the polls.

Before Desmond Meade, no one in Florida was able to do anything about it.

If this struggle has a modern-day godfather, however, it's Norris Henderson. Henderson spent twenty-seven years in one of Louisiana's most notorious prisons for a murder he insists he did not commit. In 1977, he was sentenced to life by a racially divided, non-unanimous jury and shipped into a violent hellhole despite a withheld police report that could have exonerated him. Angola, for years, housed the largest percentage of inmates with lifetime convictions of any prison in the nation. There wasn't much reason for hope, or peace. Locked away forever, Henderson started working at the prison law center, gave himself his own legal education and tried to show inmates that the deadly riots that so often made national headlines weren't the right path to improve conditions. Henderson's efforts won small but meaningful victories in the state legislature, even a seven-figure settlement from the prison's phone company for gouging inmates and their families. Then, in 2004, when his conviction was finally overturned as unlawful, Henderson walked free and founded VOTE, an acronym for Voice Of The Ex-offender. He has spent every day since, the better part of two decades, fighting to win back the civic voice of former felons. "I think what's happening is that people are understanding there is no direct correlation between a person coming into contact with the criminal justice system and his or her right to vote," Henderson says.

We're in New Orleans, overlooking the river, as Henderson walks me through the modern history of prisoner voting rights. He wears a light blazer over a plaid shirt; his horseshoe mustache extends below his lower lip, peppered with nascent grays. In 1975, he explains, Louisiana reworked its state constitution and made clear that everyone over the age of eighteen could vote, unless they were "under order of imprisonment," in which case the right to vote could be suspended. "It said your right to vote *may* be suspended," he says. "It didn't say 'shall.' No judge in this country sentenced anybody, 'Okay, you know because you stole those beans, your sentence is five years plus your citizenship forever.' No court of law. So the jurisprudence around this is just stuff they can invent out of nothing."

Indeed, subsequent legislators decided to interpret those four words "under order of imprisonment" so strictly that they paused the voting rights not only of felons but also parolees, arguing that they remained under order of state supervision. "That was never the intent," Henderson says. "We had to fast-forward almost forty-five years for people to look at this with more rational minds. People on supervision—some of them never go to jail. They walk in the courtroom and get a sentence, get it probated, and they walk right back out." But in Louisiana, they couldn't vote—and since the state for many years had the largest per capita incarcerated population, that carried political consequences. One out of every twenty-six Louisiana citizens is either in prison or on probation or parole. None of them can vote.

When that many people are touched, almost everyone knows someone affected. In his attempts to restore a spirit of fairness to the law, Henderson built the unlikeliest of coalitions—liberal reformers and prisoner advocates, sure, but also the business community and religious groups. Finally, in May 2018, years of efforts and coalition-building won a significant advance, aided by a new Democratic governor and an alliance with the American Probation and Parole Association: a bipartisan bill that restored the voting rights of everyone on probation or parole, automatically, after they'd been out of prison for five years. "In the journey of a thousand miles, we have taken two hundred really big steps," Henderson says. He hopes that the language around criminal justice issues will change as a result. "Now, having real power at the ballot box, you won't hear as many people getting on the soapbox talking about, 'Well, we're going to lock him up and throw away the keys.'"

As an inmate in Angola, Henderson vowed that if he ever got out, he would remember those still inside and carry the message that everyone has something to contribute, regardless of past mistakes. VOTE's outreach director, Checo Yancy, has spent years driving voters to the polls in Baton Rouge. It's become tradition for him to take his wife, and sometimes he's also watching his grandkids on election day. "He has to sit in the car and have his granddaughter say, 'Pawpaw, why are you not coming inside with us?' And then try and explain to her about all of these things. He won't have to sit in the car no more," Henderson says, his grin as wide as the river before us, and then repeats, "He will not have to sit in the car."

While Louisiana has the highest percentage of felons, no state has a higher number of previously incarcerated citizens than Florida. The state did offer a path for felons to regain their voting rights, only the line for registration was longer than the line for Space Mountain, and the chances of success about as likely as a white Christmas in Miami. They could apply to the state's Executive Clemency Board—a four-person panel made up of the governor, the attorney general, the commissioner of finance, and the commissioner of agriculture—then settle in for a long wait. The process allowed for two paths, one that required an in-person hearing and one that did not—and determining the proper course often took authorities more than a year. Even as far back as 2004, the *Miami Herald* noted that the number of applicants waiting for a hearing was triple the number of cases that had been heard in the previous sixteen years.[21]

Governor Charlie Crist, a Republican later elected to Congress as a

Democrat, took some steps to create an easier process during the 2000s, which helped restore the rights of more than 140,000 people during his two terms. But his Republican successor, Rick Scott, elected in 2010, slammed on the brakes. Scott increased the waiting period to as much as fifteen years after all sentencing requirements had been met. Then he slow-walked Clemency Board meetings—over his eight years, Scott's committee approved just 3,000 applications, and the backlog surged so dramatically that the League of Women Voters cautioned that, at this rate, it would take almost four decades to clear.

When an Orlando TV station asked him why the board had ground reinstatements to a halt, Scott replied that Florida had "plenty of voter turnout."[22] He told applicants at a 2016 quarterly meeting that "Clemency is, there's no standard. . . . We can do whatever we want."[23] (In 2018, a federal court called this "unfettered discretion" a violation of the U.S. Constitution and demanded that the state create a less random process; that order was then promptly stayed by a higher court on appeal.) The Clemency Board grilled those asking for their civil rights back about their dating lives, churchgoing habits, drinking and traffic violations, even pressing one applicant about whether or not he'd had sex with his cousin—creating arbitrary and sometimes cruel preconditions even for those who had paid their debt in full more than a decade previously.[24]

The committee sits in judgment high atop a flag-festooned stage. Applicants stand below at a simple podium outfitted with a box of tissues. They often need them. In June 2018, Ricardo McElroy found himself trying to explain to the state's chief financial officer an aggravated battery charge against a woman he had been romantically involved with. When his then-paramour got hold of the then twenty-year-old Ricardo's phone and discovered his conversations with other women, she became irate, McElroy claimed, began throwing his things over the balcony, and blocked the door. He said that he picked her up and moved her aside. "Were you running around on her?" asked Jimmy Patronis, the state CFO.[25]

"Well," McElroy stammered, unprepared for the question, "we weren't really, like, in a relationship. It was just like one of those friendships that comes with a little bit extra. Does that make sense?"

It did, but Patronis kept going. "So you weren't mutually exclusive? You were just dating other people?"

"I was just being young and dumb. Eighteen years later, I'm a more mature man," he stated. "I'm hoping I can get my rights back so I can vote."[26]

McElroy was one of the 3,000 lucky ones.[27] But Scott said no so often that he had his justification down to one word: "Deny." When he offered an explanation for why, it was usually that he wanted to "wait and see." "It's only been eleven years," he told one applicant. "Needs a little more time." "At this point I don't feel comfortable." "Take more time to change your life and show that you changed."[28]

Scott's reasoning was often inconsistent. He refused restoration of voting rights to several people who had been incarcerated for drunk driving when they admitted to social drinking, including at a relative's wedding. "I would never, ever touch alcohol again," the governor lectured. But then the governor would grant rights to someone convicted of DUI manslaughter or reckless driving even when he conceded he still downed "four to six" drinks a week. "There is no law we're following," he declared at a hearing in March 2016. "We get to make our decisions based on our own beliefs."[29]

His logic seems easier to understand in cases where applicants or their advocates shared their conservative politics. In March 2016, Scott agreed to reinstate voting rights after a supporting witness attested that the former felon "is the type of person we want out there," with "conservative views in all of our favor." Another quick reinstatement occurred after the applicant's wife testified to "his conservative principles." Then, in December 2013, Scott grew frustrated when an applicant admitted that he had already voted as a felon, by mistake. "I voted for you," said Stephen A. Warner, to laughter, a grin from the governor and the return of his voting rights. Rex L. Carver, on the other hand, a navy veteran, dressed in a short-sleeve polo shirt and wearing plastic-rim glasses, opened his testimony with a polite, eloquent discussion about the injustice of felon disenfranchisement and the need to protect the right to vote. He had a clean record, neat hair and a steady job, but his do-gooder politics and a handful of work-related traffic violations concerned the governor. Carver tried to explain that he drove a logging truck and was unaware that his company had loaded it above the weight limit, but Scott was having none of it. "If you look at this from our standpoint," he said, "gosh, this is an individual that doesn't worry about complying with the law." Deny.

In 2018, the *Palm Beach Post* investigated every application from Scott's two terms and discovered that he restored the rights of "twice as many whites as blacks and three times as many white men as black men," a "higher percentage of Republicans and a lower percentage of Democrats than any of his predecessors" in half a century, and restored the rights of fewer blacks than any governor since at least the 1970s.[30] According to most (though not all) academic studies, as the *Post* noted, former felons tend to prefer Democratic candidates. Preventing them from casting ballots, then, benefits Republicans, especially in Florida, which is famous for tight races that hinge on a hanging chad or an ill-designed butterfly ballot.

On election day 2018, when 1.68 million former felons had no voice, Rick Scott won election to the U.S. Senate by 10,072 votes.

Back in Alabama, Blair Bowie has set a goal of registering 10,000 of the nearly 70,000 formerly incarcerated Alabama citizens before election day. She's doing this with a staff of three, and in late July I join them in Montgomery at the Southern Poverty Law Center's sleek and heavily secured headquarters near Alabama's state capitol, steps from both a plaque commemorating Rosa Parks and the Dexter Avenue Baptist Church, where Martin Luther King Jr. organized the Montgomery bus boycott. "At first my parents were afraid of the felons," says Ellen Boettcher, a recent Boston College graduate now tasked with organizing in the Mobile area. "Now they're more nervous about the white supremacists."

The Stoneman Douglas High students—teenagers from Parkland,

Florida, who had only months before survived one of the most horrific school shootings in American history—are at the SPLC today as well, and we gather in a theater where another young organizer, Sean Champagne, explains the racist history of "moral turpitude" to them. He rattles off the numbers: 286,266 disenfranchised in Alabama, 143,924 of them black— more than 15 percent of all African Americans in the state. "That's not good," he says. "Writing bad checks? Moral turpitude. The former Speaker of the House steals a million dollars? That's not. Makes you wonder what the premise of this law is if stealing public funds is not morally turpitudi- nous. Go figure that out." Champagne has a wispy beard and a graduate student's demeanor; he disguises his outrage with irony. This issue reso- nates deeply: he grew up in Louisiana, where his father spent several years in prison. "I take it personally when the state dehumanizes someone," he tells me, "just because once they've done something wrong." Champagne wears a shirt bearing the image of Annie Pearl Avery, who greeted the Free- dom Riders, marched across Selma's Pettus Bridge and led dangerous voter registration drives across Alabama. "We're looking at the most systematic effort of white supremacy in Alabama," he continues. The activists are out to undo it, but first, he says, newly eligible voters need to know they have their rights back. The Parkland students nod, transfixed by his words and fervor. "There's still a disenfranchisement machine even though the law says otherwise. This is still Alabama. It's not Martin Luther King had a dream and then racism stopped. This has continued for fifty years."

The next day, in Birmingham, Bowie, Taylor and I set up a table outside The Hook Up, a barbershop in the Fourth Avenue North historic district. Over fifty years ago, these churches and low-slung brick buildings housed Birmingham's 1960s civil rights resistance. Today, they set the stage for another battle. "The principle of good tabling is to stand in front of the table," Bowie counsels John Paul Taylor, the Birmingham organizer. "Then hand them the clipboard sideways as they walk past so they have to turn it and engage." It's slow, but Bowie, wearing bright blue sneakers and a short- sleeved shirt covered with elephants, her hair pulled back, doesn't let anyone walk past without engaging them about the new law. "Maybe you have a family member or know someone this would help," she says, distributing pamphlets—anything to get the word out. One man who passes by had a conviction for trafficking that was later reduced to possession. He tells volunteers that he has documentation and might need more help; Bowie and Taylor, a full-service shop, make plans to assist him with the additional paperwork and accompany him to the registrar's office. "We're going to make it happen," she tells him. "You should be registered. Nice talking to you."

The day started with a 5 a.m. drive to Birmingham and concludes fifteen hours later with a stop at the Birmingham Art Museum, where Taylor conducts an information session for volunteers. As we drive back to Montgomery, through Shelby County and past a billboard reading "Go To Church Or The Devil Will Get You," with the new Janelle Monae album blasting, I ask Bowie why she does this work. The hours are long, and begin early. The three of us were on our feet most of the day—pacing outside bus stations and barbershops and door-knocking through apartment complexes—but only registered about a dozen people, if that. This is hard work and has to be done person by person. And only three months remain until election day. The organizer in her stays determined and upbeat.

"Our goal is to train 12,000 community leaders this year. Say some people don't do anything, but that they average helping three people. That's 36,000 people," she says. A League of Women Voters chapter she trained in Huntsville has already helped fifty people. A law school group at Samford University has registered another hundred. "We're going one by one. I think that these training sessions are having a ripple effect. But all these people that we signed up today? Those people would not have known all their rights had we not been there. That's just a fact. Maybe twelve votes isn't going to swing an election, but that's not what matters. There's inherent value in helping each person and helping them through something they wouldn't be able to do otherwise."

Bowie calls it "barefoot lawyering," or some combination of barefoot lawyering and organizing. Then she laughs and calls it "duck hunting":

what do you do when you want to find ducks? Go where the ducks are. "Not enough lawyers do that. We're helping people with an issue that has to do with the law and is complicated." Still, she says, "You shouldn't need a lawyer to tell you whether or not you can vote." But too many people do.

It's clear that she's driven by something more. Bowie grew up in Maryland, a slave state, and always wondered about her family history. Then she visited the new Legacy Museum in Montgomery, opened in spring 2018 by Bryan Stevenson's Equal Justice Institute on a site where slaves had been imprisoned. The museum tells a brutal story without flinching. One exhibit displays runaway slave ads from Northern newspapers, and she was horrified to find one signed by a W. D. Bowie, offering a $200 reward for a carpenter named Frank, "about five feet 9 or 10 inches high, light grey eyes, slow in speech, and very good personal appearance, about twenty-five years of age." Bowie grips the wheel a little tighter. She's off to Arizona and Nevada in the next week to continue her efforts there, a one-person dynamo for fairness and equity. This work is personal for her, too.

In Florida, however, a message of racial fairness and amends for repressive Jim Crow-era laws is a tough sell during polarized times in a perpetually purple state. After all, Scott's 2018 victory wasn't the only tight margin. Republican U.S. Representative Ron DeSantis narrowly edged Tallahassee mayor Andrew Gillum to become the state's next governor. Recounts and legal battles extended both races well into mid-November.

Alongside these cliffhangers, Proposition 4—Desmond Meade's Voting Rights Restoration for Felons Initiative—soared to victory with almost 65 percent of the vote. This was no accident. Organizers knew they needed to keep an issue infused with race and partisanship far away from those electric wires. A race-based appeal risked losing white voters. And if the proposition was seen as partisan, it could lose Republican voters.

In the years leading up to the vote for Proposition 4, the biggest nightmare for organizers was as follows: What would happen if opponents dropped a last-second TV ad along the lines of the shamelessly racist Willie Horton spot that rocked the 1988 presidential race, focused around heinous crimes by a black man and terrifying suburbanites of all parties? So they made that ad themselves, and showed the ad to a focus group just to understand what happened if voters were exposed to the scariest messaging they could imagine. That didn't necessarily matter: polls consistently showed very few undecided voters on this issue; the challenge was keeping all these strange bedfellows in the same room. "We needed to know what message people might hear that would make us lose their support," Jane Rayburn, a senior director at EMC Research, told me. This research guided one of the most internally divisive decisions of the campaign: continuing to exclude those convicted of sex crimes from voting. It also steered messaging that deliberately avoided any mention of racial equity. "This campaign is not about voting and it's not about voter suppression," Meade told volunteers in Orlando. "This is about second chances for people who have made mistakes—but those mistakes and going through those mistakes have made us much better people."

Whatever happened, they would be ready. EMC Research, a polling firm that works with Democratic clients, probed for the exact words that resonated with voters—and the ones that didn't. They tested to see if those messages were different in Miami than they were in Tallahassee or the conservative panhandle sometimes called the Redneck Riviera. They hired voter psychologists to further refine framing and even determine the right year to place the proposition on the ballot.

Initially, voters responded very well to the ideas of "fixing a broken system" and providing a "second chance"—so well that "Second Chances Florida" became the name of the campaign's website. "Letting felons vote?" This proved less popular. The word "felon," as you might imagine, polled poorly, so the researchers rephrased their copy, finally hitting on a description that worked: "returning citizens." When pollsters dug deeper to understand why the concept of "second chances" was so powerful, they found that voters across racial lines, party divisions and even religious differences especially liked that this second chance wasn't being given freely as an act of mercy, but had been *earned* by completing a sentence. Republicans, especially, liked the argument that it wasn't just the right thing to do; it was the smart thing. That led to the next layer of messaging, tested and refined into the most effective phrase: "When a debt's paid, it's paid." When I attended the August convening, pollsters had just finished an even deeper dig and learned the power of the word "eligible." The second chance wasn't simply being handed out for completing a sentence; it was an opportunity that had to be earned and then claimed.

"We want to stick to the message: giving the eligibility to vote back to people who have paid their dues," Rayburn told a large crowd of "returning citizens" at the convening. "What we know from the research is that the message we're using resonates with everybody. So anything that's not on message is off message. Even if it feels persuasive to you—if it's off message, it's off message." Rayburn's job that day was to teach a crowd of political rookies with criminal records how to talk to friends and neighbors, because polling also showed that this message worked especially well one-on-one. Maybe people don't want a rapist to vote. But John next door, who made a mistake in his twenties and paid the price? Of course he should vote.

"Personal stories are the most compelling," Rayburn told a rapt room. "They all feature returning citizens. You share that in your own words. Then you pivot to the message triangle. Our system is broken. My debt is paid. It's paid."

Rayburn tells me she's rarely seen a single word make such a huge difference. The evolution even from "second chance" to "eligibility," she explains, seems like a small nuance but actually changes everything. "It's funny," she says, "we've done four years of research to drill down on this one word. Eligibility. 'After you complete all the terms of your sentence, you can earn back the eligibility.' That one word is extremely important. I mean, that's what this amendment does, right? It does not automatically put people in the voting booth. It gives people the eligibility back."

The messaging that doesn't work? "Making it about 'the right thing to do,'" she quickly answers. "Making it a partisan issue. Because it's not. That messaging doesn't work and it's something the campaign has been really disciplined about. Across party lines, racial lines, geographic lines, people feel that if you have paid your debt, the debt is paid. We've made sure that this is an inclusive campaign."

This dedication to inclusiveness is why one of the faces of Second Chances is Brett Ramsden: thirty-six, white, confident, soft-spoken, slender, with the look of a sun-kissed Homecoming King to whom everything comes easy. Only Brett spent a decade hooked on opioids, effectively trashing what might have been a promising baseball career, feeding his addiction by stealing from his family and committing a string of break-ins.[31] He wrecked three new trucks in drunk-driving accidents. "I racked up eight felonies in one summer and didn't spend a day in jail," he said. "I should have had fifty." One judge after another saw a clean-cut white man and pushed him toward treatment. Finally, after turning up high to court dates, after passing out in a Burger King, after getting busted returning groceries to Publix with an old receipt and shoplifting fishing gear from Walmart, all for opioids and crack, he accepted help, walked into a Naples church and heard the voice of God. "Welcome back, Brett," said the voice, washing over him. "Where've you been?"

"There's value in my story," Ramsden tells me outside the hotel's Starbucks. "When you think about an ex-felon, a certain image pops into your head, you know? Maybe it's a gangbanger or a guy with pants hanging off his butt. Ultimately, it's a black guy with a gun. There's power in someone that looks like me getting up there and saying, 'This affects me too.' And it's not just me. Sixty percent of those 1.4 million people that can't vote—they look like me as well, even though a lot of us have been told our entire lives that this is a black thing."

Ramsden laughs when I ask if it ever occurred to him that his Walmart larceny spree would cost him his voting rights. That high, he says, "you can't see past the next hour." Now, however, as he struggles to get a state professional license to help other recovering addicts, can't put his name on his family's apartment lease and wants to support school board candidates making decisions that will shape his young daughter's future, he deeply regrets losing his vote. "I made very poor decisions," he says. "I'm trying to help and give back, but it's always there, for sure. For a little while longer, anyway."

No one seems to believe that Susanne Manning spent nineteen years in prison, not even her neighbors, who couldn't understand why she was asking them to support Proposition 4. "Why would you want felons to vote?" they asked Manning, who resembles a grandmotherly fourth-grade teacher, not the embezzler of $400,000 from a medical manufacturing company. She took a deep breath and told them, "Because I am one." They gasped. "I would have never known," one said. "Your yard, it's immaculate." Manning wants to start a small baking school out of her home and teach other former prisoners how to make cakes; she was amazed upon release when she discovered that Google gave her access to every imaginable recipe. "I broke the law in 1992," she says, her eyes tearing. "I was a greedy person who needed to change who I was. But did the court order me punished for the rest of my life?"

Desmond Meade grabs a chair and surveys the bustle around him. He attended his first convening a dozen years ago and it was little more than the gathering of a small email list. Now this poor, formerly homeless African American male is about to do something unthinkable—end felony disenfranchisement at its very epicenter, and maybe even point the way toward a new kind of politics. "This is a shining example of how we can get things done in this country," he says, "by shedding the partisan labels and the racial labels and coming together at that sacred space where we are all human.

"They said this couldn't be done." He smiles. "What's so beautiful is because, other than voting, this is the second purest form of democracy in action. When people take matters into their own hands." When the constitutional amendment passes with 64 percent of the vote, I'm reminded of Norris Henderson and Pawpaw in Louisiana. *No one will have to wait in the car anymore.* If Meade's wife seeks office again, he can vote for her.

In Alabama, Blair Bowie's team fell short of their wildly ambitious goal but nevertheless registered nearly 2,000 voters. Meanwhile, her legal efforts continue, as do similar cases in Louisiana, Mississippi and several other states. The Florida victory helped start a prairie fire: legislators in Iowa and Kentucky introduced bills to restore the vote to former felons. In New Jersey, proposed legislation would allow even the imprisoned to vote, as they can in Maine and Vermont. As Sean Champagne might say, pondering the demographics of those states, "Go figure that out."

Bowie, unsurprisingly, is most excited about individual stories. They reached people with no idea that the law had changed. They made voters out of people who had tried to register and had been turned away. They returned a civic voice to folks who feared theirs had been silenced forever. And every time, Bowie heard joyous, magical words. They echoed with me because I had heard them too. Take Christopher Pugh, of Mobile, who lost his right to vote in 1999 after a felony conviction. He tried to register after his release, but a registrar told him that he was not eligible. He had no idea that the law had changed. The very registrar who turned him down signed him up.[32] For good, he says. I'd heard those words before, eyes glistening, from Hailey, that morning at the Birmingham bus station. "I will be a lifelong voter," she said.

CHAPTER 2

Aboard Idaho's Medicaid Express

"I had to get off the couch and actually do something."

Forever voters are also created along Idaho's Lake Pend Oreille, which curls like a sea dragon between the Kaniksu and Coeur d'Alene national forests. On its northern shore, surrounded by three mountain ranges and wilderness, sits its largest community, the tiny town of Sandpoint, Idaho—population 8,390. This town is best known, if it is known at all, as the birthplace of Sarah Palin, whose parents taught at the middle school before moving their young family to Alaska. It's also the real-life setting for Marilynne Robinson's sorrowful novel *Housekeeping*. Robinson renamed the town Fingerbone and described how locals felt at once haunted by and drawn to the lake's glacial waters, how they could smell it on the wind, taste it from their wells. To live here, she wrote, was to feel "chastened by an outsized landscape and extravagant weather, and chastened again by an awareness that the whole of human history had occurred elsewhere."[1]

Palin and Robinson moved away long ago, but their competing visions of the wild American West, a divide wider than the Snake River, play out to this day. Conservatives and libertarians are drawn here by the freedom and open land, as near to off the grid as you can get while maintaining WiFi for your Second Amendment blog. Others find that the lake's alluring magic and natural majesty remain deep in their blood, even if they try to shake free. Sometimes they're even pulled back, and learn that a small-town argument over public education and the Lake Pend Oreille school board can turn the seductive notion that history happens someplace else upside down.

This red bastion of a one-party state accidentally kickstarted a most unlikely Medicaid for All movement that in 2018 swept across not only Idaho, but crimson Utah and Nebraska as well. It was propelled forward by three Millennial first-time activists, who led the charge in two ancient and barely roadworthy RVs painted an eye-popping bright green, utilizing door-knocking strategies they learned from books about political organizing. And it all began here in Sandpoint, with a special election over a school levy.

•••

Though taxes in Idaho have long held a lower approval rating than the wireworms and flea beetles that devour the state's famous potato plants, Sandpoint's levy had always been routine, never the stuff of pitched ideological battle. But politics here took a sharp right turn in the mid 2010s as northern Idaho attracted survivalists, libertarian refugees from liberal California, conservative Christian preppers, determined home-schoolers and other believers in the American Redoubt movement. As their numbers grew, savvy realtors photographed themselves clad in patriotic sweaters bearing semi-automatic weapons, and advertised Sandpoint properties on the Redoubt News and other blogs that covered local politics and events. That coverage helped catapult two ultraconservatives to the state legislature in 2016, in part by suggesting that a longtime Republican state senator was really just another "gun-grabbing," "liberal authoritarian progressive" in disguise.[2] In August 2016, the school levy, required to rebuild crumbling, poorly ventilated buildings from the 1950s judged "poor" or "unacceptable" for students, went down to a spectacular 65-percent-to-35-percent defeat.

The prospects for a spring 2017 levy, which would have simply maintained the previous funding level, looked similarly grim. If it failed, the district would be forced to shutter three elementary schools, consolidate two high schools an hour apart, run classes in shifts from 6 a.m. until noon and then noon through 6 p.m., and lay off some 300 teachers and other staffers.[3] That caught the attention of Garrett Strizich, who had moved back to Sandpoint with his wife, Emily, while attending medical school at the University of Idaho in nearby Moscow. Emily worked with disabled youths. Shocked by the anti-tax, anti-public school sentiment they saw in the local media, Strizich posted several pieces to his Facebook page. It didn't take long for his friend Luke Mayville to call. Mayville had grown up here as well, a skatepunk lingering outside the 7B Board Shop downtown, writing his own thrashing Tolkienesque songs about these mountains. Now thirty-two, he lived in New York, taught political science at Columbia University and had written an acclaimed study of John Adams's worries about oligarchy and inequality. As topical as those issues were in the days after a self-professed billionaire was lifted to the White House on a wave of white populist rage, Strizich's posts stirred the smell of Lake Pend Oreille from 2,554 miles away. Luke Mayville's hometown was being overtaken by the same forces overrunning the nation.

"We knew those schools well," Mayville tells me. "We went to them." And they wanted to fight for them. The anti-levy and home-school forces were dominating the letters-to-the-editor page, not to mention the breakfast conversation at hotspots like Panhandler Pies and Spuds grill, by sending targeted mailers to conservative homes. "There were a lot of people feeling helpless—and not wanting to feel helpless," says Emily Strizich. "They were looking for leadership."

Beyond standing outside the polls holding "Vote Yes" signs, however, the pro-schools forces were clueless. And, as Mayville knew from his studies, loud rallies outside the polls tend to hurt the underdog cause, because they also remind the "Vote No" forces that it's election day. He'd just read a book by two Yale political scientists, Donald Green and Alan Gerber, which identified the one tactic that changes minds—going door to door. Forget big data and big analytics and big fundraising. Knock on doors. Talk to your neighbors. Persuade the old-fashioned way. The more Mayville thought about the conundrum, the more he wanted to get involved—and election day was growing closer. He decided to spend ten days back in his hometown and put all this theory he'd studied to work. Maybe save the schools that had set him on his course. "Luke called me," remembers Garrett Strizich, "and said, 'I'm thinking about coming out.'"

Together, Luke, Garrett and Emily assembled a committee of pro-public school activists and made a plan. They aimed to knock on 3,000 doors in one weekend ahead of the vote. In the end, they fell just short of their goal, at 2,750—but they still won big on election day, which once again produced a two-to-one result, but this time in their favor. Voter turnout in the neighborhoods where their group had canvassed was triple that of nearby precincts. "We flipped the whole thing around," Mayville says. That night, as the community celebrated, Mayville and the Striziches noticed that the room was at least half Republican. They had won because they persuaded people to join their cause. When presented with a courteous argument, neighbors could find common ground. "If you read anything about Idaho politics, it's that people are way out there. If you actually get out and talk to people, you realize they're tremendously reasonable," Emily says. "Certainly people are fiercely independent. But they're also really practical and very common-sensical."

Inspired by their victory, the trio didn't want to stop. "We stepped back from that and thought, 'Wow, that was fun,'" says Mayville. Adds Strizich, "If we could organize and win in Sandpoint, why couldn't we do something like that for the entire state?" There might be other issues like public education—perhaps health care, raising the minimum wage, or preserving public lands—where a genuine consensus existed among voters, if only they could talk to one another and remove the usual stain of partisan politics.

And what kind of politics might be possible in Idaho if a statewide movement could channel the energy and empowerment, the hope, that everyday citizens gained from actually being involved? During the Sand-point campaign, it had been hard not to notice the women's marches around the entire state. In the liberal oasis of Boise, sure, but 900 people on the street in Driggs, way over in the northeast corner along the Wyoming border? As Mayville and the Striziches thought about what might come next, Congress debated a repeal and replace of the Affordable Care Act. Thousands of Idahoans who feared for their health care had no power beyond calling their senators and members of Congress, none of whom seemed likely to change their mind and vote against repeal. People were being asked to make phone calls, to think small, when what citizens actually wanted to do was make a difference. "There were people all around Idaho yearning to do something big," Mayville says. It was then that Luke, Emily and Garrett decided to bring them together. Just like that, Reclaim Idaho was born, and the quest began to identify an issue that was backed by most people of all sides but stuck in partisan quicksand.

Universal pre-K? Protecting public lands? Worthy, for sure, but this state with one of the highest percentages of minimum-wage workers had a more pressing topic. Somewhere between 60,000 and 70,000 Idaho-ans lacked health insurance, because the state legislature had refused to accept federal dollars to expand Medicaid. Prior to the Affordable Care Act, Medicaid had been restricted to Americans below the poverty level. The ACA boosted eligibility to anyone making 138 percent of the poverty level, and reimbursed states 100 percent of the costs between 2014 and 2016 (and 90 percent after that). The Supreme Court, however, ruled that states did not have to accept that money, and seventeen states largely under GOP trifecta control of the governor's office and both legislative chambers, including Idaho, refused. That created a coverage gap for anyone whose income surpassed the poverty line (too much for Medicaid) but below the 138-percent mark (too little for the Obamacare exchange).

How easy was it to fall into that gap? Put it this way: you could work a forty-hour week at $8.25 an hour and land right in the middle. Mayville knew how life-changing this could be all too intimately: his mom, a home health care aide, had contracted breast cancer just before the Affordable Care Act kicked in. Her out-of-pocket expenses nearly cost her the Sandpoint home where he was raised.

Rural states tended to have the most citizens in the gap, along with less healthy citizens, more barriers to care, and desperate, far-flung hospitals already closing at a high rate. People without health insurance also often require catastrophic care in emergency rooms, a ballooning cost which states that didn't take the money would have to cover on their own. Nevertheless, Idaho refused those federal dollars—much-needed money Idahoans had already paid as income tax. Though polls showed that Idaho voters wanted to accept the money, the legislature refused for six consecutive sessions.

Turns out, the means of breaking through that legislative blockade was parked in the Striziches' driveway. It was a 1977 Dodge Tiago RV they'd bought for $1,500. It hadn't survived a 15-mile trip to a campground earlier that year, but soon it would be painted green, christened the Medicaid Express and taken on a statewide tour. The trio didn't yet have a ballot question, or even much of an organization, so how could they roll into Coeur d'Alene or Idaho Falls and generate enthusiasm and volunteers to win Medicaid for All? Reclaim Idaho needed to separate Medicaid from any party's platform, and turn an issue into a candidate for office. And they needed a spectacle.

"I'll be honest," says Emily Strizich. "I thought [Garrett and Luke] were insane." Still, she joined an early trip. One of the first doors she knocked on belonged to an elderly woman stuck in that income gap, trying to decide between treating a disease that would kill her or bankrupting her family and making them homeless. "She's grappling with this idea: is my life worth saving?" Emily tells me.

That's not a Democratic question, or a Republican one. It shouldn't be asked in a red or a blue state. The next campaign was on. The Medicaid Express would roll.

Well, it would roll *slooowly*. "This thing is kind of like a sailboat," Luke says with a laugh, as soon as I'm buckled in for a three-day barnstorming tour from Boise to Idaho Falls, hitting Twin Falls, Pocatello and American Falls along the way. It tops out around 60. "Go too fast and it tips over." This is Medicaid Mobile 2.0, a 1989 Ford Air X reassembled with Chevy parts. "Our rule for choosing a Medicaid vehicle is when you first saw it, you had to laugh," he says. This, in the end, was the trio's "spectacle."

You can't take your eyes off this massive rolling billboard, painted Hulk green, emblazoned with "Vote Yes For Medicaid" in giant white letters and signed in black Sharpie by what looks like half the state. Mayville, plastic white sunglasses pushed atop his head, resembling Michael Cera if the actor talked more about Alexis de Tocqueville and Noam Chomsky, takes the tan upholstered seat behind the wheel. His wife, Elena, who has put her Manhattan psychology practice on hold to help win this fight, grabs shotgun. The small kitchen and all the cabinets are wood-paneled. There's a guitar resting on a small couch, one supersized spare tire inside, a broken clock stuck at 7:30, and no air conditioning. The rug is shag. As we head toward the highway, a woman working in the yard outside the Burger Belly sees this democracy-saving beast roll toward her, drops her rake and begins dancing with both hands above her head.

It's easy to get attention, but creating real political change in Idaho is a whole lot harder. Idaho is such a conservative, one-party state that it has not gone for a Democratic presidential candidate since Lyndon Johnson in 1964. Donald Trump walloped Hillary Clinton here 59 percent to 28 percent in 2016. It has elected just one Democrat, Frank Church, to the U.S. Senate since the late 1940s. One Idaho Democrat has served one single term in the U.S. House since the early 1990s. It's been sixty years since the Democrats last held a majority in the state senate, in 1958, and 1992 was the last year in which they reached double digits; the current margin of 28 Republicans and 7 Democrats shows some improvement since 2000, when the numbers were 32 Republicans and 3 Democrats. Republicans have also dominated the state house since 1960, where the only mystery has been whether they would have four, five or six times as many seats as the Democrats.

Like many bodies with absolute power, Idaho's legislature isn't much for sharing it. Unlike other western states, Idaho has had a very limited experiment with the citizens' referendum. Only a dozen have passed here since the 1930s. But after voters petitioned and overturned three controversial GOP education laws in 2012, the legislature responded by adding a new geographic requirement that makes it dramatically more difficult for citizen-led initiatives to reach the ballot. A petition drive now requires 6 percent of all registered voters—in 2018, 56,192 signatures. But no one can just camp out in Boise and collect names. That 6 percent has to come from at least 18 of the state's 35 legislative districts. A tall feat almost anywhere, but especially in Idaho—the fourteenth largest state by area and the sixth least densely populated.

Unsurprisingly, no initiative had qualified for the ballot after these tough conditions were imposed. But Mayville and the Striziches were convinced that they could mobilize both those newly energized by the 2016 election and Idaho's ignored center-right if they could frame Medicaid for All as health care for hardworking, low-income people. They spent the summer of 2017 criss-crossing the state in the Medicaid Express, not thinking about signatures yet but trying to harness energy and identify local leaders who would do that work in the months to come. "We thought people might throw Molotov cocktails at us," says Emily Strizich, about driving around a red state in a noticeably green RV pushing a reform identified with a black, Democratic president. "Instead, people would run up to us at gas stations and buy us a Coke from inside."

When they drove through wealthy Sun Valley, where media moguls and CEOs ski down the aptly named Dollar Mountain, one brand-name political operative tried to clip their wings. "She told us how many millions of dollars we needed to even begin thinking about it," remembers Emily. "Like, 'I can't believe you guys would even think about doing this.'" But as they talked to real people, they couldn't imagine what they'd need the millions of dollars for—especially if they ignored the advice of, well, highly-paid strategists who vacation in Sun Valley. "We built this group of volunteers from around the state that we're trying to activate," says Garrett Strizich. "This was the perfect thing for them to do, something concrete that they could work toward, to really make a difference."

Experts said it couldn't be done. But as Reclaim Idaho's growing network of statewide volunteers built toward the January 2018 launch of their petition drive, they were reinforcing theories of change that Mayville had read about in his political science books and was now making real in his home state. Invent a structure you've never seen before, find all the passion and talents inside the community, and harness the work that people are willing to do. The Medicaid Express became exactly the symbol of hope that Strizich had imagined it could be. When they drove through Lewiston, Rexburg, American Falls, Weiser, Post Falls, citizens realized they could become part of something larger than themselves.

"There was so much skepticism and doubt out there that it was possible to do this—and those who were skeptical put forth a lot of good reasons," Mayville recalls. "You have to organize in 18 different districts all across the state. You'd have to gather all of your signatures in the dead of winter. But as we started building teams of incredible volunteers, across the state, month after month, it just kept gaining momentum." It wasn't three Millennials who on their own collected more than 60,000 signatures statewide and qualified for the ballot by spring; their work inspired others to come forth and knock on doors. And their work created new activist networks in small towns that encouraged folks to run for local office themselves. "I've seen through all my years people not being able to afford their medications. I've never been politically involved with anything in my life," one Boise-area pharmacist told the local paper. "But I felt I had to get off the couch and actually do something."[4]

It is not easy to park the Medicaid Mobile in Idaho Falls. Downtown looks as though it's frozen in the 1980s—a board game store carries a full line of Dungeons and Dragons supplies, the Variety Mart Leathers and Pawn Shop spells out its name in what resembles red and white children's blocks—and so are the politics. Mayville allows a car to turn left in front of him and the driver waves. "We just won a vote," he proclaims. "I'm not sure if Luke's driving wins or loses more votes," cracks his wife. Over coffee with volunteers at Villa Cafe, there's discussion about how to build a bipartisan coalition in this conservative town, and a reminder about the need to stay nonpartisan at the doors. This is a Mormon community, and home to the first LDS temple built in the state in 1945. A sign outside Ferrell's Clothing that had made me chuckle at a potential double entendre—"Ask about free missionary gift"—suddenly makes a lot more sense (and seems much more innocent).

It's a brutal 95-degree summer day, but Amy Pratt fizzes with excitement as we head from downtown to a neighborhood of low ranch houses in the shadow of Interstate 15, not far from the single-spire tower of the LDS temple. We're armed with water and clipboards. Pratt door-knocked almost every day between January 6 and May 1, but hasn't been back out since the original drive finished. She hit 1,056 doors in this town, to be exact. Now we're hitting all of these doors again to begin the get-out-the-vote drive. "I'm so excited to tell them all that we made the ballot," she says. Reclaim Idaho already knows that the Idaho Freedom Foundation, well-funded through several Koch brothers affiliates, will spend millions to oppose them in the fall, positioning Reclaim as outside agitators trying to sneak Obamacare into Idaho.[5] They want to get to voters first and remind them that this is about Idahoans helping their neighbors.

We walk up a driveway where a bumper sticker on a pickup proclaims "Vietnam: We Were Winning When I Left" and the path to the door, festooned with American flag pinwheels, is the sort of green felt usually seen on a miniature golf course. I'm ready to seek friendlier ground, but Pratt holds steady, even when an older man answers the door clad in a patriotic

T-shirt that's all flags and eagles. "Why ask why? We're just the best," it reads. While I wonder if the shirt and the bumper stickers were some sort of package deal, Pratt starts a genuine conversation. Heads start bobbing. Turns out the man's aging mother falls into the Medicaid gap. "I'll definitely vote for that," he says.

"I've lived here ten years and always felt like an outsider," says Pratt, a forty-seven-year-old bus driver. "The LDS community is so tight-knit." But out here, knocking on doors, strangers fed her chocolate chip cookies in the winter, handed her bottled water in the heat, signed her petition, thanked her and promised to vote yes. "The response I got from people! It was, 'Holy shit, this could happen!' I had no idea anything like this could happen in Idaho."

"Everyone knows someone who has fallen into the gap," says Leslie Smith, a schoolteacher who helped organize the petition drive. She's one of the new activists who met Luke Mayville when the Medicaid Mobile first visited Idaho Falls and became so dedicated to the cause that she let them all stay overnight in her house. And sure enough, as we walk up to another home with Luke and Elena, we meet a woman named Teresa who's practically moved to tears. We soon learn that she's working sixteen hours a day as a home health aide even though she should be on disability, just to make enough money to push herself beyond the Medicaid gap. She's even hired an accountant to be sure she stays there, so as not to risk her insurance. "It pays $9.50 an hour," she tells us. "Not enough to pay my bills but just enough to qualify for Obama. I'm doing a lot of lifting that I'm not supposed to be doing. But, gotta do something." We canvass until dusk, and as we climb back into the Medicaid Mobile, a pickup pulls over and an elderly couple asks if we need them to sign the petition. "Good luck," she says. "Good job, guys," he adds. That's when I notice a sign outside a nearby house. "A dream you dream alone is only a dream. A dream you dream together is reality."

It's late as we roll toward American Falls, where the few motels are booked for the night. We follow a trail of stars to the Willow Bay RV camp, and Luke and Elena grab the guitar and head for a campfire. In the morning we wake alongside the stunning American Falls Reservoir to a spectacular pink and blue sky and grab coffee at the camp's cafe. Bob Dylan's "Tangled Up In Blue" provides the perfect soundtrack as we head toward Pocatello along Interstate 86. Then it's Simon and Garfunkel's "America," those gentle harmonies followed by the cascading drumroll, never grander or more romantic than when watching the lonely western sky through the giant RV windows fifty years after it was recorded, on a mission, all of us gone once more to look for America.

What we find is more than a dozen people waiting for us just after 9 a.m. at the Bru Haus Galilei coffee shop on Pocatello's dusty, charming Main Street. Chris Stevens, the Bannock County petition drive leader, found herself permanently charged up and changed after knocking on thousands of doors, hearing stories of hardship and realizing government needed to do a better job of helping. So the former school principal launched her candidacy for county commissioner. "This is the last thing I ever thought I'd be doing," she tells me. She's in her early sixties, with bright white hair, a radiant smile and the determined grit of a woman willing to found a modern dance company in Wisconsin. "Luke and others told me I should really think about it, and I said no, no, no. What are my chances in this area? And Luke actually said the thing that tipped me. He said, 'You know, Chris, winning has many faces. You've become a beacon to other people that says you're not crazy, you're not the only one, there are other people willing to work hard for a set of beliefs.' And he's right. Maybe winning here is plowing the ground."

Stevens stands before the small group, a Mike and Ike candy machine and a paperback exchange rack loaded with Sue Grafton's detective novels behind them, and outlines her big plans. They'll knock on 21,000 doors before Labor Day to get the word out. Then they'll hit those doors again before the election. At every door, Mayville adds, they'll leave literature for Stevens's race as well as the Medicaid initiative. He has the easy, calm confidence of a leader. "Remind people how big a deal this is," he tells the room. "This is the single biggest step forward for the health of Idaho's families in fifty years. We're bringing back 500 million to 600 million of our tax dollars for the well-being of 62,000 working Idahoans who need it most. 'Give us our money back!'" he tells them. "It appeals universally to people. We're already paying for it, twice." Heads start nodding. "First, when our federal taxes go to other states, then again with the shamefully inefficient catastrophic health care fund."

He's training these regular folks first on messaging, then on closing the deal. "Ask for their vote," he says. "Can we count on you to vote for this? The political science says that triggers accountability. They've promised a real flesh-and-blood person." Mayville has a room full of grandparents prepped for door-to-door combat. He tells them about a long drive from Emmett to Salmon, across five hours and two national forests, when a 1,500-pound cow stepped in front of the Medicaid Express. "That might be the stiffest resistance we faced," he says, winning a laugh. "Everyone we talk to—Republicans, Democrats, independents—sympathizes with this issue and eagerly supports it."

Four months later, he will be proven correct, as Idaho, along with Nebraska and Utah, adopts Medicaid for All by a big margin: 365,000 yes votes, just under 61 percent. "The people of Idaho went out, did the work, and then delivered, and then it happened," an overwhelmed Garrett Strizich will tell supporters that night.[6] But that day in July, there are doors to knock on. It is sweltering, we are high in the hills of Pocatello and Mayville could not be happier. "This is what Alexis de Tocqueville called the art of association," he says, and sets off jogging up another driveway, clipboard under his arm, a big grin on his face, battling inequality in a way John Adams might only imagine, one neighbor at a time.

CHAPTER 3

The Defeat of the Voter Fraud Myth

"The fix was in."

This grin is different. It's boyish and giddy, but certain. Kris Kobach wears the aw-shucks smile of the star quarterback on prom night, naturally winning the approval of his date's demanding father, the doors of power and privilege swinging wide. *Just as he knew they would.* Kobach's enthusiastic beam says, "I belong here, never doubted it."

It was November 20, 2016, just twelve days after Donald Trump's surprise victory, and the Kansas secretary of state stood confidently alongside the president-elect at his exclusive New Jersey golf club, one of many gilded transition sanctums. Kobach had been exchanging emails with Gene Hamilton, the Trump transition official overseeing the administration's immigration policy, plans for a Muslim travel ban and appointments to Homeland Security and Justice. In them, Kobach, the architect of the nation's strictest voter ID and anti-immigration measures, assured Hamilton that he had already begun writing amendments to the National Voter Registration Act that would "make clear that proof of citizenship requirements are permitted."[1] That day, he carried a brown leather portfolio case with one paper-clipped document visible. Cameras captured its title: "Kobach Strategic Plan For First 365 Days."[2]

Kobach took his place on the portico next to Trump, with the assembled international media looking on, his view all flashbulbs, manicured lawns, a spectacular tiered fountain. The next president held his left arm on Kobach's back, and with his right he pointed at him with a gesture that said, "Not me, this is the real man, this guy right here."

Sure, the media had mocked Kobach's claims about voter fraud, like the time in 2010 when Kobach declared that almost 2,000 dead Kansans were still registered to vote and that at least one of them, Albert K. Brewer, had in fact cast a primary vote that very year, despite having been buried in 1996. While Kobach told the press that he was "still trying to achieve confirmation of this," the *Wichita Eagle* sent a reporter to the registered address and found Albert K. Brewer doing yard work.[3] "I don't think this is heaven, not when I'm raking leaves," he said.[4] His dad, also Albert K. Brewer, had died in 1996, his preference in the state's 2010 primary and any other election forever unknown.

But Kobach pressed eternally forward, deaf to fact-checkers, as one can be when every media profile notes your degrees from Harvard, Yale and Oxford. In 2016, he found that at Bedminster, his ideas—once dismissed, then brushed aside—had gained currency at the center of power. The "Kobach Strategic Plan"! Aides opened the giant white doors for the secretary of state and the president-elect. Kobach beheld the staircase where Ivanka Trump and Jared Kushner took their wedding photos, and entered a clubhouse where the initiation fee alone ran upward of $300,000.[5] To him, on that night, anything must have seemed possible.

Trump emerged from his meetings with Kobach convinced that he would have won the national popular vote if it wasn't for voter fraud, and when the media asked how he explained the missing 2.8 million votes, the White House pointed to Kobach for the proof. Then Trump soon appointed Kobach, along with vice president Mike Pence, as co-chairs of a presidential commission to investigate election integrity. How could Kobach know, as he felt the hand of the next president of the United States on the small of his back, that over six weeks in the summer of 2018 a nerdy, easily dismissed pal from Maine and a young lawyer with a background in improv would pull all of it down? First in a Kansas courtroom, and then before the nation, Kobach's very rationale for voter ID, his entire case for fraud and then his facade of election protection would be shredded, decisively, and even seen as fraudulent itself, like some exclusive, glittery Trump Vineyards label pasted over a bottle of Two Buck Chuck.

Far, far from Trump National sits the secretary of state's suite in Augusta, Maine, tucked upstairs in a brick building that feels like nothing like a clubhouse and more like a long-retired elementary school. Enter Matt Dunlap's office and you're greeted not with a colossal chandelier or fancy marble floors, but a giant black bear rug.

The rug makes for a rather jarring sight. As Maine's secretary of state, Dunlap is responsible for administering elections, the state archives and the department of motor vehicles. His office runs student mock elections and the Eighth Grade Citizenship Awards. You'd expect a rug displaying the state seal, perhaps walls covered in license plates—especially since Dunlap, balding and bespectacled, *looks* like a secretary of state. The actor who played Kevin on *The Office* could portray him in the movie. But it was Dunlap who brought this bear down himself through superior patience— waiting weeks, months, ramrod-straight and silent in a tree stand just ten minutes from his home until the ideal moment to strike presented itself.

In the end, the beast never saw Dunlap coming. Neither would Kobach, having underestimated the focus and determination behind those shirtsleeves and 1950s frames. Kobach's impressive-sounding Presidential Commission on Election Integrity was to be the front through which a cabal of shadowy Republican activists and oft-debunked academics, backed by misleading studies, laundered their phony voting fraud theories into a justification for real-world suppression tactics such as national voter ID and massive coast-to-coast electoral roll purges. It failed spectacularly, felled by arrogance, cartoonish incompetence, even a shadowy right-wing researcher arrested for child pornography. The commission's disingenuous creation and private White House emails were laid bare thanks to the courage of Dunlap, the small-state hunter they underestimated.

"It was a dishonest effort from the very beginning. It was never really meant to uncover anything," Dunlap tells me, more mournful than outraged. "It was meant to backfill an unprovable thesis that there's voter fraud—then to issue a fake report justifying laws or executive orders that change the fundamental nature of how we run elections. I think that might have been the real danger that we averted."

Though many critics recognized the commission as a show trial, steered by Kobach—an Inspector Clouseau who gazes into his mirror and sees Sherlock Holmes—toward confirmation of his own false theories, Dunlap nevertheless wanted to serve. Kobach understood that the commission needed to be bipartisan, on the surface, at least. Dunlap accepted his appointment knowing that he'd be criticized for lending legitimacy to a pseudoscientific charade. Nevertheless, he thought a committee that lacked perspectives like his own might be more dangerous if left unchecked. He also thought Maine had a story to tell about clean elections run entirely without voter ID; this appointment might give him the opportunity to share it before the national media. Then, if Kobach went too far, Dunlap thought he might be a valuable counterweight. Dunlap never expected to star in Kobach's show, but he had no idea just how passive and "supporting" his role was intended to be.

The first clue came in June 2017, when Kobach, in the name of the commission, demanded voluminous voter data from all fifty state election officials, including Social Security numbers, party registration and voting history. This came as a surprise to Dunlap and other commissioners, who'd reminded Kobach on a conference call just the day before how zealously secretaries of state protected that data. Even officials from Trump and Kobach's own party saw the dangers in handing over such personal information. "They can go jump in the Gulf of Mexico," replied Mississippi secretary of state Delbert Hosemann, a Republican, to Kobach's request.[6]

Then, in September of 2017, just before the commission met in New Hampshire, Kobach published an opinion piece on *Breitbart News Network*, a conservative media organ once run by Steve Bannon, suggesting that it was election fraud that cost Trump the state's electoral votes and the seat of GOP senator Kelly Ayotte.[7] Kobach's reasoning in his essay was creative: more than 6,500 people had voted on election day 2016 with an out-of-state driver's license and only 1,014 of them had obtained a New Hampshire license since, cinching in his mind that the remaining 5,486 votes were fraudulent Democratic ballots that tilted the results. "I issue driver's licenses!" Dunlap says. "Making an equation between voting and not updating a driver's license is like saying if you have cash in your wallet, it's proof that you've robbed a bank."

In October 2017, a shockwave rattled the Election Integrity commission, when a staff researcher was arrested for possessing child pornography on his phone. Dunlap and others on the commission were unaware that the commission even had a researcher. Dunlap learned about the staffer, and the arrest, when the *Washington Post* connected the bust to the commission,[8] and his inbox erupted with media inquiries. Then he learned about a potential late fall commission meeting only after a conservative voting group boasted that it had been invited to give testimony.

Was there a forthcoming meeting? What was the deal with this researcher? Dunlap's emails to Kobach were ignored. Voice mailboxes at the White House were too full to accept new messages. Dunlap had had enough. He wrote a formal letter to the commission. "I just want to know what's going on," he tells me, saying that he still saw himself as a team player. "I want to know who we're talking to. I want to know what we're talking about. I want to know what our reference materials are. And most of all, I'd like to get a handle on our schedule."

Instead, his letter got no reaction from either Kobach or the vice president's office. "Silence," he says. "If they had handed me a bunch of binders, I probably would have been satisfied. But they didn't do that." Ten days later, he got an email from Pence's office. They were reviewing his request with legal counsel. For the first time, but not for the last, Dunlap wondered if he was even actually on the commission.

His letter, however, did catch someone's attention in the "deep state." One fall afternoon, Dunlap returned from a meeting in Bangor and decided to take the afternoon off and "button up my yard." His cell phone buzzed: a Facebook message from a well-connected friend in Washington. The tone was urgent: call me, but on my cell. What followed played out like a scene from *All the President's Men*, akin to Bob Woodward rearranging plants on his balcony to signal a meeting with his secret super-source Deep Throat. Dunlap's friend said that he carried a message from the chief of staff of a United States senator who wished not to be named. "He said, 'Matt, look, people are talking about you down here.'" They'd noticed the letter and wanted to help. Better even than Dunlap, they knew the kind of resources he'd need. "You're not going to be able to take on the Department of Justice and the White House alone.'" Dunlap, chilled, didn't realize that was what he'd done. "You need attorneys. I'm going to give you a name and number. You ought to give them a call."

Terrified, Dunlap hung up. He had merely asked when his commission met next. He didn't want to go to war with Washington or reenact *Three Days of the Condor*. Still, unsure of what he was doing or whom he might be calling, Dunlap climbed into his car for privacy and left a message at the number he'd been given. "My name is Matt Dunlap. I'm the secretary of state for the state of Maine and I was given your name by a third party who wishes to remain anonymous. I think I might be in some kind of trouble." He'd reached a new nonprofit, American Oversight, a world-class assemblage of legal talent dedicated to high-impact litigation and investigation. "It's like having a company softball team and all of a sudden Dustin Pedroia shows up," he cracks, referring to the Boston Red Sox all-star. The group knew more about the commission's workings than Dunlap—and, fatefully, Kobach. Dunlap would learn that the commission was subject to something called the Federal Advisory Committee Act, which requires that any such presidential commission embrace diverse viewpoints and a broad spectrum of political views, maintain open public records and be conducted with complete transparency. American Oversight wanted to bring a lawsuit immediately. Slow down, said Dunlap, spooked and unsure whom he could trust. "I'm from Maine," he said, where there's a certain circumspect way of doing things. "I'm glad you like the apple sauce, but I really need the Mason jars back."

Folksy Vacationland wisdom aside, there was no time to lose. Dunlap didn't want to go to war, but he was determined to know what was going on behind the scenes. In mid-November, mere weeks after that stomach-churning call, Dunlap and American Oversight filed suit. They alleged that the commission's "superficial bipartisanship has been a facade" and that Dunlap and other Democratic commissioners were being "excluded from the commission's work."[9] The panel's operations have "not been open and transparent, not even to the commissioners themselves," they charged. Dunlap still hoped the suit might wake people up in the vice president's office and put things back on track. Perhaps Pence aide Andrew Kossack would return his phone calls and even apologize. Dunlap understood what it was like to run a busy office, after all. He just wanted his schedule. Instead, Kobach called Dunlap's suit "baseless and paranoid," and insisted that Dunlap was "making assumptions about commission business occurring without his knowledge."[10] Kobach said he looked forward to refuting it all in court. Three days before Christmas, however, a federal judge quickly found in Dunlap's favor, ruling that the commission's "indefensible" position "ignores the law."[11] They could not exclude Dunlap from a presidential advisory commission of which he was a member.

The court ordered the commission to turn over thousands of pages of documents, ensure genuine transparency, and also to include Dunlap as a full participant in all deliberations and activities. "I said to the attorneys, 'I half wonder if they don't pull the plug on this now,'" rather than accede to the court's demands for balance and transparency, says Dunlap. It was a good hunch. The White House waited for cover, a moment when the Beltway media was distracted. That soon arrived, with the publication of Michael Wolff's salacious Oval Office tell-all *Fire and Fury*, loaded with gossipy tidbits—such as Steve Bannon's description of Ivanka Trump as "dumb as a brick" that created a cable news and Twitter tinderbox. "Sure enough," says Dunlap, "January 3, we got the email that they dissolved the commission." Kobach had surrendered. But he wasn't ready to be stuffed and mounted quite yet.

It would take Dunlap a while to figure it out, but Dale Ho knew from the very beginning that Kris Kobach was all hat and no cattle.

Ho, named one of the nation's top Asian American attorneys under forty, directs the ACLU's Voting Rights Project, and has won crucial courtroom victories in an era when they've been difficult to come by. But when the U.S. Supreme Court eliminated the full protections of the Voting Rights Act in 2013's *Shelby County v. Holder*, ending the requirement that states with a history of racial discrimination receive approval from the Justice Department before making changes to their election procedures and laws, Ho's job became noticeably more difficult.

Prior to the early 2010s, the voting rights arc in America—including the Motor Voter Act in 1993, the Help America Vote Act in 2002, and the unanimous reauthorization of the Voting Rights Act in the Senate as late as 2006—was bending, slowly but steadily, toward justice. Ho believes the election of a black president changed its direction. After Obama's historic victory in 2008, Republicans swept the 2010 midterms, expanding their complete control from the South and Midwest into purple states such as Michigan, Ohio, Pennsylvania, North Carolina and Wisconsin. Before the 2012 elections, GOP legislatures in nineteen states had enacted some twenty-five new laws that made it harder to register to vote or more difficult to cast a ballot. After the *Shelby* decision, that trickle became a torrent. More than 500 bills creating new voting obstacles appeared nationwide, some mere hours after the *Shelby* decision,[12] suggesting that one side was raring and ready to go.

"You don't get an electorate that looks like that, and you don't get a president that looks like that, unless there's fraud, right?" asks Ho, sarcasm thick and dripping. It's a steamy summer day in New York City, and a tattoo pokes out from Ho's shirtsleeve. "That's the bedtime story some folks on that side started telling themselves. We're losing our country. Our country is changing. Not because that's just the future, natural demographic trends, but because of some nefarious plot. Before that, guys like Kris Kobach weren't getting elected secretary of state on a voter fraud platform."

In 2013, Kansas and Kobach took direct aim at the Motor Voter Act with a stringent new registration process called SAFE, short for the Secure and Fair Elections Act. The Motor Voter bill directed states to make registration as easy as possible, and, indeed, Kansas only required residents to check a box attesting to U.S. citizenship. That ease of access ended with SAFE. Now applicants needed to prove their citizenship first with a passport or birth certificate, otherwise they'd land on a "suspense list" until they presented the proper paperwork or were booted off the rolls.

All this caught Donna Bucci, of Wichita, by surprise.[13] She thought she'd register to vote when she renewed her driver's license, but her expired license wasn't proof of citizenship. She didn't have a passport, and, as a minimum wage worker in a Kansas prison, she couldn't budget the twenty dollars needed to get a replacement birth certificate from her home state of Maryland. Kobach insisted that the new law was necessary to prevent noncitizens from voting in Kansas elections. Critics argued that, in practice, it targeted poor people and minorities who either couldn't afford or no longer had their birth certificates, and young people who move frequently. Indeed, one study found that one in seven Kansans, overwhelmingly young and of color, who tried to register to vote after the law's passage were barred because they lacked acceptable forms of ID. Ho and the ACLU filed suit on behalf of Bucci and five others. They won a temporary stay of the law prior to the 2016 election. Then, in March 2017, the case went before a federal judge in Kansas City, an appointee of George H. W. Bush. Kobach, the voter fraud philosopher-king, would have his day in court to prove that fraud existed and that these restrictions were necessary.

"It was his *chance* to prove it," Ho gently corrects me, "*if* he had any facts."

Ho says he starts every case thinking not about how he can win, but about what he can prove. His team started with the birth certificate requirement and news reports that tens of thousands of Kansans had their registration blocked. "That's really bad," he says. "That's not just some liberal belief that we ought to make voting easier or that obtaining documents, in theory, is onerous because it costs twenty dollars." With actual evidence and real-life stories of Kansans who had been prevented from voting by Kobach's law, Ho and his team moved on to step two: was there any evidence of noncitizens voting in Kansas that might justify toughening the registration requirements? "Best we could find was rumors of some hog farming operation in the late 1990s that supposedly bussed in noncitizens to vote in some local election." They knew the legal standard: under the Motor Voter law, states could not demand that people do anything more than sign an oath, under penalty of perjury, that they are citizens. "We had to bring this case now," Ho tells me. "And it's against one of the nation's chief purveyors of lies about fraud. This wasn't just a chance to take out a really pernicious law, but to change the entire narrative on these issues." The idea of voter fraud itself would be on trial.

Kobach put a brave face on the demise of the Commission for Electoral Integrity, claiming that the panel had indeed discovered fraud and suggesting that the battle would move into the Homeland Security department, away from pesky Democrats. But just nine weeks later, it would be harder for him to spin the embarrassment he suffered at the hands of Ho, inside a federal courthouse in Kansas City named after a very different breed of Midwestern Republican, longtime Kansas senator Bob Dole.

Exuding supreme confidence in his own competence, Kobach decided that he would defend the SAFE Act himself rather than bring in experienced trial lawyers. Maybe it was arrogance, or years of Fox News softballs and friendly campaign crowds, that made Kobach believe his case for voter fraud had become self-evident. "He's been puffed up as this genius, right?" says Ho. Either way, it was a fatal mistake. Kobach may be a wily politician but he is not an experienced litigator, and in Ho he faced a tenacious, rigorous opponent. Given months to build his evidence, Kobach instead flew blind. He proved to be unprepared for rules of evidence stricter than the editing process of a *Breitbart* op-ed, unready for cross-examination tougher than questions from *Fox and Friends* hosts. Finally, if he thought the GOP-appointed judge hearing the case would, like Trump, place her hand on his back and put politics before facts, well, Kobach's calculations landed as far afield as his estimates of noncitizen voting.

Ho and the ACLU tore down Kobach's experts and exposed their studies as partisan junk science. By the end, a judge would describe Kobach's two key academics, including the Election Integrity commission's Hans von Spakovsky, as "misleading," "disingenuous" and "credibly dismantled," and place "no weight" on their opinions.[14] It was as if Kobach had prepared his case inside an ideological vacuum, making the rookie debater's mistake of failing to anticipate where Ho would poke and probe, even when his experts' weaknesses could be identified with a simple Google search.[15]

For example, Jesse Richman of Old Dominion University, who attained notoriety as Trump's favorite political scientist when the president used an op-ed Richman wrote for the *Washington Post* to argue that voter fraud had helped Democrats rig elections.[16] Richman made his case by extrapolating data from the Cooperative Congressional Election Survey (CCES), a study of 32,000 voters from 2008. Forty of those 32,000 online respondents reported that they had voted as a noncitizen. Richman multiplied those results against the entire electorate and concluded that, given those percentages, anywhere from 38,000 to 2.8 million illegal votes may have been cast overall. Hundreds of political scientists, including the Harvard professor who ran the CCES, signed a letter rejecting the legitimacy of Richman's methodology.[17]

Kobach and Trump took Richman's fanciful research one step further. They assumed Richman's largest number was correct, transposed 2008's numbers to 2016, then assumed that every one of those potential 2.8 million noncitizen voters had pulled the lever for Clinton.[18] When, in the courtroom, Ho played the video of Kobach making that argument on Fox News and asked Richman if that was a reasonable argument, the professor paused, swallowed hard and admitted that "I do not believe that my study provides strong support for that notion."

Except Richman used this same questionable methodology for a report he submitted to the court about noncitizen voting in Kansas: he turned incredibly tiny sample sizes—as small as one voter—into several sweeping conclusions about tens of thousands of noncitizen voters in Kansas. For example, in one study, Richman examined Kansans with temporary driver's licenses and found that 16 percent of them had tried to vote. Therefore, he concluded, the same percentage of adults in the state of Kansas—18,000 people—might have illegally registered or attempted to join the voting rolls. Kobach agreed with those findings. Richman's entire study, however, included just thirty-seven people. The number of people who said they had attempted to register to vote? Just six. Ho deflated this dodgy pseudoscience with one question on cross-examination: Were any of those six people actually on the Kansas voting rolls? The answer was "no."[19]

Ho also brought the Harvard professor who had conducted the CCES research, Stephen Ansolabehere, to the stand. The scene resembled the moment in Woody Allen's *Annie Hall* where Allen's character overhears a tweedy blowhard at the movies mansplaining Marshall McLuhan's theories about film to his date and silences him by presenting McLuhan himself. "You know nothing of my work," McLuhan tells him. "How you got to teach a course in anything is totally amazing." Because of the small sam-

ple size, Ho asked Ansolabehere, would it be accurate to say that noncitizen voting in Kansas might also be "not statistically distinct from zero?"

"Correct," Ansolabehere replied.[20]

Kobach, meanwhile, tried some fancy math of his own with his most
important evidence: thirty-eight noncitizens in one county alone, Sedgwick County, had attempted to register to vote since 1999. Kobach had
tried to slide this evidence past Ho and the ACLU lawyers in discovery
by summarizing the cases in a spreadsheet. Ho demanded the underlying
documents. His team could hardly believe what they found: almost every
case was an administrative error. One of those thirty-eight people had even
sent the voter registration card back to the county with "mistake" written
on it, because the person was not a citizen. Someone else noted, "Please put
in the record I am not a citizen. I cannot vote." Another person filled out the
line for a Social Security number starting with the "A" from his alien registration number.[21] On several other forms, in response to the question "Are
you a U.S. citizen?" people checked no. In cross-examination, it emerged
that only thirteen of those thirty-eight people made it onto the rolls; just
five cast a ballot over the course of nineteen years. "We're just like, 'This is
what you have?'" Ho says now, still astonished.

On the stand, Hans von Spakovsky clung to Kobach's Sedgwick
County spreadsheet, insisting that "Kansas clearly has had a problem with
noncitizens registering to vote." Ho was "chomping at the bit to go after
him," he says. On cross, Ho demanded to see the evidence underpinning
this claim. Von Spakovsky had none. He had based his entire claim about
tens of thousands of fraudulent votes on Sedgwick County.

Ho's performance was a star turn from a virtuoso who had spent three
years before law school training to be an actor, complete with eye-rolling,
sometimes with his back dismissively to the witness, punctuated by laughter and disbelief. "I let a lot of normal decorum fall away," he admits. "I
didn't mind conveying to people in the courtroom how absurd this was. I'm
not going to get him to admit that he's a liar, because that will never fucking work, right? I'll just show everything that you omitted, every piece of

evidence contrary to your opinion that you glided over, that you mischaracterized, places where it looks like you actually plagiarized a Kris Kobach press release in your expert report, used the exact same language. I'll just put it all up on the screen. I felt like I was hitting a punching bag just waiting to go in there."

Kobach, on the ropes, maintained the fraud he'd identified was merely the "tip of the iceberg."

In June 2018, Judge Robinson viewed it differently. "The Court draws the more obvious conclusion that there is no iceberg; only an icicle, largely created by confusion and administrative error."[22] The ruling noted that this trial was Kobach's opportunity to produce credible evidence but he "failed to do so," she wrote, refusing to accept "extrapolated numbers from tiny sample sizes and otherwise flawed data."

Robinson dismissed the Kansas citizenship requirement as a violation of the Motor Voter Act, but she didn't stop there. She also declared it unconstitutional, violating Fourteenth Amendment guarantees of equal protection under the law. That decision foreclosed Kobach and Trump from trying to push a similar bill through Congress. And then she ordered Kobach back to school, demanding that he complete six hours of legal education on Kansas's civil rules of procedure and evidence.

"We had a chance to put the voter fraud myth on trial," Ho says. "Not on Fox News, but in a courtroom. And to see what he had. He had nothing."

Maine's secretary of state Matt Dunlap wasn't going away, either. He, too, wanted to see what Kobach had and what the Electoral Integrity commission had been doing behind the scenes prior to its dissolution. Government attorneys argued that ending the commission ought also to end the battle over its records and void Dunlap's right to the documents. Dunlap, however, dug in and kept his case alive. First, he won a temporary restraining order to keep Kobach and others from shredding papers and wiping email servers. Then, in August 2018, he received all the documents and immediately posted all 8,000 pages online. Dunlap revealed exchanges between high-level White House aides; back-channel conversations between right-wing researchers, Kobach, and then-attorney general Jeff Sessions; and email chains limited to Kobach cronies and commission conservatives.

Kobach had been running an inquisition, not a commission, and his Keystone Kops weren't even bright enough to keep their tracks off email. "I've served on a lot of task forces. You work in good faith and try and find your way to yes," Dunlap says. "How naive. It wasn't until I actually read these documents that I realized how much of a fix was already in on this thing."

The emails[23] show that Kobach, from the very beginning, was so determined to have his preordained conclusions dominate the panel that he insisted that the word "diverse" be stricken from a description of the perspectives and experiences which the commission would represent. Von Spakovsky, meanwhile, advocated for keeping Democrats off the panel altogether, in an email that was forwarded to Sessions (the original recipients of the email were redacted). In late February 2017, before the commission had even been named, von Spakovsky said that including Democrats would "guarantee" an "abject failure," arguing that "[t]here isn't a single Democratic official that will do anything other than obstruct any investigation of voter fraud." This is either willful ignorance of the law surrounding presidential commissions, or disregard of it. A Republican commissioner, Christy McCormick, endorsed a Department of Justice statistician for the committee by noting she was "pretty confident that he is conservative (and Christian too)."

Kobach's focus was so relentless and monomaniacal that at 2:59 a.m., one June morning, Kobach informed Andrew Kossack, Mark Paoletta and Matthew Morgan in the vice president's office that he was revising, one more time, the order of the questions the commission would be sending to secretaries of state. The change was more than revealing. "I don't think voter intimidation should be listed before voter fraud. That is a secondary or tertiary concern of the commission."

Kobach and Pence's office also used vagueness and misdirection so that secretaries of state would not know exactly how the commission intended to use the requested files of voter data that they requested, so controversially, at the beginning of their work. Drafts suggested that Kobach wanted to vacuum large amounts of personal information—even of those excused from jury duty due to death, criminal convictions or citizenship status. And Kobach's intentions were not difficult to discern; he had created a program called CrossCheck which he used to determine, for instance, whether someone had voted in several states (the system generated more false positives than anything else, flagging people with the same last name, birthday, or last four digits of their Social Security number). The official request stated that the information would be used by the commission to "fully analyze vulnerabilities and issues related to voter registration and voting." Kobach's team hit on that language, however, only after several revisions. Early on, for example, they had hardly obscured their intentions at all, making it very clear that "the Commission may compare voter rolls to federal databases of known noncitizens residing in the United States to identify ineligible noncitizens." They appeared to be laying the groundwork for a massive campaign of intimidation, even deportation, all triggered by a Spanish-sounding last name.

Dunlap's lawsuit even unearthed a draft of the commission's final report, circulated by Kossack, which staffers had started writing in November 2017, after just two meetings. It's titled "Evidence of Election Integrity and Voter Fraud Issues," but it offers no more than a blank list of categories—"instances of fraudulent or improper voting," "noncitizen voting," etc.—that Kobach and his allies couldn't fill with any evidence at all. "Glaringly empty," Dunlap observes. In a letter to Pence and Kobach after he had reviewed those 8,000 pages, Dunlap named the larger problem: "That the Commission predicted it would find widespread evidence of fraud actually reveals a troubling bias," he wrote. "A very few commissioners worked to buttress their preordained conclusions shielded from dissent or dialogue."

Good thing Dunlap had that bullhorn, after all.

Kobach's year would only get worse. In November, he'd lose the gubernatorial election in Kansas.

Dunlap doesn't get those late-night calls from Kobach on his cell phone any longer. I ask him if he has ever thought about why Kobach personally recruited him onto the commission, why he spent so much time courting him to join. Did Kobach imagine that Dunlap would merely roll over and play Democrat, allowing the Republicans to have their way?

Dunlap opens his hands wide and points at the bear rug spread across his floor. "I'm a Democrat and I hunt and I have guns," he says. "It's weird to him. They probably saw this guy who's got a reputation for being non-partisan. Not a lawyer. From a small state. Can't be very smart. He won't give us too much trouble." Dunlap pauses and allows a small laugh. "Then I gave them trouble. They didn't know what to do with that."

Dale Ho, meanwhile, still wonders why Kobach "put on such a crappy case." In the end, Kobach's arrogance and ineptitude destroyed the voter registration bill he hoped would become a national model. Maybe that's it, he concludes. "They're bullshitters. They're just grabbing whatever threads they can to try to weave something together, to show you a picture they've already cooked up in their heads, regardless of the facts," Ho says. "They're not even that good at it. You don't need to be a detective to see through this bullshit. All you need to do is hold it up to the light." But as we'll see in North Dakota, Utah, North Carolina and many other states, however transparent and easily disproved these fraudulent claims might be, determined partisans continue to make them.

CHAPTER 4

Native Americans Battle Back

"There will be a lot more Native voices to hear from."

The driver's license office in Rolla, North Dakota, is open on the first Wednesday of every month, from 10:20 a.m. until 2:35 p.m., except from noon until 1 p.m., when it's closed for lunch. This is about as north as you can go in North Dakota, the last town along Route 30 before you reach the Canadian border, just 14 miles and one right turn away. The DMV is a small stand inside the combined city hall and public library. Downtown Rolla, dusty and low against a wide western sky, population 1,280, looks much as it did when it was first laid out in 1888. These days, you don't miss the homemade caramel rolls or the malted waffle at North 40. The fashions at the Golden Rule remain flannels, fleeces and flags. There's been one movie a week at Curt's Theatre for the past 103 years.

But something has changed in North Dakota that's made the three hours and fifteen minutes each month that this office is open for nearby residents to get a driver's license quite important. North Dakota is such a small state that it doesn't bother with voter registration. Precincts are small; everyone knows everyone. The method has worked so well that the nonpartisan Pew Charitable Trusts ranked the state best in the nation in its Elections Performance Index in 2008, 2010 and 2012.[1] Voter fraud, according to the secretary of state, was "virtually nonexistent."[2] There was one apparent instance in 2012, a teenager who appeared to have voted twice, once at college and then at home via absentee ballot. Officials gave him a stern talking-to and declared him "scared straight."[3]

In 2012, Heidi Heitkamp, a Democrat, captured one of North Dakota's U.S. Senate seats by just 2,996 votes, aided by particularly enthusiastic support from Native Americans, the state's largest minority group. The state legislature responded swiftly. In April 2013, and again in three consecutive sessions, the Republican-dominated body tightened North Dakota's voter ID law into the toughest in America.[4] The new law, written by state representative Randy Boehning of Fargo, required a valid state identification card complete with a street address. A passport, an expired out-of-state license, a utility bill, a military ID—all of these forms of ID, which had been perfectly acceptable to this point, were no longer good enough. Legislators also eliminated what had been called "fail-safe" backups that allowed poll workers in tiny towns to vouch for a resident they'd likely known their entire life. These new barriers—expensive, time-consuming and requiring long weekday trips during an extraordinarily limited window—struck Native Americans the hardest. Republicans said they were necessary to prevent fraud; Native Americans said they would prevent them from voting.[5]

And that's what happened. Lucille Vivier, a member of the Turtle Mountain Band of Chippewa Indians, arrived at the polls in November 2014 with her tribal ID. It had always been sufficient, but not this year. Vivier had tried her hardest to meet the requirements, but the voter ID law set a standard that was impossible for her to meet. The reservation doesn't have street addresses, or even mail delivery. Nevertheless, she spent $120 for a ride to the nearest Social Security office to try get the paperwork she needed, as well as another $40 for childcare for her five kids, including three with special needs. But that Social Security office wouldn't accept her tribal ID. On election day, the poll workers wouldn't either, turning her away even though one of them had known her since kindergarten.

Navy veteran Richard Brakebill, another member of the Turtle Mountain Band, proudly voted in nearly every election before he, too, was refused a ballot at the Rolla City Hall. His license had expired days earlier and his efforts to get a new one failed when he couldn't produce his Arkansas birth certificate. His possessions and paperwork had been destroyed in a house fire. Meanwhile, at the local Knights of Columbus hall where Elvis Norquay had voted for decades, save Novembers spent serving his country in Vietnam, another Native American left the polls frustrated and sad. The address on his ID did not match the homeless shelter where he'd been living. "It kind of brought me down, you know?" Norquay says, his Presleyesque jet-black hair pulled back into a long ponytail.

More than 5.2 million Native Americans currently live in the United States, and they call some of the most remote and difficult-to-access parts of the country home. Their road to the ballot box has always been a challenging one: Congress only granted America's original residents citizenship in 1924.[6] Their voting rights, however, had to be won state by state. It was not an easy fight; it took another three decades for some states to extend the franchise to Native Americans. New Mexico held out until 1962. Since then, voting hasn't gotten much easier. Indeed, throughout the mid-2010s, without the protections of the Voting Rights Act, intentional voter suppression techniques targeting Native Americans that might have been commonplace, if still shocking, fifty years ago have proliferated rapidly across North Dakota, Utah, Arizona and many other states.[7] As William Faulkner once wrote, "The past isn't dead. In fact, it's not even past."

The tactics have only become more surgical and disingenuous: demands for street addresses which legislators know Natives lack, or shuttering voting precincts on tribal land ostensibly for noncompliance with the Americans with Disabilities Act. Some western states have moved to voting by mail—well aware that many Native Americans might not be able to translate the language of ballot questions, for instance, or that Natives might receive mail at a post office box an hour away—accompanied by "ballot harvesting" laws that make it a felony for a fellow tribal member to drive a completed ballot back to town on behalf of an elder or someone without a car.

These purposeful barriers, however, have been met with determined resistance from optimistic tribal members and dedicated attorneys. In December 2017, a federal court in Utah would end a brutal racial gerrymander that had endured for decades, corralling a Navajo majority in San Juan County into one district and ensuring that the white minority controlled the other two seats. Nevada, under court order in 2017, added early voting locations on the Walker River Paiute and Pyramid Lake Paiute reservations after local election boards had closed polling stations and forced Natives to drive more than 100 miles to vote.[8] Meanwhile, Richard Brakebill, Lucille Vivier and Elvis Norquay were among the lead plaintiffs challenging the North Dakota voter ID law, which unleashed some of the most unexpected political aftershocks of 2018. Voting "means to make our country better," says Norquay, a lifelong Turtle Mountain resident who speaks inclusively and optimistically, and demands nothing more—or less—than to have his voice heard. "If you don't vote," he says, "you don't get to look forward to anything."[9]

For decades here in Utah's vast San Juan County, along the state's southeastern border, members of the Navajo Nation could look forward to only one of the three seats on the county commission, no matter how many of them cast ballots. The county is majority Navajo, but more than 90 percent of the Navajo have been packed into one of three wildly gerrymandered districts. That guarantees the white minority the other two seats and control of the board.

San Juan County is Utah's largest county; in terms of square miles, it's larger than New Jersey and Massachusetts, and nearly the size of Connecticut, Delaware and Rhode Island combined. This is stunning country. Everywhere you look are breathtaking canyons and red-rock formations so awe-inspiring they might drop you to your knees (or make you pull over every few miles to take a photo). The desert captures the majesty and trascendant allure of the wide-open American West, yet feels so otherworldly, more Martian than earthly, that it could be another planet altogether. Appropriately, it provided the backdrop for classic John Ford westerns like *The Searchers* and *Stagecoach*, but also the ethereal vistas of Stanley Kubrick's *2001: A Space Odyssey*.

It's very much two worlds. To the south, San Juan County is impoverished and majority Navajo. Nearly 72 percent of the residents are unemployed, and the only roads between far-off towns become impassable in rain or snow. Most homes lack running water and electricity, there are just three post offices over all these miles and you might drive hours without seeing gas or food, save for the small roadside stands selling jewelry and fry bread.

In the north of the county sit Blanding and Monticello, its two most populous towns, settled by Mormon missionaries in the late 1880s. Blanding's broad streets, as legend has it, were designed by Brigham Young to be wide enough for a driver to turn around his team of oxen without cursing.[10] When the Mormons arrived, they forcibly removed the Navajo and other native tribes, pushing those who weren't killed far south, into the desert beyond the San Juan River. They took the Natives' land, then they claimed all the power.

Only in 1957 did Utah allow Native Americans to vote, under court order. It was another three decades before the first Navajo won elected office. Until the mid-1980s, San Juan County's white voters took advantage of the oldest trick in the book: at-large elections. By allowing the entire county to vote for all three seats on the county commission, at-large elections assured that the powerful white voting bloc won all three. Mormon candidates from Blanding and Monticello received a further assist from county clerks who refused to register Navajo voters, knocked Navajo candidates off the ballot, and printed ballots only in English so that most Native Americans would find them impossible to navigate. The Department of Justice finally took notice in 1983[11] and forced the county to scrap the patently discriminatory at-large system and replace it with three districts, assuring the Navajo of a voice in county affairs. The districts the white minority drew, however, guaranteed themselves the largest voice. Blanding and Monticello were placed in separate districts, with 93 percent of the Navajo majority in the third—enforcing power through gerrymandering. Little changed for the Navajo. "We've been lied to and we've been messed with for years and years," Leonard Gorman, executive director of the Navajo Nation Human Rights Commission, tells me. New schools and libraries opened in the north, along with a publicly-funded community center with a golf course. Meanwhile, even into the 1990s, county officials denied they had any responsibility to educate Navajo students. When the U.S. Department of Justice examined the disparities, horrified investigators concluded that they "hadn't seen anything so bad since the '60s in the South."[12]

As I drive to meet Kenneth Maryboy, one of the Navajo county commissioners, who lives only about a mile off the main road, my rented SUV feels like a roller coaster as it bounces through potholes more like small trenches. I can't imagine what a school bus ride feels like. "It's like living in a hellhole," Kenneth tells me at his home outside Bluff, with rolling red mesas and green sage as far as you can see. The only noise is the sound of barking dogs. His tiny yellow ranch-style house is decorated with plastic pumpkins and cobwebs for Halloween; bloody handprints on the front door spell out "Help us," as if zombies have gotten to everyone inside. Only help doesn't come regularly to the Navajo in San Juan County.

County officials didn't bother redistricting after the 1990, 2000 or 2010 censuses. They claimed that the consent agreement with the Department of Justice prevented them from altering the lines, but really they wanted to preserve a permanent two-to-one edge and hoped that no one would notice. The county commission even pulled an ugly bait-and-switch on Gorman in 2011. He and the county had reached a deal, under which both the Navajo and the commission would draw a set of maps, then both proposals would be sent to a judge for consideration. The commission agreed, then simply acted as if their maps were the only ones, ignoring the Navajo proposal altogether and denying that the deal meant what it said.

Later, the commission told Gorman that the 1980s arrangement with the federal government was in perpetuity. "Instituted forever and ever," says Gorman. "On one side," he says, with amazing equanimity, "the story is forever changing. On our side, we're forever baffled."

In 2016, the Navajo Nation sued the county, alleging that the districts violated the voting protections in the Fourteenth and Fifteenth Amendments. County officials railed against "predatory attorneys" preying on "one of the poorest counties in the nation" and imagining a "racial divide that simply doesn't exist in San Juan County." But a federal judge decided enough was enough. "Keeping an election district in place for decades without regular reconsideration is unusual in any context," wrote U.S. district judge Robert Shelby. In the context of San Juan County, however, "it offends basic democratic principles." He ordered the county commission districts, as well as those of the school board, redrawn by a neutral "special master," in the name of "binding precedent, common sense and the interest of justice."[13] When this was done, two of the three new districts had a Navajo majority. Maryboy, whose older brother was the first Native American elected to the county commission after the districts were installed in 1986, announced his candidacy for one of them. Suddenly no one from Monticello or Blanding even wanted to stand against him. Maryboy ran unopposed.

"There's nothing easy for the Native American in San Juan County," says Maryboy, his eyes fixed on the far horizon. "But nevertheless, we won. They fight us all the way to the end. We have to fight for everything. Everything. This is the only way we do things in San Juan County."

So, perhaps unsurprisingly, the next battle was just beginning.

⬤

Willie Grayeyes meets me at the Recapture Lodge in tiny, artsy Bluff. This is the gateway to Bears Ears National Monument, and Grayeyes has led the Navajo struggle to preserve the full 1.35-million-acre landscape. Local officials and the Trump administration have battled to reduce it by as much as

85 percent. Grayeyes's 2009 Nissan Altima has more than 400,000 miles on it and feels like a hotel room itself, filled with water bottles, toothpaste tubes and multiple changes of clothes. He is seeking the most competitive seat on the county commission, district two, and his Republican opponent is the father of San Juan County's attorney. It's less than two weeks until election day, so the Recapture Lodge and this Altima have become home—it beats the more than three hours and 135 miles across the desert to his home in Navajo Mountain. That's a torturous trip even in good weather: there is no direct road across Monument Valley. You have to drive southwest into Arizona, then backtrack north across the Utah line. There's no mail service, either, and the closest post office boxes are inside the General Store off Highway 160 in Tonalea, Arizona. (More on that later.) Just try running a political campaign here. "This is not walking down one street and knocking on doors," Leonard Gorman tells me. "No, no, no. You knock on one door, drive down the road twenty minutes, maybe someone's home. We employed that for five months."

This is the essence of what the Navajo endure in San Juan County: Grayeyes's lodge is named after Recapture Canyon, which is prized for its ancient Native American artifacts and delicate archeology. The 2nd district seat is currently held by Phil Lyman, who was once convicted and jailed for leading an ATV caravan through the canyon, whooping and waving American flags, to protest federal land management. It's a sign of what's now possible in San Juan County that Grayeyes could claim Lyman's seat. "They've been in control for I don't know how many years," Grayeyes tells me as we approach the Twin Rocks Cafe, a diner that sits at the base of a stunning red-rock canyon, the majestic dual formations rising like conjoined twins. "Probably ever since the county was established."

We both order the blue corn cakes and coffee, and as we wait for breakfast, Grayeyes describes the line between San Juan County's conservative, Mormon towns and the Democratic-leaning Navajo Nation as the "invisible wall." Where Maryboy's frustration boils into anger, Grayeyes appears unflappable, his wiry silver hair pulled back into a ponytail, then wrapped into a bun. He notes that the county receives federal dollars based on its size and population, but then "water, natural resources, education dollars—they all stop there." Nothing flows south over the invisible wall. "It does not matter how many miles we have, or how many people." He's running to change the county's behavior, he says, to be sure that resources reach the underserved and the unemployed. "Where are the roads? Health services? Public safety? Telecommunications infrastructure? We need to break that wall down, one stone at a time." After that, Grayeyes calmly says, he'd love to run a professional audit of the county's financial records.

Unsurprisingly, this does not sit well with county leaders, already angered by outsiders drawing new districts and threatening their long-held power. Grayeyes has spent fifty years living on Navajo Mountain. His family is there and, by Navajo tradition, his umbilical cord is buried there. He'd been registered to vote there for the last thirty-four years, and hadn't missed an election since the early 1990s. But on March 20, 2018, Wendy Black, a Republican candidate for the 2nd district seat, sent a note to the county clerk, John David Nielson. It has "been brought to my attention," she wrote, that Grayeyes "may" live in Arizona.[14] Remember that Arizona mailing address, necessary since Navajo Mountain lacks delivery or street addresses? Black and Nielson had no proof. But they thought this might allow them to disqualify Grayeyes from the race. Had they followed the law, an official complaint would have triggered a letter to Grayeyes within forty-eight hours, asking for proof of residency. Instead, Nielson called the sheriff and asked him to send a deputy down to Navajo Mountain to investigate. Then on April 16, according to court documents, long after that two-day window had closed, the clerk reached out to Black and asked her to file her complaint in writing. By this time, Black had lost the Republican nomination to the ironically named Kelly Laws, the father of the county attorney, and remained bitter. But, she emailed Nielson, "I REALLY don't think Willie should be there." Black stopped by city hall, and together they worked out the complaint, which claimed that Black had made the trip to Navajo Mountain herself and found Grayeyes's house "not livable, windows boarded up. Roof dilapidated. No tracks going into house for years."[15]

There were just a few problems with this. First, there's no proof she actually made the trip. Second, Black and the county clerk conspired to illegally backdate the April complaint to March 20, after the deadline had been missed by weeks. Third, when they finally notified Grayeyes, he responded with his years of voting records, Google Earth images of his house, documentation of the cattle operation he runs on that land, and a public invitation to Nielson to visit. Nielson sent the police instead. Grayeyes wasn't home when they arrived and, on May 9, the clerk accepted that unanswered knock as sufficient evidence to disqualify him from the race. The San Juan County attorney—the man whose father was seeking the office himself—even sent this half-baked case to an outside prosecutor for possible criminal charges against Grayeyes. The prosecutor refused to file them.

When Grayeyes sued for reinstatement, the entire Keystone Kops conspiracy unraveled. His attorneys deposed Nielson, who admitted everything.

"The second page of this shows it being completed and signed on March 20, 2018."

"Yes."

"That is false. Correct?"

"Yes."

"And you signed it as her having signed on the 20th of March."

"Yes."

"That was false, too. Correct?"

"It was."[16]

It took no time at all for the outraged federal judge to place Grayeyes back on the ballot in August, ruling that "virtually no aspect of Nielson's handling of this matter was legal or within the scope of his role." The state of Utah decided it needed to send election day watchdogs to San Juan County, to guard against additional shenanigans. Grayeyes's attorney, Steven Boos, compared the county's actions to a case from the early 1970s, when election officials intentionally misled a Navajo candidate about filing deadlines. "The Grayeyes stuff makes it seem as though in the last half century nothing has changed," says Boos, "which is a sad commentary."

Perhaps the only person unsurprised by all this was Grayeyes himself. "Clean politics," he observes wryly. "Those things don't bother me. They seemed to be digging around to see where I sleep, or where I hang up my clothes and stuff like that. I don't get angry. It's not my doing. It's theirs. Whatever they do, it's just a game, a political game. The only way to address it is not to give up."

But even maintaining the basic faith that things can get better is hard in San Juan County. Gorman, of the Navajo Nation Human Rights Commission, walks with a stoop and his goatee has gone gray, every step and every strand betraying the battles not just against the power structure but within his own community, as he tries to lift spirits and maintain hope. "Unfortunately, the majority of my people have been repressed for a long, long time. They're convinced that there will be no change. That repression is still going on to this day in San Juan County government, like the sheriff's office. It's a very difficult thing to overcome when we try to send the message that change is on its way."

Yet it is. Grayeyes went to bed early on election night, so it wasn't until the next morning that he learned he'd been elected to the San Juan County commission. First, he'd defeated those who had twisted the laws for their own gain, and then he knocked off Kelly Laws, claiming the seat by 159 votes and almost 10 percentage points. When he and Kenneth Maryboy took their seats, Navajos had control of the commission for the first time.

"The challenges we face every day will no doubt continue," Grayeyes says. "The opposition has also been displayed here and there throughout the county. . . . But changes are already taking place—and it's starting with the redistricting."

The suppression efforts that nearly removed Willie Grayeyes from Utah's ballot and kept Richard Brakebill, Elvis Norquay and Lucille Vivier from casting theirs in North Dakota share the same roots: they are attempts to maintain power by manipulating the rules. In San Juan County, the silencing of the Navajo had become part of the culture, a structure of privilege and superiority imposed by Mormon settlers some 140 years ago and now just another reason why this land feels so haunted and raw. But while Native Americans in North Dakota have hurdled many barriers to the ballot, the state's current voter ID bill—demanding residential street addresses that Natives simply do not have—is a thoroughly modern and surgically targeted creation. North Dakota's legislature considered tightening its election procedures in 2011, but eleven Democrats and twenty-seven Republicans joined together to reject new ID provisions, citing concerns that they could keep Native Americans and others lacking official identification from voting. The number of voter fraud prosecutions after the 2012 elections here was a memorable round number: zero.

Something else, then, pushed voter ID to the top of the North Dakota GOP legislative agenda the following year. Legislators didn't conduct a single study, hold a public hearing or investigate the issue at all. So what motivated them to enact one of the nation's strictest voter ID laws, in a state with no voter fraud? What drove a bill that demanded the one thing—a street address—a Democratic-leaning swing constituency did not have? Honest Republican legislators openly conceded that the victory by Democrat Heidi Heitkamp spurred this legislation. "I think that shined a light on it in a way that it was decided that now we should fix the issue," says Dan Ruby, a Republican representative in the state house. But Ruby insists that he didn't want to keep anyone away from the polls. "We hear the other side say that, 'They want to suppress the Native Americans from voting,'" he told *The Nation*. "Nobody said that. I've never heard one person say, 'Yup, we need to keep certain people that vote against us out.'"[17]

Perhaps not. But plenty of people, inside the legislature and out, warned them that that would be the real-world impact. Tribe members couldn't provide addresses they did not have. Norquay and other homeless people were effectively disenfranchised as well. On election day 2014, it showed. It wasn't just Brakebill, Norquay and Vivier who were prevented from voting: Native American turnout plummeted, even as statewide turn-out held steady from the previous midterm, in 2010. Turtle Mountain saw its turnout dip by double digits, from 45 percent in 2010 to barely 33 per-cent in 2014.

Republican legislators responded by turning the screws tighter. In 2015, the legislature toughened the ID law, disallowing college IDs. They also eliminated most every "fail-safe" provision that allowed a poll worker to grant a provisional ballot if they could vouch for that person's identity. A federal court paused the new law until lawmakers reinstated the "fail-safe" backup plan, allowing citizens without an ID, but with a valid address, to swear an affidavit and vote provisionally. The court noted how targeted the law appeared, and that, in order to obtain the ID the legislature required, it "helps to have a computer with Internet access, a credit card, a car, the ability to take time off work and a familiarity with government and its bureaucracy. The typical Native American in North Dakota without ID lacks all that."[18]

The new law, the court found, imposed burdens that outweighed any reasonable state interest. It also solved a problem that didn't exist—voter fraud—while creating a voter suppression problem that the state, which had until recently not even required voters to register, had never had in the past. There is, Judge Daniel Hovland wrote, "a total lack of evidence to show that voter fraud has ever been a problem in North Dakota."[19] The affidavit provision enabled some Native Americans to vote, but the pure number of them provided new evidence of what an obstacle the new ID law had become—and whom it affected most. In 2016, the number of requested affidavits nearly *tripled* from 2012. They soared by 750 percent in the three North Dakota counties with the largest percentage of Native Americans, and they dropped by 11 percent in the three counties with the smallest.

The response from Republican legislators? That's right: they tripled down on voter ID and moved to reduce the number of affidavits, not by loosening the ID restrictions but by tightening conditions under which even a provisional ballot could be counted. Under the new law, a voter without ID could cast the provisional ballot but, for it to count, he or she would have to produce the necessary ID—with the street address that, again, often did not exist—to a county clerk within six days of the election. In private emails, Republican officials gloated, knowing that very few voters could meet such a standard. "Many individuals who cast them will not likely come into your office later to verify their qualifications," wrote Jim Silman, the deputy secretary of state, in an email to a county auditor.[20] "Since these voters don't return to verify their registration status, the cost for a ballot and an envelope is a small price to pay."

Judge Hovland, fed up, put an end to the chicanery once again. His injunction pointed out that the new law "still requires voters to have one of the very same forms of a qualifying ID in order to vote that was previously found to impose a discriminatory and burdensome impact on Native Americans. . . . No eligible voter, regardless of their station in life, should be denied the opportunity to vote."[21] This time, however, the 8th Circuit overturned his ruling, conceding that while Native Americans could be harmed, that was outweighed by the state's interest in guarding against voter fraud. By the time the case reached the U.S. Supreme Court, just weeks before the 2018 midterms, the justices decided not to get involved, on the grounds that it would confuse matters close to an election.

If the courts would not protect the voting rights of North Dakota's Native Americans, the tribes would need a creative new plan—and fast.

In South Antelope, South Dakota, O. J. "Oliver" Semans's phone blew up with messages. Oliver and his wife, Barb, are the founders of Four Directions, America's leading nonpartisan Native voter engagement and protection organization in the nation, and as Judge Hovland's positive spring ruling morphed into the disappointing fall punt by the U.S. Supreme

Court, all hopes turned to them. The courts and the North Dakota politicians had suggested it would be easy for Native Americans to obtain a street address. The secretary of state's office said that all they needed to do was dial the emergency services, describe their location, and the sheriff's office would have an address assigned within an hour. Natives, uneager to engage with law enforcement, didn't love that option. But those who were willing to try found it much harder than that. One woman on Standing Rock reservation spent several days trying to reach the sheriff on the phone; he seemed to be out every time she called. A tribal elder named Terry Yellow Fat finally reached the sheriff and received an address. Turns out, the address was for a bar. Yellow Fat worried that if he used an address on his ID that he knew was wrong, he might get arrested for voter fraud.[22]

As Semans heard the stories from Standing Rock and other locations, he had an idea: what if the tribe mapped their land and assigned street addresses, then printed new tribal IDs that included them? It would be a complicated and expensive project, and they only had twenty-five days. Semans called a longtime ally, Jean Schroedel, a political science professor at Claremont Graduate University in California and one of the nation's leading experts on Native Americans and the vote. "People don't pay attention to it because it's in these rural areas that are a long ways away from population centers. Folks say, 'Oh, who cares about Indians? They're a very small group.' Yes," Schroedel says, passion and agitation in her voice, "but they're small for a reason. It's not a good reason."

Schroedel doesn't draw maps, but she sent an urgent email to her colleague Brian Hilton, a professor at Claremont's Center for Information Systems and Technology and an expert in GIS mapping software. Right away, they were looking at maps. Standing Rock reservation has a little under two thousand roads or road segments. They needed to be named, and the structures needed numbers. "Then we would have to sit down with the people and figure out where they actually lived," Schroedel tells me. "It's not feasible. You would have to have massive resources. We didn't. But we could do rough estimates. It's not perfect, but it's the best we could do."

Hilton used a program called RGIS that allowed him to bring in multiple layers of information from satellites and maps. He could zoom into certain areas, see what streets actually existed, then toggle back to the satellite imagery and see if there were any homes on those streets. In each precinct of the tribal land, he created quadrants, and each quadrant received an address. "It's somewhat laborious," he told a GIS industry publication.[23] But Hilton kept at it for days, and managed to create a spreadsheet of addresses and precincts for Standing Rock, Spirit Lake and Turtle Mountain. That was overlaid onto a PDF map, and addresses were assigned.

Then the frantic push began to put IDs into as many hands as possible. When more than 250 people showed up at Turtle Mountain's tribal government building one day, the ID machine actually burned out. Semans's team quickly ordered four more. News media deluged the small Four Directions office in Fort Yates, the capital of Standing Rock. Volunteers met reporters at the Family Dollar store and led them to Four Directions, which, sure enough, lacked a street address accessible by GPS. The musician Dave Matthews and the actor Mark Ruffalo came to town for a fundraiser. Readers of the progressive Daily Kos website crowd-sourced another $400,000 in small donations. "People mobilized," Prairie Rose Seminole, the director of Native Vote, tells me. "If you live along a rural road, they're numbering the houses. Tribes are meeting the demand for addresses and ID. People are knocking on doors. Do you need an ID? Do you plan on voting? Do you need a ride?"

In every community, Seminole says, "it's desperate lengths." Canvassers spread out across the vast lands—some reservations stretch over millions of acres and several counties—going door to door, even when it could be miles between doors. They wanted people to match the location of their homes to a precinct on the new map, if WiFi service allowed it. Not everyone wanted to talk, or believed their vote mattered. But others hadn't heard about the new requirements and hopped in the van for a ride to tribal headquarters, where the cost of a new ID had been waived. "If we're not doing this," asked Cesar Alvarez, on NBC, battling back in Four Beats Village with just a clipboard and faith in democracy, "who will?"[24]

An Episcopal priest for two churches in towns close to Standing Rock stepped up as well. The Reverend John Floberg used the 911 system to get street addresses for his churches, then announced he would use them as homeless shelters during election week. Native Americans were welcome to stay and claim the church's address as their own. "Is this finding a loophole?" Floberg asked a public radio reporter, rhetorically. "If the state of North Dakota wants to play games, then we'll find ways to do that."[25]

Danielle Lang, an attorney with the Campaign Legal Center in Washington, DC, wasn't ready to give up either.[26] Lang had won key victories, which few had imagined possible, for voting rights in Alabama and Arizona. She noticed one line in the circuit court's decision: the judge vowed that courthouse doors "would remain open" if any voters were prevented from casting a ballot. She took that as a personal invitation to find a plaintiff. She dropped everything, grabbed a flight to North Dakota and drove to Spirit Lake. Lang understood the street address problem intellectually. Then she tried to drive on tribal lands. A street would be labeled one thing on Google Maps, something else on Bing, then have an entirely different name on the state's official map, and perhaps a fourth name on a street sign, when a sign existed. "Nearly everyone I met used their P.O. boxes for everything," she recalls. "Driving around the reservation, it was easy to understand why." Lang calls it Kafkaesque, the bizarre need to prepare a legal argument for why a residential address requirement didn't make sense in a land where no one had them.

Lang and the tireless Native Americans Rights Fund found a plaintiff in Dion Jackson, whose 2018 absentee ballot had been rejected because the residential address he used was ruled invalid. While the address worked just fine for FedEx deliveries, he says, it wasn't in the North Dakota Department of Transportation's database. Jackson, Lang says, thought that was that, just another indignity of reservation life which he didn't have any power to address. But when he signed on to the lawsuit, Jackson found his voice. He began speaking out in the media. "To me, it almost seems like the state does not want Native Americans to be heard, they just expect to take advantage of us again." Terry Yellow Fat joined the case. So did Leslie and Clark Peltier, who live on trust land just north of Turtle Mountain, in Belcourt. They've been in the same house for a dozen years, and received almost as many addresses from the state. In one election, poll workers told them they should not be voting in Belcourt, but in nearby St. John. Their 911 address is in Belcourt, but the secretary of state's office says it's in St. John. "We are trying to follow the state's program as much as possible, but the addresses don't match," says Leslie Peltier. "I'm afraid that I may not be able to exercise my right to vote on election day because of the discrepancies."[27] A concerned Judge Holland ultimately decided he could not halt the ID requirement days before an election, but Lang and NARF won a court order ensuring that Dion, Peltier, Yellow Fat and other plaintiffs could vote.

"Before we are done," Lang says, "there will be a lot more Native voices to hear from."

That road might be long, but the journey is underway. North Dakota's voter ID law threatened the right of Native Americans to vote. But on election day, Native Americans turned out in massive numbers to protect it. The state didn't make it easy, but the tribes met every challenge. In Sioux County, home to Standing Rock, turnout surged to 52.5 percent, the highest since 2008—a 105 percent increase over the 2014 midterms and a 17 percent jump over the presidential election year of 2016. Benson County, where Spirit Lake is located, also had presidential-year turnout for a midterm. Turtle Mountain reached its highest level in more than a decade—up 62 percent from 2014 and more than 33 percent from 2016.[28] "We topped the highest turnout since 2008—pretty cool," Semans marveled. "I didn't think we could do it. But when I started working with the youth council— they put this together in four days. I saw the enthusiasm."[29]

The Native American surge couldn't save Heidi Heitkamp, who lost her bid for a second term in the U.S. Senate. But it was a different story in Fargo. Remember Randy Boehning, the legislator who wrote the original voter ID bill? He not only lost his bid for a fourth term, but fell to Ruth Buffalo, the first Native American Democratic woman ever elected to North Dakota's state house. "It's crazy that it happened that way," Buffalo tells me, still amazed seven months after taking office. Buffalo had family and friends living on tribal land whose voting precincts were shut down, ostensibly for budget reasons. "Which is hard to comprehend," she told the *New York Times*, "because they're in the middle of oil country."[30] They had to drive around the Little Missouri River, an extra forty-five minutes, all the way to Killdeer. But they voted.

"The harder the odds, the harder you need to fight back," says Semans. "You don't give up."

CHAPTER 5

Michigan's Redistricting Revolution

"We were tired of sitting on the sidelines."

Long odds and hard fights don't intimidate Katie Fahey either. Lin-Manuel Miranda writes *Hamilton* songs about the likes of her: young, scrappy and hungry, and not throwing away her shot. As the results of the 2016 presidential election became known, Fahey's Facebook page was a cesspool of gloating Trump supporters, horrified liberals researching Canada's immigration policies, and friends and family members at one another's throats. Trump's 10,912-vote margin in Michigan included Fahey's parents and many close family members, and the fury on her feed made her anxious about having to dodge flying mashed potatoes and airborne cranberry sauce during Thanksgiving dinner.

Fahey, then twenty-seven, had scored a ticket to Hillary Clinton's victory party in Manhattan, donned her best red pantsuit, and flew from Detroit to New York City to celebrate with the first woman president. Now all she wanted to do was curl up in sweatpants and mourn. She'd watched, inspired, as friends who never got involved researched the finer points of childcare policy and had debates at birthday parties, or waited hours to see a candidate speak. Now her feed was full of recrimination and despair: friends calling each other evil or, worse, wondering why they'd bothered at all.

All that vitriol shook Fahey out of her own malaise. At around 8 a.m. two days after Clinton's defeat, before heading to work at a recycling non-profit, Fahey took to Facebook herself. "I'd like to take on gerrymandering in Michigan," she wrote. "If you're interested in doing this as well, please let me know." Then she added a smiley-face emoji, for charm. An optimist and a doer by nature, Fahey recognized what bound her Facebook friends together, even as they screamed at one another: a sense that our political system was broken. Calls for a political revolution to drain the swamp, to do away with a malfunctioning Electoral College: all denoted the hollowed-out beams of the same rotting infrastructure. "If that's really it, why don't we start there?" she tells me. "I wanted to talk about fixing stuff—not candidates or political parties." Fair electoral maps, she thought, would at least reinstill the belief that every vote counts.

She wasn't the only one. At the time, it seemed ridiculous that a Facebook post could save democracy rather than sow more dissension and disinformation. Fahey had posted a similar call to action three years earlier, which generated no replies at all. But this one would be different. By the time she reached the office, her post had started to go viral. The likes were adding up, shares were mounting and direct messages were pouring in. "I remember calling a coworker and saying, 'There are thirty or forty people who want to do this. Do you think we should really do this?" says Fahey, a dark-haired dynamo with an easy smile, as she gives me a tour of her parents' all-American suburban ranch house, where she wrote the post. They checked Ballotpedia and learned that a ballot initiative would require 315,654 signatures gathered in 180 days. That seemed impossible. But if they could turn those thirty people into 3,000, that would mean just fifteen signatures a week per person. "I'm a Millennial. If my friends' dog needs surgery, they crowdfund it," she says. Why not fix a gasping democracy the same way?

Fahey had never organized anything other than the Grand Rapids Improv Fest. But that training had taught her how to jump in with a hearty "yes and . . . ," the up-for-it attitude of any good improv actor. She was already the friend people called to complain about their boyfriend or job and hung up with a four-part plan to fix their life. So that afternoon she launched a Facebook group, Michiganders For Nonpartisan Redistricting Reform, and sent out invitations. Anyone could join after agreeing to a few simple rules. They had to represent themselves, not a party or politician. They had to keep the conversation among just the group, so that everyone could talk freely. They had to agree that the mission was to create a system that worked for all voters, not to manipulate the game for either side. Finally, sneering stories about the new president were banned. "Nope! You can do that anywhere else on the Internet," Fahey says, "but not here."

Google spreadsheets organized volunteers, schedules and strengths. Strategy calls took place over Google Hangout and video conferencing. Strangers became friends. Committees formed: policy, communication, outreach, fundraising, education and field operations. They got to work crafting the language of a state constitutional amendment and collecting signatures to put it on the ballot. All the while, experts told them it couldn't be done here—but they ignored them. They did eventually choose a catchier name, though: Voters Not Politicians. Over the next two years, they built a volunteer citizen army to conquer gerrymandering and the powerful, well-funded interests that had turned Michigan into one of the least representative states in the country. Deep-pocketed opponents tried to stop them at the Michigan Supreme Court, controlled 5–2 by GOP appointees, but failed. The state Chamber of Commerce wanted to drown their proposed amendment in dark money and negative ads, but overwhelming public support made them think twice. Finally, the Michigan Freedom Fund, part of the conservative DeVos network, spent well into seven figures trying to derail it at the ballot box.

Katie Fahey and her Facebook friends crushed them all.

"It's easy to complain," former California governor and anti-gerrymandering crusader Arnold Schwarzenegger tells me, marveling over Fahey's gumption. "But then to go up and say, 'I'm going to do something about it! That's what she did."

Gerrymandering sounds wonky. It reminds people of falling asleep in high school civics, and if it didn't already mean rewiring democracy, you could easily imagine marketing an insomnia cure under that brand name. Voters know better in Michigan, however, which became ground zero for one of the most radical gerrymanders in the nation. Republican strategists—including a visionary named Bob LaBrant, a Chamber of Commerce mastermind who taught the GOP the importance of smart districting—armed with infinite resources and patience, captured both houses of Michigan's state legislature in 2010 as well as the governor's office. Complete control of government granted them unfettered dominance over the decennial redistricting that followed in 2011. Republicans remapped aggressively and penned Democrats into 5 of the state's 14 congressional districts, then drew themselves such an advantage in the state house that the GOP managed to keep control in 2012, 2016 and 2018 even when they won fewer total votes than Democrats. The legislature, emboldened by unbeatable districts, then passed an emergency manager law that allowed the state to take control of cash-strapped municipalities, a measure so unpopular that citizens repealed it the following year. The impervious legislature reinstated it, with a provision that citizens could not remove it again. Then an emergency manager in Flint, looking to save a little money, switched the city's water supply to the Flint River, contaminating the water, raising lead levels and perhaps unleashing a deadly outbreak of legionnaire's disease.

Nevertheless, Voters Not Politicians expected a tiny crowd for their first public meeting, on March 4, 2017, in Marquette, a small town in the state's often-forgotten Upper Peninsula. They got seventy people: standing room only at the public library for a talk about redistricting that had only been announced three days before. "That's when I knew we were on to something," Fahey tells me. Over the next thirty-two nights, Voters Not Politicians held another thirty-two meetings. The audiences kept growing.

Hundreds of people turned out in urban Lansing and Detroit, collegiate Ann Arbor, and small-town Pentwater and Monroe. Fahey had the instinctive savvy to understand that this crusade needed to be nonpartisan. She described gerrymandering as an "assault on our fundamental rights" as voters. "It's not one party doing it to another," she'd say, again and again. "It's the game that's flawed."

People in Michigan wanted new rules. The game could be flawed, but at least it should be fair. Suddenly, those 3,000 volunteers and 315,654 signatures seemed like less of a dream. Everyone who attended a meeting received a survey on which they could suggest ideas for fixing the problem. More than 1,000 people provided input to the VNP policy committee, chaired by Nancy Wang, an environmental law professor, and also including retired judges, a veterinarian, and a birthing doula. They opened the committee to anyone who wanted to participate, Wang says, because "we wanted to make sure we created something that was by and for the people of Michigan."

Months of discussion and debate led to a proposal for a model commission that they would take to the ballot: thirteen members that would be comprised of five independents, four Republicans, and four Democrats, selected through a random application process and far removed from any political connection. It would force consensus, mirroring the politics so many would like to see, by requiring not only majority support to pass a map, but also buy-in from at least two members of each group. No faction could conspire with another to disadvantage anyone else. And it would guarantee transparency, public input and impartiality.[1]

Earnest language and smart proposals, however, meant nothing if VNP couldn't take it to the people. That would require some 315,000 signatures, collected over just 180 days, across this state of 10 million people. "We had a plan," field director Jamie Lyons-Eddy told the *Atlantic*. "We needed 3,000 people to get ten to fifteen signatures a week."[2] They also needed to hire lawyers to vet the proposition's language, and make alliances with the NAACP, the League of Women Voters and other key organizations.

National organizations who hadn't wanted any part of an expensive fight in Michigan—a difficult state where good initiative ideas go to die—slowly watched this effort blossom and came on board. And in August 2017, when the secretary of state's office approved the text of the proposition, 4,000 volunteers—including Fahey's conservative mom and dad—fanned out statewide, to every local fair, farmers' market, highway rest area, Labor Day parade, college football tailgate, even the Cheeseburger Festival in Caseville, to collect signatures. Bob LaBrant, meanwhile, eyed the young activists with as much amusement as interest.

"I was very skeptical. Volunteer efforts generally crash and burn," LaBrant told me over coffee at the Grand Traverse Pie Company across from Michigan's state capitol. The mastermind behind the GOP's original campaign to remap Michigan soon realized that this one was different. "But when they got their petition approved and went into the field, you knew by October that it would garner enough signatures. They were out en masse, week after week after week. They were meticulous about dotting their i's and crossing their t's. This is probably the cleanest petition drive people have ever seen. It's very impressive."

In Michigan history, only one group ever attained ballot access without resorting to paid signature gatherers: anti-abortion initiatives sponsored by Right to Life of Michigan. They did have paid staff, professional organizers and an easy-to-activate network of churches. Voters Not Politicians had none of those advantages, yet blew the number away with all volunteers—gathering more than 434,000 names—and reached the target with seventy days to spare.

"I remember learning about democracy—one person one vote, how great our government is—and then you learn about gerrymandering," Fahey says. "I remember asking my fourth-grade teacher, 'Why don't we do anything about this?' Why don't we fix it if we know that politicians cheat? We're taught about the spirit of democracy. I was the sucker who believed it.

"We were tired of sitting on the sidelines," she says. "If we want an end to gerrymandering, we the people have to do it."

On a rainy Tuesday in September 2018, the Voters Not Politicians office in Lansing, located on the upper floor of a former school building in Old Town, has even more activity than the kickboxing parlor across the hall. Election day is less than seven weeks away, and volunteers busily cut "turf"—the neighborhood that door-knockers will hit that evening—while canvassers load clipboards with pamphlets and other materials. A giant homemade tapestry puzzles together Michigan's gerrymandered districts out of brightly colored fabric swatches, surrounded by patriotic images of flags, farmland and Fords. "All political power is inherent in the people," it proclaims, quoting the opening words of the state constitution. In bright blue "Slay the Gerrymander" or red "Yes on Two" T-shirts, volunteers of all ages and races download the territory they'll cover that evening onto an iPhone app called Minivan, which guides them straight to the likeliest supporters and key persuadables. While the activists dread a dark-money onslaught of negative TV ads, they've decided the best course of action is to talk to as many people as they can—knocking on an astonishing 30,000 doors statewide some days. "When you get a chance to explain it to them, people are really quite keen," says super-volunteer Karen Twyman.

I head into the field with Twyman and Gail Harvey, another volunteer, and we drive toward Michigan State University. "When I stopped crying after Hillary lost, I thought, I have to do something about gerrymandering," Twyman says. Later that month, a fellow church member mentioned that there was a meeting about that coming up in Dewitt, about fifteen minutes away. That Saturday was freezing, and there had been a snowstorm the night before. Twyman thought the meeting might be canceled, but a hardcore team turned out, including Fahey. Twyman signed on to circulate petitions.

"Remember where I parked the car!" she says as we head out to finish a turf before sundown. These leafy streets are friendly. We meet people who signed the original petition, and while not everyone knows what Proposition 2 is—the canvassers mention it by name so voters will know what to look for—all they have to say is "gerrymandering" and everyone is on board. "That's what's fun about it," she says, "when you meet people you don't know and they're for it. Oh, my heart!"

Everyone adjourns to nearby Zoobie's Old Town Tavern for pizza and beer after the evening canvass, along with something else all-American: nostalgia for the old days. "We were all too motivated and fired up to know that we couldn't do this," says Walt Sorg, a retired veteran of the state commerce department, his gray hair neatly parted to one side. "All the pros told us, 'You're doing it backwards.' Which we did! We did do it backwards. But we worked the *Field of Dreams* philosophy. If you build it, they will come."

Volunteers even figured out how to make do-it-yourself recycled clipboards. Canvassers needed almost 5,000 of them, custom-sized to hold the petition papers, and at between five and seven dollars each, that would have been a sizable early expense. On Facebook, a woodcarver volunteered to make them from Masonite hardboard in his workshop and to connect the group with others who hated gerrymandering and had access to professional-grade saws. The group bought large pieces of hardboard at Lowe's and designed exactly the clipboards they needed. The average cost? Ten cents apiece.

Susan Skidmore, a former pharmaceutical sales rep trained to be motivated by numbers, helped pass those clipboards out, then led everyone in signatures collected. Her secret: highway rest areas. She even mapped out the various turnpike stops by peak traffic flow. "I'm used to making my numbers," she tells me. "But I literally became insane." She gathered more than 3,000 signatures. "Thanksgiving, instead of eating turkey dinner, I drove to Detroit, collected signatures at the Turkey Trot, and then hit the rest area on the way home. Pens were freezing. People were posting that it was like *Game of Thrones*: 'Winter is coming.'"

Watching all this unfold, LaBrant still couldn't believe the grass-roots intensity. He spotted the signature gatherers at a rest stop along Interstate 96 in Howell, and told a local NBC affiliate that VNP was "making the petition management industry look bad." He marveled that "Wherever two or more are gathered, they've been there."[3]

Behind the scenes, strategists with ties to the Chamber of Commerce, the Michigan Freedom Fund and the state GOP worked the angles. Could they design a lawsuit that would knock Proposition 2 off the ballot? Could they, at least, delay it from reaching voters until 2019, booting it into a low-turnout off-year and away from a cresting blue wave? Might all this be decided by Michigan's Supreme Court, an elected body funded generously by the state Chamber of Commerce, in which Republicans held a 5–2 edge? As spring neared, their counter-strategizing intensified. One morning, the Chamber even hosted a big-dollar fundraiser for two GOP bench nominees, including a justice named Elizabeth Clement.[4] A group called Citizens Protecting Michigan's Constitution appeared, and challenged the Proposition, arguing that it was so broad that it represented a fundamental change to the state constitution and required a constitutional convention. The group's number one funder, documents quietly revealed, was Michigan's Chamber.[5]

Then Bob LaBrant found himself someplace he'd rather not be: back in the news. One of the Republican mapmakers or aides had been careless and held onto emails from the 2011 redistricting. Turns out that those strategists had done a lot of explicit boasting about how effectively they'd gerrymandered Michigan.[6]

In public, Michigan Republicans had long denied that partisanship had anything to do with the congressional districts they drew after the 2010 census, a map that has locked in 9 of the state's 14 congressional seats for the GOP in every election since, even in years when Democrats earn many more votes statewide. They insisted that Voting Rights Act requirements and the state's political geography—Democratic voters clustered in Detroit and Ann Arbor, Republicans spread more efficiently throughout the state—baked in its red edge naturally and inevitably.

Behind the scenes, however, some were making very different claims. "In a glorious way that makes it easier to cram ALL of the Dem garbage in Wayne, Washtenaw, Oakland and Macomb counties into only four districts," wrote Jack Daly, chief of staff to then GOP congressman Thaddeus McCotter, in a note to mapmaker Jeff Timmer (a former executive director of the state GOP) and LaBrant, who was then senior VP of political action for the Michigan Chamber of Commerce. Another email celebrated a vulgar contour on the map that looked like an extended middle finger, and how it would ratfuck a Democratic incumbent. "Perfect," a colleague wrote Timmer. "[I]t's giving the finger to sandy levin [sic]. I love it." Timmer's firm, the Sterling Corporation, won the contract to draw the maps by ensuring they had the legislative ties to pass the maps, the necessary relationships to keep the congressional delegation happy, the smarts to make the maps hold up in court—and the fundraising ties to make the GOP caucuses pay for it all. "We not only provide invaluable expertise, we pay for ourselves," Timmer and a colleague wrote in their proposal. The emails, revealed during a federal lawsuit challenging both the state's legislative and congressional maps, helped convince a bipartisan panel of federal judges to strike them all down as an unconstitutional partisan gerrymander in April 2018.

All this broke the first rule of master Republican mapmaker Tom Hofeller, the "Michelangelo of the modern gerrymander."[7] Hofeller first recognized how sophisticated new GIS (Geographic Information Systems) software and powerful new data sets provided an opportunity for the GOP to gerrymander itself into decade-long advantages in the U.S. House of Representatives and state legislatures nationwide—and how the grade-school maxim "loose lips sink ships" could bring it crashing down. Hofeller trained state legislators and line-drawers with a PowerPoint so old-school that it looks like it might have been designed on a Commodore 64.[8] There were no special effects to clutter the message: "Avoid recklessness." "Always be discreet." "Emails are the tools of the devil." "Remember—A journey to legal HELL starts with but a single misstatement OR a stupid email!" "Remember, the court record is already open." "Remember recent email disasters!!!"

This would be the latest email disaster. Michigan voters read the embarrassing details, observed the rank partisanship and became convinced that reform was necessary. The emails—disclosed as part of a federal court challenge to the constitutionality of the Michigan map by the League of Women Voters—reveal the entire sordid story of GOP operatives, mapmakers and congressional staffers determined to design maps that would provide Republicans with a full decade of dominance. In another exchange, LaBrant told Timmer that national Republicans had suggested a map with 10 Republican seats and just 4 for the Democrats— and then boasted over email about how they would be more careful than that: "We needed for legal and PR purposes a good looking map that did not look like an obvious gerrymander." LaBrant later observed that "we've spent a lot of time providing options to ensure we have a solid 9–5 delegation in 2012 and beyond."

With well-funded opponents schooled in brass-knuckle politics, the ragtag reformers needed someone to step up and provide some muscle. Media-savvy anti-corruption crusaders from the organization RepresentUs decided that if the Michigan Chamber of Commerce and its allies wanted to undercut the anti-gerrymandering initiative, they'd have to pay a political price. The RepresentUs volunteers marched on the downtown Detroit headquarters of Deloitte Consulting, located in the swanky GM Renaissance Center.[9] Mark Davidoff, Deloitte's managing partner in Michigan, chaired the Chamber board. Since the Chamber was funding the legal assault, Davidoff seemed an appropriate recipient for thousands of signatures asking him to back off and let the people vote. Fresh-faced, clean-cut college students carried boxes of petitions, while grandmothers in comfortable sneakers chanted "drop the suit" and placards accused the Chamber of cheating and stacking the deck. Davidoff, unamused, refused to accept the petitions and called in three different layers of security as the protesters marched closer to the Deloitte lobby.

"When we saw this historic, anti-gerrymandering measure going into the hands of a court with five judges connected to money on one side of the case and two not, we knew something had to be done to level the playing field," says Dan Krassner, the political director of RepresentUs. "There were two justices in Michigan on the ballot this year and they needed to hear from their voters how important the right to vote on anti-gerrymandering was to the people of Michigan. It had to be politically toxic for the justices in Michigan to do anything but rule on the facts of the case."

Krassner knew the Chamber's soft spot, because he had been an officer with the Florida Chamber of Commerce before switching sides and joining the reformers. "I know how state Chambers work," Krassner, a smooth operator in a rumpled package, says with a grin over breakfast near the nonpartisan organization's western Massachusetts office. "They're front groups to do the dirty political and lobbying work." At the Florida Chamber, Krassner tells me, lobbyists would bring the legislators checks, then bills they had written. His team would sit in the committee rooms, on BlackBerrys, and message the legislators what to say and how to vote.

The Chamber staff, Krassner knew, got paid big salaries to brush aside the occasional attack. The companies that make up the organization, however, pay a little more attention to bad publicity—especially when that means a video of grandmothers with bullhorns accusing the company of rigging the political system and disenfranchising voters. "Anyone who is fighting a state Chamber or a national Chamber should peel the onion back and look at where the money is. Who's funding that group?" says Krassner. "We wanted to tell the community what they were doing behind closed doors."

Davidoff deleted his Twitter account. The Chamber removed the names of other board members from its website. So RepresentUs took out ads targeting Chamber members in their hometown newspapers, and used Facebook ads to shame Davidoff and two other board members— West Shore Bank CEO Ray Biggs and Grand Hotel managing director Ken Hayward—where they lived and worked.[10] They also directed a clever digital campaign at West Shore Bank's customers, Grand Hotel guests and anyone in Deloitte's office tower. Arnold Schwarzenegger, Sarah Silverman and other celebrities amplified the ads on Twitter.

In late July, the court delivered its verdict: Voters Not Politicians made the ballot, barely, in a narrow 4–3 decision. "We are stewards of the people and must faithfully abide by the decision they make through the laws they adopt," David Viviano, a Republican-backed justice, wrote in the majority opinion. Justice Elizabeth Clement joined him as well.

When Fahey called me the next morning, she was still riding high. Her lawyers had told her they were right on the merits, but nevertheless had stood only a fifty-fifty chance of success. The legal bills were mounting: Fahey even swallowed hard and accepted $250,000 from the National Democratic Redistricting Commission, knowing that gave critics an opening to call her organization partisans in disguise. But they would owe $800,000 to the lawyers alone; if they did not make it onto the ballot, how would they raise that money?

Fahey had to project a cool face, knowing that thousands of volunteers were looking to her for stability and guidance. "The cool thing is, it really felt like the decision was putting the rule of law ahead of the rule of money," she said. "There's just so much cynicism out there, and since day one we've been doubted—because of our own lack of money and political connections. We were biting our nails along with everybody else. We knew the law was on our side, but . . . I hope this is a powerful message for a lot of campaigns, now and forever."

The Chamber appeared to quietly back away. Voters Not Politicians had expected as much as $33 million would be spent against them, but the public pressure dissuaded anyone from mounting an aggressive campaign. "The downside reputational risk was too great," veteran Lansing consultant Sarah Hubbard of the Acuitas firm told the website *The Bridge*. "Who else is going to come up with the money? There isn't a grass-roots movement in support of gerrymandering out there."[11]

It's after 10 p.m. on an endless Wednesday less than two weeks before the election. Fahey's day has already included four cities, a funder's meeting, the opening of a new office in Detroit and several national media interviews. As we head for a late-night drink in a Livonia strip-mall pub, it's clear that the pressure is on, no matter how easy she makes it all look. "We're this underdog story that the nation's paying attention to," she says. "You're like, 'Oh shit, if I make a decision that screws this up, I'm letting democracy down.' Which is terrifying!"

After the court's decision, Fahey struck gold with big funders. More than $10 million arrived from major donors, some of whom wanted to attach strings to the cash. "It would have been very easy to sell out to the industrial nonprofit complex," she says, but she wouldn't bow down to anyone. Real people were knocking on doors to end gerrymandering in their state. This campaign was not going to be handed over to partisans or professionals.

"It was interesting going into this being young and optimistic," she says. "When I think about having to ask the people of Michigan to help us raise money for attack ads? Or for a Supreme Court case when I *know* we wrote the proposition right? When we know that the law's on our side, but the opposition has been quoted saying they think they can beat us more easily in court? That is so wrong. It is wrong."

But Fahey looks at her volunteers and sees future leaders who now know how to organize, citizens who understand that their voices can be heard. All of them understand that when people speak together, their voices echo everywhere. "The coolest part for me has been seeing how many people didn't know they had power and have stepped into leadership. It's insane—a group that came from a Facebook post. We had no idea what we were doing, but we researched the hell out of everything and put our own grass-roots spin on it. We have this quirky story, that a bunch of Internet strangers tried to fight for democracy together."

Six weeks later, the drink of choice was champagne. These strangers who found one another on Facebook, who crowd-sourced their ballot initiative and convinced hundreds of thousands of fellow citizens to join them, earned more than 61 percent of the vote. Voters, not politicians, would now draw district lines—the basic building blocks of democracy.

"I knew we could do it. It feels perfect," Fahey told supporters that night.[12] A few days later, still celebrating, she told me, "I knew that there were thousands of us that had worked as hard, and as passionately as we possibly could. I feel like I believe in democracy still—because part of starting this and doing it this way was a belief that the people could come together and make change happen."[13]

CHAPTER 6

Redistricting Goes National

"There's got to be a better way to do democracy."

Katie Fahey wasn't the only exuberant democracy warrior on election night 2018. While Republicans lost the U.S. House, the beating extended to the system that had put many of them in office. It hardly mattered where: red states, blue states, purple states, Trump states. Turns out all Americans hate gerrymandering. The irrepressible Fahey made Michigan's story irresistible. But citizens also forced—and won—statewide initiatives in Colorado, Utah, Ohio and Missouri—five for five. That gerrymandering sleep aid? It wouldn't sell anywhere. These states appeared fully woke—and enraged. And while each of those five states found a different path, with its own solution, they all became examples of how determined citizens can unrig ratfucked politics.

The first victory came in May, in Ohio, where fired-up citizens forced recalcitrant lawmakers to make a deal on redistricting by mounting a petition drive that would have put an anti-gerrymandering initiative on the ballot in November 2018. That pushed nervous politicians to the table: the legislature offered a bipartisan deal on a redistricting commission that required minority-party support to pass a map if reformers held off on their initiative. More than 70 percent of Ohio voters approved the new commission in a runaway May 2018 referendum.

The reform push began on the long bus ride home from the 2017 Women's March on Washington. "We wanted to have something positive to work toward. It wasn't always reacting to whatever Trump did," says Sara Sampson of Ohio Indivisible 12 as she awaited the results, sixteen months later, at an Ohio State ballroom. Her group helped kickstart the petition drive. They witnessed gerrymandering's chilling effect on democracy when they bird-dogged their own congressman, Pat Tiberi, with daily phone calls and weekly sit-ins and still couldn't get his attention. "Why won't he listen to us?" they asked on the group's Facebook page. "Well," says Sampson, "he doesn't have to listen to us." In Ohio, the Republican Party wins around 52 percent of the statewide congressional vote, but in 2011 drew maps that packed most of the state's Democrats into 4 of its 16 seats; they maintained that 12–4 edge in 2012, 2014, 2016 and 2018.

Sampson worried that the compromise commission might not do enough to create fair representation. But both sides had reason to make a deal: Republican legislators didn't want to gamble on the Democrats gaining complete control, while reformers knew that the fight to pass a ballot initiative would cost millions of dollars, attract deep-pocketed opponents and become not only super-partisan but an ugly, and potentially losing, battle. "What ended up passing is not as strong as what we were proposing," Sampson says, "but it won. And winning with more than 70 percent shows that people are serious about this, paying close attention and demand change."

"It's a beautiful story to think that they collected these signatures, and then they moved the legislature to action," says Catherine Turcer, the longtime Ohio anti-gerrymandering crusader who led Fair Districts Ohio. She coordinated the petition drive from a small office in a Columbus highrise with watermarks in the ceiling that resemble Ohio's multi-tentacled congressional districts, and an elevator that actually traps us on the way to the victory party. "Yes, they did move them to action. But not because, 'That pulled my heartstrings and now I have a conscience.' The politicians made a calculation that it wasn't a good risk for them."

Money also forced a compromise in Colorado, but in a much different way. It's certainly the most unusual success story of the 2018 cycle, filled with mistrust, unlikely alliances and slippery partisan intrigue, especially among the Democrats. Colorado is purple, and deeply independent: unaffiliated voters here outnumber both Democrats and Republicans. In reality, however, the state's politics are trending blue: Democrats have held the governor's office since 2007, and since 2005 have controlled both the state house (except for 2011–12) and senate (save 2015–18). Democrats were not eager for change. Indeed, many wouldn't even use the word "gerrymander" to describe the process here.

Yet that's exactly what it was. Colorado's state legislature draws the congressional map, and a commission of politicians and political appointees sets out the state house and senate districts. Here, it was Democrats who played hardball in 2011 and rolled right over an unwitting GOP. Three Democratic congressional aspirants drew the districts they'd soon represent. A horrified academic, appointed by Republicans, later described "a marionette show," with prefabricated testimony presented by paid or partisan witnesses, and commissioners presenting maps drawn secretly by anonymous party operatives fueled by an endless supply of dark money. "Democracy in action," proclaimed former Denver mayor Wellington Webb, a Democratic commissioner, chuckling at the naive "comments of a political science professor."[1]

The road to reform rose in early 2016 at Katie Mullen's Irish Pub in downtown Denver, where four "has-been" state legislators, two Republicans and two Democrats, all bearing redistricting battle scars, downed just enough lunchtime cheer to grab napkins and begin sketching out a plan.[2] Rob Witwer, one of the conservative old-timers around the table, had also served on that ugly 2011 commission, when his suggestions for a nonpartisan, Iowa-style process were greeted with "crickets" by Democrats and fellow Republicans. No one at this lunchtime caucus planned to seek higher office again. They could be honest about all the ways in which gerrymandering corrodes the electoral process, and how partisan redistricting breeds not only a more extreme caucus but also hard feelings that oftentimes make it a challenge for legislators to work together at all. Most importantly, they kept meeting and working after that initial lunchtime buzz wore off. They branded themselves as Fair Districts Colorado, recruited every living former governor to the group, both Democrat and Republican, and launched a bid to put an initiative on the 2016 ballot.

Not everyone liked the group's plan or trusted its members. "Our job was to squash them," admits Curtis Hubbard, a strategist with the liberal Colorado firm OnPoint, which was hired by a coalition of Democratic and progressive groups to keep this reform far away from the 2016 ballot. When we talk, Hubbard describes Fair Districts Colorado as a "Republican group," and I have to interrupt the spun narrative and remind him that one of the key organizers that day at Katie Mullen's was a progressive Democrat and the state's first openly gay House Speaker. "Well, they didn't give a lot of thought to what they were getting involved with," he says, adding that some of the Fair Districts members' "hearts were in the right place" but that their friendships with Republicans suckered them into "a really bad policy proposal." Democrats and civil rights groups cast the Fair Districts proposal as a GOP Trojan horse that would diminish minority representation. It wasn't, necessarily, but the overwhelming whiteness and insularity of the Fair Districts effort made it easy to portray that way. Hubbard and the Democratic groups ultimately beat back Fair Districts, not on the merits but on a technicality. The Fair Districts opponents convinced the state Supreme Court that because the initiative would reform both state legislative and congressional redistricting, it violated a clause in the state constitution that limited ballot initiatives to a single subject. "We were able to kill it," says Hubbard, "but we knew they'd come back again in 2018."

When they did, Hubbard's team was ready—with two initiatives of their own. The Democratic group pushed their plans for congressional and state legislative redistricting under the umbrella of People Not Politicians. If they'd been honest, they would have called themselves Politicians Confusing People. "Essentially it was mutual assured destruction, right?" Hubbard says now. "You were going to have just too much for voters to wade through." The debate grew bitter and divided customary allies: the League of Women Voters signed on with Fair Districts Colorado, while Common Cause backed People Not Politicians. Some accused People Not Politicians of being a progressive front group, its real agenda being to stall reform and hand Democrats the pen for the 2020 cycle. Meanwhile, Fair Districts struggled to diversify beyond the state's white political establishment. When a progressive former lawmaker involved with the effort tweeted that the group's latest proposal included "extensive outreach to solicit input from minority indiv/grps for months," state senator Jessie Ulibarri asked, pointedly, "Which ones signed on? . . . I'll wait." Frank McNulty, a conservative former state house Speaker, didn't do Fair Districts any favors with his response, "I can't help being born white, bro," or his hashtag, #bornthisway.[3]

Both organizations' plans were bound for the ballot, or for nasty litigation. And a pitched battle over reform would be every bit as toxic as the polarized politics produced by gerrymandering. Enter Kent Thiry, gajillionaire CEO of a Denver kidney dialysis company, who first learned about gerrymandering as a small-town Midwestern boy attending Stanford and found it so preposterously un-American that he was sure his professor was lying. "I sent a letter home to my parents wondering if I should switch schools," he says with a laugh. Thiry's decision to bankroll Fair Districts all but guaranteed the proposal would go to the vote, which nudged both groups to meet and come up with a single bipartisan proposal. They could work together for real reform, or he'd start funding primary battles.

"There was not a lot of trust in that room. People showed up basically to say they were there and they had made an effort," Hubbard says. But Thiry used his wealth to keep the conversation moving, sometimes cajoling, sometimes with a threat to get voters involved. "It was a really incredible moment, because you had people from the right, people from the left, who had some distrust in one another, and it took a long time to bring everyone along to agree on the foundational principles of what we were pursuing." Over what Thiry describes as seventy meetings and dozens of drafts, they not only worked out a compromise everyone could support—an independent commission comprised of four Democrats, four Republicans and four unaffiliated voters, with multiple layers of checks and balances—but one that sailed unanimously through both the state house and senate and onto the fall ballot.

"Six months earlier," Thiry says, still sounding amazed, "the legislature would have voted against it." It was a sweet next chapter for Thiry, who had actually backed off from funding redistricting reform in California in the late 2000s when "my company was threatened with so much retaliation that I had to drop out." This time, he wielded the hammer. "This is a full contact sport. It's not a civics lesson," he tells me. "We wanted to be sure that certain legislators knew that an overwhelming percentage of their district favored this—and if they opposed it, we would make sure the voters knew. That changed the conversation immediately. Good old-fashioned, legal, straightforward above-board politics."

Maybe it required a little fear to coerce Ohio and Colorado politicians to surrender their gerrymandered spoils. The real lesson of 2018's great unrigging, however, is how regular voters—the most conservative Republicans, wild-eyed progressive Democrats and deeply frustrated independents alike—all worried enough about representative democracy's future that they were willing to back fair-minded reforms and a better political process even at the expense of their own party's prospects, and even in crimson Utah and Missouri.

It's fewer than 10 miles from Salt Lake City to the Holladay headquarters of Better Boundaries Utah. My short late-autumn trip is the perfect reminder of why this ballot initiative exists. I cut across three different congressional districts, weaving in and out of Utah's 2nd and 4th districts twice, as Foothill Drive curves around the University of Utah, past Cauldron Park, venue for the opening and closing ceremonies of the 2002 Winter Olympics, and finally lands me at Holladay's 3 Cups coffee, which is located, appropriately enough, in the 3rd district. This wealthy suburb of 30,709 people, Mitt Romney and family among them, offers breathtaking views of Alta, Gobbler's Knob and Grandeur Peak. Shell out the $2.79 million to become Romney's neighbor along Walker Lane, and the former Republican presidential nominee will be your U.S. senator. It might require closer study to determine your other representatives. Holladay isn't just one of the most exclusive havens in Utah, it's one of the most gerrymandered. These mere 5.3 square miles have been carved into intricate puzzle pieces: two congressional districts, two state senate districts, and a staggering four state house seats. Holladay's maps have been tended as precisely as the landscaping here. They're as carefully designed as the bookshelf in Romney's study, which swivels out to reveal a secret room, a man cave hidden within an enclave.[4]

"You live in a town for a reason," says Catherine Kanter, who based the Better Boundaries campaign in a nondescript Holladay office plaza—just down the hall from Inner Guidance coaching and The Anatomy of Wellness, two more common concerns in this wealthy town—which straddles two congressional districts. Kanter is well aware of that mighty symbolism.

When you're fighting gerrymandering in a one-party state—only 12 percent of Utahans are registered Democrats, the smallest percentage in any state other than Idaho—you can't exactly argue that tilted maps skew outcomes. So it's helpful to have a real example of how lines as jagged as the nearby mountain peaks affect Utahans' everyday lives. "You're connected, and therefore you should have a collective voice," Kanter tells me. "A town is where your kids go to school, where you worship, you may work there. You have affinity with your neighbors." Gerrymandering, she argues, dilutes all that community interest for incumbent self-interest. It's the ultimate conflict, Kanter proclaims, for politicians to choose voters, slicing, dicing and julienning their hometowns into shapes that better resemble the fancy toppings that line the overpriced duck confit taco at Taqueria 27, where we have lunch. But they hardly resemble meaningful representation. "That's the part I felt needed to be fixed. It doesn't make any sense."

Kanter has the polish and poise of a TV-procedural defense attorney, and needed every bit of it to win this tight, improbable victory in a state that's the same shade as Taylor Swift's lipstick. Utah's anti-gerrymandering initiative squeaked to victory with 50.34 percent of the vote. That's by far the narrowest margin of the five otherwise wildly popular 2018 propositions nationwide: just 6,944 votes of the 1,017,492 cast statewide. Winning here, however, even by a whisker, sends a powerful message: The fight against gerrymandering isn't just some liberal thing. Meaningful change can emerge from a state associated with neither bipartisanship nor political reform. Gerrymandering doesn't just carve up Democrats and Republicans, or dilute the votes of minorities in a state less snow-white than this one. It divides neighbors, fellow parishioners. It dilutes the power of the people to fight for what matters closest to home.

Victory in Utah required careful, effective messaging, respected Republican co-chairs for the ballot initiative campaign, and a surprising mascot: Ronald Reagan. But it only happened because one quixotic citizen tilted at a windmill, certain that her state could do better. Kanter lowered her lance not long after narrowly losing a 2016 race for the Salt Lake County council. As a first-time (strike one) Democratic (strike two) candidate running for a countywide, at-large seat (you're out), she never expected to win. What Kanter didn't imagine was that she'd encounter such frustration and exhaustion with politics as she knocked on door after door, weekend after weekend. It didn't matter whether she talked to Republicans, independents or even those rare Utah Democrats. They all told her that they couldn't bear hyperpartisanship for another moment, that their choices all seemed too extreme, that they felt powerless and lost. Some complained that the joy had been drained from voting itself. After she lost, Kanter curled up with her dogs and mourned her own defeat, naturally, but felt more despondent about elections themselves.

As she searched for explanations for this small-d democratic malaise, Kanter realized that redistricting not only shaped politics in faraway swing states wired red by Republicans after the 2010 census, but in natural one-party states like her own. A light switched on. Here was something structural that led to disconnection and dysfunction—and something structural could be fixed. She discovered that a group called Better Boundaries planned to circulate a citizen ballot initiative that would do exactly that: create a seven-person commission to redraw the state's 104 state house and senate seats as well as its four U.S. House districts, following strict guidelines and an open and transparent process. The commission could not use partisan data, or favor any incumbent or political party. A variety of options would be submitted to the legislature; they'd select one, without altering it, with an up or down vote.

Kanter had not only a law degree, but a superhero-level knack for fundraising. First, she oversaw the drafting of the initiative's language, making sure that the text was as accessible and clearly stated as possible. Then, when the campaign manager unexpectedly abandoned this nascent effort at a crucial moment in the signature-collecting process, Kanter faced a choice. She could either take charge or let the entire cause collapse. "I'm a redistricting reformist. I'm not a Utah redistricting reformist," she says. "I live here. That's why I'm doing it here. I want a better process here. But I also hope that we can be some kind of a beacon. This is a problem all throughout the country. If we don't tamp it down, the technology just gets more sophisticated, the big data gets more precise, and the gerrymandering gets worse and worse."

As Kanter would soon discover, nothing about this would be easy or inexpensive. Though Utah was the second state in the union to establish a referendum process, back in 1900, only five initiatives passed in the 118 years since. Legislators made it almost impossible to place an initiative on the ballot, first by restricting how petitions could be collected, and then by setting an extraordinarily high numerical bar. State law requires initiative supporters to gather signatures amounting to 10 percent of the votes cast in the most recent presidential election. In 2018, that was about 113,000.

It also requires that 10 percent level to be reached in 26 of the state's 29 state senate districts, many of which are sparsely settled and larger than entire New England states. As if that doesn't make things hard enough for reformers, opponents of the measure can request the name and address of every petition signer and then spend thirty days convincing them to rescind their support. Knock off a handful of signatures, push even one of those far-flung counties under the 10 percent mark, and the pesky initiative is gone. (Another 2018 ballot initiative, which would have created a more open primary process, failed by 100 signatures in two counties after opponents waged a determined rescission effort.)

Volunteers went to every corner of Utah and collected 193,000 signatures. Their enthusiasm and hard work vindicated everything Kanter believed, even as she solicited money from national organizations to fund redistricting reform in Utah—which often resulted in perplexed reactions over the apparent pointlessless of the effort. But it all made sense to her. Utah's a red state, and it will probably always be a red state. Partisan control of the state legislature wouldn't change whether her proposition passed or failed—which made it risk-free for voters to support fairness. Republicans would still hold the legislature and be heavy favorites to hold at least three U.S. House seats, if not all four. But the winners of those seats would be more accountable to their electorate, and the communities they represent would be kept whole. Only incumbent legislators would feel threatened by that.

Kanter needed an easy way to signal to Republicans, in a Republican state, that they could be anti-gerrymandering. This campaign was not a trick or a liberal plot. It had to be removed from any partisan narrative. So what better mascot for such a mission than Ronald Reagan? The GOP icon had hated gerrymandering, after all, and repeatedly referred to it as "undemocratic" and a "national disgrace." Better Boundaries created powerful ads using footage of the Gipper, reassuring Republican voters that fair maps were good for everyone. Kanter calls those TV and radio ads "a really important piece," as Reagan's words "were the trigger that told

Republicans it was OK to be for reform." Some present-day Utah Republicans would help as well.

Two respected Democrats signed on as Better Boundaries co-chairs: two-term Salt Lake City mayor Ralph Becker and former U.S. congresswoman Karen Shepherd, whose years after Congress included appointments at Harvard University, the Council of Foreign Relations and the national Chamber of Commerce. Alas, Utah Democrats can probably hold their state convention at any medium-sized Starbucks. For Proposition 4 to pass, Republican support would be absolutely necessary. No state party leadership, Republican or Democrat, wants to reform away its power. If Better Boundaries wanted to win, it would need leadership from the Republican business elite and friendly faces from the Mormon community. Exceptional citizens stepped forward.

Jeff Wright could spend his Tuesday evening anywhere other than St. Luke's Episcopal Church, where he presides over a town hall–style discussion over the proposition. Wright founded the private equity firm Actium Partners, earned advanced degrees from Oxford and the London School of Economics, and has an Andy Warhol portrait of Theodore Roosevelt hanging in his Park City home. He served as the finance director for former Utah governor Jon Huntsman's presidential campaign, and it's easy to imagine him as a governor or senator himself. Instead, as one of two Republican Better Boundaries co-chairs, he's debating Proposition 4 with a right-wing think tank operative and a conservative state legislator and local rancher who's still in his boots from "running sheep." The hedge-funders, media moguls and big-time developers who live here, at least part-time, are environmentalist and cosmopolitan, and move easily through Aspen and Davos. Their quintessence would be moderate businessmen like Huntsman or Romney. They may not be the majority in Utah, but they write the checks and have a certain familiarity with getting what they want.

They also happen to be good salesmen. Wright's opponents at this community gathering have a nearly impossible task. It's difficult to oppose a measure that would curb something as widely loathed as gerrymandering. They try anyway. The state representative takes the approach that legislators aren't going to listen to the ballot initiative anyway, and will change it the first chance they get. "It's likely to be open season," he says mournfully, referring to his party's leaders. "To say they won't do anything, that would be a lie." (Presumably he also lets his sheep roam free; the coyotes would just find a way in regardless.) The think-tanker shakes his head sadly and argues that Proposition 4 will just lead to lots of lawsuits over the maps— hoping that folks hate trial lawyers more than they hate gerrymandering. Wright, in an immaculate pinstripe suit, outclasses them with simple, winning themes. "This is a moral issue," he says. "We fundamentally believe voters should pick their politicians. This is not about the past, but how we choose our future leaders."

St. Luke's is so Park City that the complimentary coffee and bottled water comes with a $10 "donation request." Over that exorbitantly-priced cup of Folgers after the event, I'm determined to figure out Wright's motivation, to understand why someone worth nine figures wouldn't just stay home and watch that evening's World Series game in high definition and gaze at his Warhol. Why get whacked by Democrats, who might think this commission leaves the legislature too big a role in the end? Why take heat from fellow Republicans, wondering why he'd screw up the good thing they've got going? Is it political ambition? A frustrated end run on a legislature more socially conservative than he might prefer? No, and no again. Wright insists his view is much more global. "I suddenly realized the impact I was having was small," he says. Yes, he's helped fund homeless shelters, scholarships and arts programs nearby, but he wanted to take on something larger-scale.

"I do business internationally," he tells me. "I really see this binary world between representative democracy and everything else. Everything else is starting to get momentum. If you're a country right now saying, 'What's the best model?,' democracy is a mess! Who would look to the United States as a beacon right now?" Instead, countries might look to China or authoritarian regimes with booming growth numbers, while our democracy goes through a midlife crisis. "As imperfect as we are, the world needs America. That starts in our community, it starts in our states, it starts in our Congress. And our Congress"—Wright shakes his head—"is just so broken. The businessman in me would do a SWOT analysis"—that's MBA-speak for a flowchart of strengths, weaknesses, opportunities and threats—"and one of the key threats would be gerrymandering."

Wright is calm, a careful listener, and while he shrugs aside any awkwardness or personal price—"I'm an independent businessman, luckily I'm not beholden to the legislature"—there's some righteous anger underneath. He's still bothered by the state legislator this evening who matter-of-factly suggested that the legislature would simply override the people if Proposition 4 passes. "It's arrogant, and it's entitled. I hope the legislature respects the will of the people," he says. "I know we're on the right side of the famous arc of history that bends toward justice."

The next day, at a lunchtime debate at the University of Utah, Wright's crafty opponent, the aptly named state senator Todd Weiler, may be the most outspoken foe of the proposition. Maybe it's Utah nice, but Wright indulges only in some gentle eye-rolling and almost imperceptible head shakes as Weiler argues that "everything is about partisanship." Wright would never admit it, but in that moment I think I see his exact motivation: to strip politics of that dangerous and polarizing notion before it chokes democracy entirely.

When Blake Moore greets me the following morning at the Cicero Group, a boutique management firm in Salt Lake City's trendy high-tech district, he could easily pass for one of the college students at the debate. He's a tall glass of whole milk, aglow like the good guy in *Pretty in Pink*. As a Utah high school student, Moore's flawless GPA, three-sport excellence, Eagle Scout perfection—his capstone project was collecting books for a local homeless shelter—earned him the national Wendy's High School Heisman. (Yes, that's actually a thing.) After an overseas stint with the

State Department, Moore landed at Northwestern University for his graduate degree in public policy and had his sense of American politics rattled when he started researching gerrymandering. Two days after submitting the paper, he texted a liberal friend about starting a petition drive to end gerrymandering in Utah. The friend told him about Better Boundaries; a Cicero colleague put him in touch with Kanter. They had breakfast, then a week later Moore became a statewide co-chair. Utah's Golden Boy had his next good deed.

"I get asked a lot, 'You're a Republican in a red state. Why do you care so much? Why is this something you'd put time and effort into?'" Moore tells me. His answer is a simple one: no one will defend gerrymandering or pretend that it's not a conflict for politicians to draw their own districts. If Republicans are going to win anyway, who needs it? "I want fiscally conservative principles to win on a level playing field," he says. Now, however, the legislature looks like a shadowy body that has manipulated rules for their own benefit. So make it stop. Let an independent commission draw the lines. Republicans will still win and create the sound policy Utahans want. Then criticism of the legislature disappears. "All of a sudden you have a win-win," he says. "Good policies get passed and there's no more criticism that the process has been nefarious."

Reform is good for Utah Republicans. But it also might impress blue-state Democrats. "Utah, being a red state, can show the country that a) gerrymandering is ridiculous, and b) if we're able to do this here, what's stopping you, Maryland? Why are you digging your heels in, Massachusetts?" Utah, he suggests proudly, will become a good-government beacon, modeling the kind of politics we should have—the best we can be. "It's a better approach and will make a lot of the strife and division in our communities unnecessary," he says. "I have neighbors that think completely different than me, and we still break bread. That should be taking place in our political system too."

Utah's majestic capitol, with its stunning neo-Corinthian columns, soars above Salt Lake City, a monument to what politics might be. Over 1,200 miles east in Jefferson City, it's as if the Missouri state capitol is rising from an actual swamp, on the banks of a waterway actually known as the Big Muddy. If Utah's victorious reformers took pains not to criticize the legislature, appealing to a more virtuous politics that citizens could proudly look up to, Missouri activists would have happily declared this a toxic Superfund site desperately needing decontamination. No one confuses "Jeff," as the capital city is known, with Vegas—the Applebee's down Missouri Boulevard is an actual hotspot for legislator and lobbyist mingling—but politicos have the same sense that what happens here, stays here. Imagine a place that's a freshman-year frat party, eternally. It's two or three hours away from home. No one is checking up on you. Beer flows, everywhere. Someone else picks up the bill—even for the nachos and wings. "We've heard stories about legislators calling lobbyists who weren't even at the Applebee's," says Sean Soendker Nicholson, who led the Clean Missouri initiative drive, when we met. "'Can you fax your credit card number down and pick up the tab?'"

In 2017, Missouri legislators broke their own record for the most goodies accepted from lobbyists—just under $1.1 million in free food, drinks, tickets and random gifts and perks.[5] That's a lot of neighborhood beef nachos and double-crunch buffalo wings. Sometimes, they'd legislate while they partied. One afternoon at the capitol, Nicholson noticed that a committee had posted notice of an off-site public hearing at 1436 Southridge Drive. He recognized that address as Das Stein Haus, a German bistro and nightclub, where lawmakers might start with the escargot bourguignonne before moving onto Helmut's special Chateaubriand flambé for two. Nicholson and a colleague grabbed a camera and decided to attend, discovering a quorum of lawmakers and a handful of lobbyists literally in a back room.

An even niftier loophole in the state's campaign finance laws allows almost all these shenanigans to be reported anonymously, as gifts to caucuses, committees and other groups, effectively shielding who's taking what, and from whom, from the general public. It's nice work, if you can get it. Alas, you probably can't. Missouri insiders draw the state legislative districts, which helps explain why more than 90 percent of these frat boys (more than three-quarters of them are men) get reelected by double digits. It works well for everyone in Jeff: Republicans, as one might expect, hold big legislative majorities. Democrats, without real hope of control, go along because it keeps their own seats safe. Life in the minority isn't quite so bad when it comes with easy reelection and the keys to the St. Louis or Kansas City political machine.

Nicholson wanted to clean up the entire mess. But how? Redistricting reform had no natural political base: most Republicans enjoyed the status quo, and many influential black Democrats worried that more competitive districts would be drawn at the expense of spreading African Americans across more districts, perhaps improving the party's chances but making victory more difficult for specific incumbents. Many black politicians enjoyed having a district packed with 75 percent black voters and didn't want to jeopardize their own easy reelection. Stronger campaign finance, ethics and transparency provisions didn't stand a chance when one party held all the power and gerrymandered away any fear of defeat. Consulting firms were unwilling to sign on to the enterprise, telling Nicholson that "structural pieces, like democracy, people just don't feel that in their guts."

Nicholson and Clean Missouri disagreed and placed a nervy bet: they believed that even in this era of fierce fealty to team red or team blue, the idea of clean government might transcend partisanship, race and self-interest. "Rigged," after all, is the one word that unifies Bernie Sanders and Donald Trump loyalists. Fortunately—or unfortunately—reformers didn't have to search far to discover bipartisan examples of bad behavior. Why not collect all of these reforms? The Clean Missouri initiative would ban lobbyist gifts over $5. No Mizzou tickets or fancy dinners. It demanded that the legislature operate under the same open records statutes as everyone else in state government. It curbed the revolving door from legislator to lobbyist. And it fundamentally reshaped how state legislative maps would be drawn, appointing a nonpartisan state demographer to do the technical line-drawing in consultation with an independent commission. Its criteria would both protect the political power of minority communities and create truly competitive districts that reflected the state's partisan makeup, as shown by an index of the most recent elections for U.S. president, governor and the U.S. Senate. "People got it," says Nicholson. "It was not a hard sell at the doors. People understand there's got to be a better way to do democracy. The only place, even now, that this was controversial is in Jefferson City."

Nicholson explained the proposal, line by line, to Republicans and Democrats, to Tea Party conservatives and the NAACP, to anyone fair-minded who might come aboard. There were long phone calls, and multiple lunches, all to build a nontraditional coalition. His coalition would take the time to listen and earn support. "The catch," says Nicholson, "is that there was no catch." Nicholson, a progressive activist, and state senator Rob Schaaf, a conservative Republican, had been on opposite sides of many issues. But after sixteen years in the legislature, Schaaf realized something was deeply broken. "I've seen the corrupting influence of big money," Schaaf says, casually adding an allegation that should rattle citizens. "The legislature, most of the time, I would say, doesn't do the wishes of the people. It does the wishes of the big donors."[6] Across party lines, the reformers built relationships and trust, not for an outcome but for a better process. "People are so used to being rooked in political deals," says Nicholson. "You have to show that this protects everybody."

Then, as volunteers spread across the Show-Me State to collect signatures—more than 347,000 of them—for the petition that would put the initiative on the ballot, the state's governor, Eric Greitens, was indicted on a felony charge of invasion of privacy. Already facing a potential four years of prison time, the governor resigned after an investigation uncovered shocking allegations of sexual assault, nonconsensual sex and threats of "revenge porn." Suddenly, it became a good year to upend Jeff. "We had seen what a total lack of ethics looked like," says Nicholson, "and just the raw desire of power with nothing behind it."

Of course, Missouri's power establishment would not give up without a fight. The state Chamber of Commerce bankrolled a lawsuit against the initiative, arguing that it violated the state constitution's requirement that any initiative must be single-issue. "Ethical government," they maintained, the single issue the reformers claimed, was too big an umbrella for campaign finance reform and a redistricting overhaul, let alone the new transparency guidelines for the legislature. The Chamber and its allies funded business as usual, trips overseas; they likely little minded a late-night call from Applebee's after a Dollarita-fueled caucus meeting. When, in mid-September, they found a judge who agreed, the Clean Missouri initiative was removed from the ballot for a week. But an appeals court reinstated it, and the state Supreme Court upheld the decision. Nicholson showed me examples of the ugly dark money campaign that targeted digital ads at conservatives and African Americans, using the opposite message but the same clip art. Conservatives were told that if Clean Missouri passed, George Soros and out-of-state Democrats would draw the state's districts, while urban Missourians were told that the "white man" would control the pen and dilute their districts. But the coalition that Nicholson built, one line at a time, one meeting at a time, one unexpected ally after another signing on, held strong. "This wasn't about parties. I don't care about the parties," he says. "The current system is unfair to voters, because voters can't say, 'This representative is not doing what we sent them there to do.' The system right now is set up so that we can't fire a politician who's in Jefferson City doing what their donors want."

Not anymore. On election day, in the midst of a national blue wave, Missouri voters once again favored Republicans up and down the ballot. They elected a Republican governor and ousted a Democratic U.S. senator. Yet Clean Missouri passed with more support than any statewide politician received, soaring to victory with more than 62 percent. Let the cleanup of the Big Muddy begin.

Democracy was on the ballot in these five states, and democracy won big. After the 2018 clean sweep, more than a third of all congressional districts will be drawn by commissions, not politicians. That's a big deal: more than three-quarters of the congressional seats that changed hands in 2018 were drawn by either commissions or courts. Fairer districts led not only to more competitive races, but also to election results that were responsive to a shift in public opinion. In Pennsylvania, Florida, Virginia and California, for example, as the electorate moved toward the Democrats, they won more seats. That hadn't happened in California prior to its commission; incumbents lost exactly one election over an entire decade loaded with political waves. It didn't help just one side, either; the only three GOP congressional flips in 2018 happened in courts-or-commission states as well.

As historic as 2018 was, the number of states where voters have the ability to alter redistricting through a ballot initiative is dwindling. In Arkansas, home to the very first redistricting initiative in 1936, attorney David Couch plans another in 2020, after the state attorney general disqualified his 2018 effort on a technicality. Oklahoma and Florida could be next. Democrats redistricted Arkansas to their benefit for years; now it's Republicans set up to abuse the process. "When I first filed the initiative, the governor was like, 'Well, that's not fair. The Democrats got to do it for so long, it's our turn to cheat the people,'" Couch says, laughing over the phone from Little Rock. "It polls well—quite well, for Arkansas, in the high 60s. It's very popular with Democrats, popular with independents. Moderately popular with Republicans even, because it's got that anti-politician ring to it."

When voters are given a choice, fairness wins. Perhaps that's why they're not often given the option. Voters have to wrestle away a better future, themselves. If it can be done in Utah, it can be done anywhere. But in states where initiatives are not allowed, a different strategy is necessary.

● CHAPTER 7

Donald Duck and Goofy No More

"The map was smoking. The map made it easy."

Pennsylvania's vicious partisan gerrymander was undone first by hundreds of crude, sexist emails, and then ultimately defeated by a brilliant mathematician who explained a genius-level probability theory to a state judge using an analogy about cab drivers and bad restaurants.

Between the misogyny and the math prodigy came rival state Supreme Court justices determined to bring each other down; a builders' union that spent megamillions to flip the court toward Democratic control, deploying ruthless tactics to clear the field for the union president's brother to claim a seat on the bench; and a determined band of public interest lawyers who decided they could beat the most aggressive GOP map in the nation by telling a story about Disney characters and a steakhouse that straddled two congressional districts.

It's also the unlikely tale of a youth pastor turned statewide anti-gerrymandering evangelist, a piano teacher who decided to draw her own state legislative map, a cartoonish cabal of Harrisburg legislators who couldn't keep their conspiracy straight, and a high school civics teacher who returned from a deployment to Guantánamo Bay angry to find his hometown congressional district drawn into the shape of a barbell. Before it concluded with a giant victory for reformers—and a new legal path for fair maps nationwide—Republican legislators and even a U.S. senator would cling to tilted maps by pushing for impeachment of the state Supreme Court justices who declared the districts unconstitutional.

In the end, the court's decision came down to six idealistic words in Pennsylvania's state constitution: "Elections shall be free and equal."

"An election corrupted by extensive, sophisticated gerrymandering and partisan dilution of votes is not 'free and equal,'" wrote Justice Debra Todd, striking down maps that had embedded a 13–5 Republican advantage in 2012, 2014 and 2016 by cramming a statewide Democratic majority into a handful of overwhelmingly blue districts, while keeping the other 70 percent of the seats safely red. "A diluted vote is not an equal vote, as all voters do not have an equal opportunity to translate their votes into representation."[1]

New court-ordered maps, drawn by a neutral "special master," transformed Pennsylvania's political landscape—and the nation's. In 2012, the gerrymandered map helped Republicans win 13 of the 18 seats even though Democrats won more than 51 percent of the total vote. Smart Democratic candidates and funders got the message: these seats wouldn't be budged any time soon. Indeed, Republicans romped to the same lopsided advantage in the following two elections. But the creation of competitive districts spawned real races, and a responsive map allowed Democrats to turn a majority of votes into four additional seats in 2018. Fair maps produced a fair result.

"It shows that it's not so hard for judges to rule partisan gerrymandering unconstitutional, and to strike down a map and order a new one," says Daniel Jacobson, one of the victorious lawyers. "It was seen as, 'Oh, this is so impossible to do.' It's actually what courts do best: evaluate evidence."

They didn't need the perfect democracy-saving theorem. They just let the maps speak for themselves.

Master Republican mapmaker Tom Hofeller always warned legislators to remember that "a journey to legal HELL starts with but a single misstatement OR a stupid email." As we learned in Michigan, legislators didn't always listen. Still, Hofeller probably never considered having to give the same caution to judges. But during early 2010, just as Chris Jankowski and savvy GOP strategists began targeting Democratic state legislators and raising the $1 million necessary to flip both Pennsylvania chambers and lock in Republican control of redistricting, the state's elected Supreme Court justices planted the seeds of the map's eventual destruction. And they did so in spectacular fashion.

Seamus McCaffery, the court's gun-packing, Harley-riding tough guy, once leapt from the bench and slammed a defendant to the floor with a headlock Hulk Hogan would have applauded.[2] A former Philadelphia police detective, McCaffery handed down huge fines to drunk football fans, threatened to imprison activists ahead of a protest, and wrote the court's ruling that law enforcement officers no longer needed a warrant to search cars during routine traffic stops. He proudly proclaimed that his favorite four-letter word was spelled J-A-I-L.[3] But in late 2014 his emails became enmeshed in a statewide scandal dubbed Porngate, and 245 sexually explicit emails, more than 700 attached photos and 45 different videos suggested that he might prefer another four-letter word best.

When McCaffery's colleagues issued disapproving statements, the robed bad-ass placed a call to another justice he knew also had an email problem, because they'd been on the same chains with quizzes about Thai transsexuals and cracks about Southern Comfort as "liquid panty removal." That justice, Michael Eakin, later told investigators that McCaffery told him he "was not going down alone."[4] Eakin held fast to his public position, and the next day his emails, many from a private Yahoo account under the alias "John Smith," found their way into the media and lit the state's judicial boys' club on fire. McCaffery said Eakin misinterpreted the call and that he never released anything to the media.

A later investigation uncovered dozens of racist and sexist memes shared among Eakin and his golf, fantasy football and strip club buddies, which included prosecutors, prospective lower-court judges and other prominent officials. Most of the emails dated back to 2009–12, but the timing could not have been worse for Pennsylvania Republicans, who were already reeling from the disbarment of another justice, Joan Orie Melvin, for having her judicial staff do political work. In the closing weeks of the 2015 Supreme Court campaign, front pages statewide looked a lot like "Judges Gone Wild"—a lurid peek at what happens when the robes come off.[5]

The boys' club shared jokes about domestic assault with the punch-line "you see how much keeping your mouth shut helps." They guffawed over a cartoon about why robot golf caddies were painted silver instead of black: "Four of 'em didn't show for work, two filed for welfare, one of them robbed the pro shop, and the other thinks he's the President." They fantasized about potential sleeping arrangements if they vacationed with Eakin's female aides, and looked forward to an actual weekend away. "I've got a stake of fifty ones and a titty-deficit that needs cured," one justice wrote.[6]

Meanwhile, Pennsylvania's most influential labor unions had a bigger pile and maybe even a more desperate desire. After all that was happening with "Porngate," 2015 was a good year to be a Democrat seeking a seat on the state Supreme Court. Republicans controlled both chambers of the state legislature with giant majorities, as well as having an edge on the court. John Dougherty—better known as Johnny Doc, leader of the International Brotherhood of Electrical Workers, Local 98, and one of the most powerful men in state politics—looked at states like Ohio, Wisconsin and Michigan, where similar GOP trifectas had led to right-to-work legislation, limits on collective bargaining and the ability to organize, and similar policies anathema to unions. He knew the Pennsylvania legislature might not be friendly to labor for a decade. So Dougherty placed a $10 million bet on the state Supreme Court instead. If Democrats swept the three open seats, labor might have a Supreme Court veto over the legislation it feared most. Just as important, Democrats on the court would be able to select the all-important fifth member of the redistricting commission responsible for drawing the state legislative lines in 2021. "These decisions are decisions that could change our whole world in one moment," Dougherty told the *Philadelphia Inquirer* in 2018, even as an FBI investigation zeroed in on the union's political network, its contributions to candidates and allegations of workplace intimidation.[7]

But back in 2015, Dougherty's financial prowess was crucial to flipping all three seats and giving Democrats a 5–2 edge on the state Supreme Court. Dougherty and the IBEW helped raise and bundle much of the $15.8 million spent, largely on wildly negative attack ads, which set a record as the most costly judicial election in American history. One of those seats went to Dougherty's brother Kevin, a lower court judge. Privately, Pennsylvania labor higher-ups suggested to me that at least one opponent found himself brass-knuckled out of the race, as in, some friendly advice that it might not be such a good idea to run this year, *if you know what I mean.*

If Dougherty and other Democrats had a redistricting strategy that revolved around 2021, there were other Pennsylvanians who had no interest in waiting that long for change. They didn't believe it had to be a partisan battle, either.

Amanda Holt didn't understand why so many different people represented her neighborhood. Holt, then twenty-nine, taught piano lessons in Upper Macungie Township, just outside Allentown, and served on the local Republican town committee. But when she talked politics with neighbors in 2012, even one who lived right down the street, everyone was surprised to learn they weren't represented by the same person in the House or the Senate. "We couldn't figure out why," Holt said, so they took a look at the maps. Their small town, population 21,194, had a district line running down the middle of a suburban street. Chaotic zigzags separated neighbors and divided towns intentionally.

Some people saw those district lines and thought, "Politics as usual," but that wasn't acceptable to Holt. She looked in the state constitution for the rules governing redistricting and found these words: "Unless absolutely necessary, no county, city, incorporated town, borough, township or ward shall be divided in forming either a senatorial or representative district." Then she redrew the lines herself, using just U.S. census data and her own graphic design skills. The politicians' map at that time split counties in 42 of 50 state legislative districts, and divided municipalities in 75 of 200 state house seats. Holt's map split only 12 counties statewide, and slashed the number of divided towns to 23. "When you start to break those [municipalities] apart, it starts to break that representative voice," she said. In September 2011, Holt explained her map to the redistricting commission. They listened politely then ignored her ideas, ultimately settling on a map that split more than twice as many communities as Holt had.

Politics as usual, right? Holt wouldn't stand for it. Alongside attorneys from the state's Public Interest Law Center, who were impressed by her simple constitutional argument, she battled the legislators' map to the state Supreme Court—and won. The court, finding Holt's arguments and homemade maps "powerful evidence indeed," ordered the legislature to try again. "It is enough that the Holt plan here overwhelmingly shows" that the maps "made subdivision splits that were not absolutely necessary," the justices ruled.[8] Newspapers statewide named her the citizen of the year. "The constitution was put in place to help protect our voice," Holt says. "When it's disrespected, our voice is disrespected."[9]

If the piano teacher struck the match, a Philadelphia youth pastor with a literature PhD poured the gasoline. Carol Kuniholm had never heard of gerrymandering, had never been to the state capital and didn't even own a suit. She simply wanted to understand why her state's education funding formula favored wealthy suburban schools over poorer urban ones. So in spring 2015 she joined the League of Women Voters, landed on an electoral reform commission and started asking questions. A colleague told her she "had gerrymandering under control." By that, the colleague meant there was a conference call every other Saturday morning when whoever was interested would talk about reform bills. This "solution" had been going on for years.

"They had no plan," Kuniholm tells me three years later, on a spring evening over pizza across from the state capitol in Harrisburg. Kuniholm has long, straight white hair, parted evenly down the middle and sometimes pulled back tight, as if she's stepped out of a photo from Philadelphia's colonial days or an early constitutional debate. Republican legislative leaders had spent the day gutting her bill for an independent redistricting commission, actually managing to use it as a vehicle to make gerrymandering worse by allowing the legislature to create districts for seats on the state Supreme Court. It's not the first time her training as a pastor has allowed her to stay calm. A glass of wine doesn't hurt either.

Back in 2015, however, none of the would-be reformers had met with a legislator. The group didn't have a name, let alone any presence on social media. Thankfully, Kuniholm knew something about organizing from her pastoral work. She picked a name that sounded tweetable—Fair Districts PA—and when the so-called experts told her that it would take eight months of study to determine a strategy and another six months to fundraise, she hung up the phone, bought the Fair Districts domain name, and started holding meetings in church basements.

Kuniholm built the website and soon emails started to arrive from concerned citizens who thought democracy was broken and wanted to understand what had gone awry. She started a weekly conference call to educate activists and build a roster of volunteers. National experts told her that change wasn't possible in Pennsylvania, since the state constitution didn't allow for citizen initiatives. But Kuniholm just kept going. Then Donald Trump captured the White House with 2.8 million fewer votes than Hillary Clinton, and the Monday afternoon call exploded from twenty-five people to seventy-five. "The whole thing was so weird," Kuniholm says. A union organizer encouraged her to hold an event in Philadelphia, so she booked a historic church downtown, one block from city hall. It was a freezing Wednesday evening, and she arrived for the talk to see 450 people already in line. More than 800 people eventually showed up. Night after night, statewide, the same thing happened. "I was taking care of grand-kids, spending time in my backyard, and kayaking," she recalls. "And then I wasn't kayaking anymore. I was spending my time in Harrisburg. With crazy people." She bought a suit.

These days, Kuniholm jokingly refers to the capitol rotunda as her office. Fair Districts PA held over 400 events statewide in eighteen months. They have a mailing list of some 30,000 names. More than 8,000 volun-teers led discussions in local Rotary clubs and libraries, blanketed newspa-per op-ed pages with letters, won endorsements from the councils of more than half of the cities and towns in Pennsylvania, and marched on Harris-burg again and again. They drafted a reform bill that would take the power to draw both state and U.S. congressional district lines away from legisla-tors and collected 110 cosponsors in a 203-member house, more than any other proposal that came before Pennsylvania lawmakers in all of 2017 and 2018. When hundreds of volunteers for Fair Districts PA first rallied at the capitol in 2017, they didn't know the rules, didn't know if they could just walk into their legislator's office and request a meeting. When thousands showed up in 2018, Kuniholm says, "we owned the place."

I sit with Kuniholm in the senate gallery as her bill goes down to defeat. She stays focused on the fight ahead, and takes solace in the knowledge that thousands of people statewide now know how to read a bill and how to fol-low a legislative schedule, and know they can speak loudly and be heard. "We might not win this round right now. But we will work like crazy," she says. Fair Districts activists are super-voters and are not going anywhere. She allows herself a moment of frustration after months of watching the legislative sausage-grinding up close. "The problems are deeper than I'd realized. The duplicity is deeper than I'd realized. The desperate attempt to maintain control is deeper than I'd realized. Sure, there have been days where I just feel emotionally exhausted. And then," she says, "you take a breath, and then you go on. And then you do more."

Just as the Pennsylvania state senate ambushed Kuniholm's newly woke swarm of grass-roots activists with a judicial redistricting poison pill, cracking coalitions and delivering a blunt-force reminder that rooms this smoky would not be fumigated easily, the voting rights crusaders at the Public Interest Law Center reminded citizens of that crucial phrase from the state constitution: "Elections shall be free and equal." Pennsylvania's 13–5 congressional map, drawn to ensure election results long before voters head to the polls, rigged the game and violated that fundamental guarantee. Three dedicated attorneys set out to make those six words matter.

The Law Center is located on a busy stretch of Benjamin Franklin Parkway in downtown Philadelphia, on the second floor of the United Way building. Nothing fancy or sleek gives away the high-powered work that's done here. This is the nerve center of the most important redistricting litigation of 2018, a case that not only forced Pennsylvania's map to be redrawn immediately, but also pointed a way forward for other states at a time when the U.S. Supreme Court has refused to require a national solution. The walls are covered with handmade posters drawn by schoolchildren as thanks for the Law Center's battles for public education access and funding. Chairs for visitors are piled high with file folders. We grab coffee in homemade "I Heart PA-07" mugs from the case—the heart is a bright red recreation of the nation's most infamously gerrymandered district, resembling Donald Duck kicking Goofy—and create our own conference room in the middle of the office.

Legal director Mimi McKenzie went to see Bernie Sanders speak at the Philadelphia library in January 2017, and it kicked the law school lecturer out of a post-election malaise. "Stop moping! Get to work! There are serious things to be done!" Sanders implored, and the next day she received the PILC job offer. She joined Michael Churchill, an irrepressible, bow-tied, gray-haired eminence who won the first Holt case, and Ben Geffen, soft-spoken and determined, preternaturally gifted at taking the most complicated topics and breaking them into ABCs, and fresh from a giant victory in striking down Pennsylvania's stringent voter ID law.

On McKenzie's first day, executive director Jennifer Clarke handed her files on the federal suits challenging gerrymandering in Wisconsin and North Carolina. Pennsylvania, Wisconsin and North Carolina regularly shared the top three spots on lists of the nation's most gerrymandered states, the way Alabama, Clemson and Ohio State pass around the highest rankings in college football polls. Pennsylvania's congressional map, which rigged a competitive, bluish state outrageously red, hadn't budged from 13 Republicans and 5 Democrats over three electoral cycles. The outcomes were as predetermined as a game between Alabama and the Little Sisters of the Poor. But while three consecutive elections made the empirical reality of a rock-solid 13–5 map clear to all, it was now 2017. The Wisconsin and North Carolina cases had begun five years earlier, and while there had been many victories, appeals to the U.S. Supreme Court trapped them in glacial legal machinery. Could anything be done to unrig Pennsylvania's map? More importantly, could it happen quickly enough to restore fair congressional elections the following year? "We got really inspired by Wisconsin. They had the machete and they blazed the trail," says Geffen. "But the thing that became apparent to us as we started thinking about a case was that it might be too late."

A federal suit, they saw immediately, would take too long. Geffen and Churchill, however, had already won robust voting rights decisions under the state constitution. The Holt decision and those 400 Fair Districts meetings, meanwhile, had made gerrymandering both a household name and a public enemy in Pennsylvania of Tom Brady-esque proportions. "There was a glimmer of hope that we could get a decision in time for 2018 if we went into state court," McKenzie said. The state Supreme Court had a different look, thanks to Dougherty's efforts, and redistricting had become a hot topic on Philadelphia talk radio. Angry callers, pissed off and carved up, would vent about living in Goofy's finger, in districts so cracked, stacked or packed for one side that they felt powerless and voiceless. "In 2012, when we talked about Amanda Holt's case, people's eyes would glaze over. 'What the hell is this issue?'" says Churchill. "This was a very different experience." McKenzie realized that they could find plaintiffs in every congressional district, from Goofy's armpit to the far end of a barbell, all of whom could describe specific harms and drive home how very unfree and unequal the state's congressional elections had become.

They'd need those personal stories, because there was one huge problem with filing in state court: Pennsylvania's legislative privilege protection is so broad that politicians can keep almost all of their communications secret. Reformers in other states, like Michigan, had the benefit of boastful and vengeful emails in which greedy legislators and rapacious mapmakers vividly confessed to their antidemocratic misdeeds. Here, there would be no access to the back rooms or the draft maps. In Pennsylvania, the maps themselves would need to be the smoking gun.

"It was the wildest case I've ever worked on in my life," says Jacobson, an attorney at Arnold & Porter in Washington, DC, and the PILC's pro bono partner.

They filed in June 2017 in Pennsylvania's Commonwealth Court, the state's trial court for election law cases, and requested an expedited schedule. The two lead defendants, senate president Joseph Scarnati and House Speaker Michael Turzai, both Republicans, sought to slow things down, requesting that the case be paused until the U.S. Supreme Court decided the cases from Wisconsin and Maryland. The Pennsylvania attorneys found that "obviously ludicrous," says Jacobson. Why would a state court, asked to make a finding on its state constitution, wait for a federal ruling? But judges at many levels are reluctant to weigh in on something as obviously partisan and political as gerrymandering. "I'll never forget," says Jacobson, "Judge [Dan] Pellegrini says, 'It is impossible for you to get resolution for this case in time for 2018. You're delusional if you think that's possible." The Commonwealth Court agreed with the legislative leaders and put the case on hold, pending guidance from the U.S. Supreme Court. "At the time, it seemed terrible," says Jacobson. "It turned out to be the best thing that ever happened."

That's because Pennsylvania's state Supreme Court has the authority of "extraordinary jurisdiction," a power related to the even more awesome-sounding King's Bench Power. While it's very rarely used—the first rule of the King's Bench Power is that you try not to use the King's Bench Power—it allows the Supreme Court to claim any case in any state court. The lawyers could have appealed the Commonwealth Court's stay and crossed fingers for a speedy timeline. Instead, they threw the legal Hail Mary and hoped Pennsylvania's Supreme Court would share their urgency. "What did we have to lose?" says Jacobson. Two days after the November elections, which included the reelection of three incumbent Supreme Court justices (two Democrats and one Republican), they got news both good and bad. The court would take the case—but they found it so urgent that they did not want to wait until 2018 to hear it. They ordered a careful-what-you-wish-for trial in early December. As in, the December that was just a few short weeks away. "Keep in mind, nothing has happened on this case at this point," Jacobson tells me. The Arnold & Porter offices, in Washington, are the opposite of the PIRC. It's the kind of Roald Dahl creation where you check in downstairs, only to be ushered through another security check upstairs before gaining access to the fancy internal elevators. "We haven't done any discovery, no experts, no nothing. Which, for lawyers, it usually takes years to do in a case like this. They told us we had six weeks."

It was time to start cramming for finals. McKenzie discovered perfect plaintiffs: a civics teacher back from fighting the war on terror only to come home to a debased democracy; a woman from the third largest county in the state, which was in dire need of federal funds for sewage treatment but was carved into so many pieces that no one in Washington gave a damn; a voter from urban Chester determined to talk to her congressman about gun violence, only to find her home carved off from the rest of the city, an afterthought attached to a suburban district whose representative didn't care about shootings at all. Geffen, meanwhile, had come across an article in a math journal—yes, he even read those—about real-world applications of a probability theory called the Monte Carlo; among other things, the author, Wesley Pegden of Carnegie Mellon University in Pittsburgh, thought the Monte Carlo might be useful in detecting gerrymandering. Geffen picked up the phone. Meanwhile, the attorneys asked a local political science professor with the all-American name of John Kennedy to untangle the GOP maps, to go street-level and explain how the twists and turns that looked chaotic on paper were actually more precise than military time.

The savvy teams in Philadelphia and Washington knew they would need every bit of ammunition they could find. They were skeptical of any single-bullet argument, having watched the Wisconsin team pin its hopes on the efficiency gap and win in the federal courts, only to have their mathematical approach derided by U.S. Supreme Court Chief Justice John Roberts as "sociological gobbledygook," and by Justice Samuel Alito as an unproven theory by a "young researcher." No magic number would convince the court or prove the maps were rigged. Instead, they decided to tell multiple stories, all with the same ending. The power of their case came from the collective weight of all these stories, how they all pointed to the same conclusion. Not every judge understands advanced probability theory, but all judges understand weighing a preponderance of evidence and coming to a fair-minded conclusion based on where it leads.

The Republican legislators, meanwhile, went back to the gerrymander playbook: they tried to rewrite the rules. The day before a crucial pretrial conference in Harrisburg, an emergency motion was filed to force the case out of the state court and into the federal system. Defendants, if they all agree, have this option whenever they believe there's a basis for federal jurisdiction. Scarnati filed the motion, saying that Turzai would shortly notify the court of his agreement to it. When the email notifications arrived at PILC and Arnold & Porter that afternoon, after 3 p.m., "we go into complete panic mode," Jacobson says. Everyone worked through the night on a motion to remand the case back to the state court.

If they'd lost, it might have been game over once again. "I filed our petition at 2:30 a.m.," McKenzie remembers. When court opened at 9 a.m., they received word that a federal judge would listen to arguments at 1 p.m. "We're suiting up," Jacobson and his partners said, and boarded an Amtrak to Philadelphia.

They were in an Uber to the courthouse when word arrived that the senate president had changed his mind. Scarnati, apparently anxious that the judge would find his motion frivolous, informed the court that, though he had thought the Speaker of the House agreed with him, there was now some confusion. "It was just bizarre," says Churchill. "They didn't hesitate to say whatever was convenient at the time without thinking through long-term strategy and consistency." The federal judge sent the case back to the state court—and then things got even stranger. Turzai filed notice that he had never agreed to the motion and that Scarnati had misled the court. The next morning, Scarnati accused Turzai of mistruths. But while the opposition splintered, the state court judge demanded that everyone dance in double time: expert reports would be due in ten days. It was almost Thanksgiving. No one was ready. "Panic attacks. Late night calls," says Jacobson. "Full madness mode."

Fortunately, the story the experts needed to tell was crazier still.

Creed's Seafood and Steaks is sandwiched between the Pennsylvania Turnpike and the County Line Expressway in the town of King of Prussia, Pennsylvania. It's consistently rated one of the five best steakhouses in eastern Pennsylvania, but it's become known for more than just the Lancaster ribeye. My book *Ratf**ked* popularized Pennsylvania's 7th congressional district as Donald Duck kicking Goofy, a Disney brawl spread across 50 miles—a chiropractor's dream that corrals parts of Philadelphia before twisting and turning north and west all the way to Reading. A 510-foot zag through the Creed's parking lot formed Goofy's Adam's apple, one of the byzantine contortions separating the 6th district from the 7th. But while a cartoonish kick in the pants looks funny on paper, it took John Kennedy to demonstrate the real-world violence it inflicted on eastern Pennsylvania communities. We walk along an undramatic cartographic crime scene, populated mostly by Audis and BMWs parked for a businessmen's lunch, within a concrete frame of interstate entrance ramps filled with eighteen-wheelers. In court, however, a photo of this parking lot—exhibit 81—evinced gasps out of *Perry Mason* or *My Cousin Vinny*.

"Mr. Kennedy, what is this?" Jacobson asked, projecting a photo of the parking lot with the district line laid on top. "A steakhouse. Creed's Seafood and Steaks," Kennedy replied. "That's the size of the connection at that point." Then he explained why that mattered. The 7th district, over the last six decades, had been based around Delaware County. The map drawn in 2011 started there, then meandered into Montgomery, Chester, Lancaster and Berks counties, bringing together Amish communities and Philadelphia suburbs with nothing in common, forcing two essentially separate districts into one linked only by a thin corridor running through this parking lot. Kennedy narrated each ludicrous twist, aided by aerial maps overlaid by the crazy lines and color-coded to show political performance. "In the courtroom," says Jacobson, "it was devastating."[10]

Kennedy had had less than four weeks to bring these maps to life. He had political science classes to teach, exams to grade, a family. But he took the four days over Thanksgiving and barricaded himself in an upstairs home office with state almanacs, microfilmed news stories, dusty history books and decades of congressional maps—feverishly building his own documentary that told the story of how communities that had been together forever were suddenly cleaved apart.

Kennedy had never testified as an expert witness before. The evening before the hearing, he paced the floors of the Harrisburg Hilton, feeling the pressure. His wife sat directly in front of the witness stand, and afterward said that he made eye contact with her at least a half-dozen times. Kennedy didn't recall seeing her there at all; he was too focused on showing how Goofy's toe finds Donald's backside in a medical facility along Route 30.

Goofy's armpit? That's along the border of the 1st congressional district, and he demonstrated the precision with which the seemingly random line had been drawn. He described the map precinct by precinct, detailing its effect on neighbors in Chester and Swarthmore, now divided by red and blue as the lines pushed college "gown" into the 1st district and reddish "town" into the 7th, all with the goal of diluting Democratic votes. He delivered a tour de force of the state's political geography.

"The map made it easy. The map told the story," Kennedy humbly tells me, tucking into a salmon burger. His head is shaved and he has the solid build of a high school halfback. He collects vinyl and loves the Beach Boys. And he's an evangelist for the communities of this state. "I've lived in Pennsylvania most of my life. These communities are important to me. It's important that the Lehigh Valley"—Allentown, Bethlehem, Erie—"have its identity intact. That it has its own congressional district. That it's not splintered, or just a political tool to maximize political gain."

After all, he points out, the local baseball team is the Lehigh Valley Iron Pigs, not the Allentown–Hershey Iron Pigs. It's the Lehigh Valley Transit Authority, the Lehigh Valley International Airport. There's no nonpolitical reason to split these cities, he says, though many of them were stripped for red and blue parts. When Republicans wanted to divide blue-collar Reading, grabbing most of it for the new 16th district and separating it from its appropriate home in Berks County, they took everything except the bluest part, the county seat. "They lassoed it," he tells me. The string of the lasso? A small path no wider than a malt shop and a service station. "They split counties that had never been split before. There was no consideration for communities of interest or the interests of the citizens—who might have to drive through 30 miles of one district to get to another, or it's 80 miles to the nearest district office. The only consideration was to maximize the number of Republicans" in Congress.

The 2011 map, Kennedy told the court, "carves up Pennsylvania's communities of interest at an unprecedented level and—and contains more anomalies than ever before."[11] He put it even more directly to me. "It's a laughingstock. How can you justify it?" These are the howls of an outraged citizen, not a partisan, still furious over the way politicians put their own interests ahead of those of the people they are supposed to represent. "It's like they had so much confidence in their ability to do whatever they wanted—and that the public was never going to catch up to it."

One thing's certain: the politicians never imagined that Wesley Pegden, a six-foot-five-inch, 150-pound young mathematician, would deposit his lanky frame into a tiny Harrisburg chair and undo their maps, turn by turn, with a mathematical theorem that was virtually unknown when they were crafted. Or that the Carnegie Mellon professor would explain this fancy math—known as the Monte Carlo method, or a Markov chain— to a bewildered judge with a simple metaphor that he'd come up with just that morning.

The Monte Carlo method calculates probability when there is a huge range of potential outcomes. Think of it as a way to show whether or not one configuration—or one set of congressional districts—is an outlier compared to all of the other possibilities. Confused? Here's how Pegden introduced the idea to the court. You've just arrived in a new city, and you ask the cab driver to bring you to a restaurant that captures the local dining scene. He does—and the food is awful. Does this mean that every restaurant here is bad? Did the driver dislike you? You could test this theory by dining at every restaurant in town. That might take a while. Or you could sample the food at other places nearby. Find something you like? Great! Still hate them all? You've learned something important about the dining scene.

Pegden's academic paper, which Geffen discovered, suggested that this would be a perfect method for rooting out gerrymandering. The number of possible maps is incredibly large. But a Markov chain, he explained, removes the need to draw all of them to determine whether one particular plan is infected with partisan bias. Just take that map, make a sequence of small, random changes to it and observe whether the partisan bias decreases, or even evaporates.

One after another, Pegden made a trillion small changes to the map. Quite quickly, he noticed something: the partisan bias began to disappear. "We start with this map of Pennsylvania and we start making these small changes, right?" he testified. "Goofy and Donald are getting fuzzier. . . . What we observe is that with those small changes, the districting quickly becomes fairer."[12]

It turned out that 99.99999 percent of the maps created by those trillion tiny changes had less partisan bias than the original. Almost *any* change made the existing map fairer—revealing just how crafted the Republicans' work had been. "The Republican bias of the maps decreased after one step and never returned to that initial level in a trillion steps," Pegden tells me over breakfast in North Carolina with another key figure from the case, University of Michigan political scientist Jowei Chen. "So in some very extreme sense, it shows the lines are very carefully drawn, right? They wanted the lines exactly like this. When you make these little changes, I could almost hear the mapmakers in my mind shouting, 'No, no! That's what we wanted! Exactly that!'"

The mapmakers had optimized the districts to maximize the number of safe Republican seats. Pegden showed what they did by reverse-engineering it, one twist at a time.

Chen took a different approach. He used a computer to draw 500 maps that rigorously followed the state constitution's precise requirements: compactness, keeping counties together, minimizing splits of municipalities. The legislature's plan could then be compared with other maps that might reasonably have been drawn. The result was similar. In the words of Supreme Court justice Debra Todd, who wrote the majority decision that eventually struck down the GOP maps, Chen's work "reveals torturously drawn districts that cause plainly unnecessary political subdivision splits."

"We see the same thing consistently with every single one of the non-partisan criteria that I'm looking at," Chen says. "Put all that together. What does that collectively tell us? It tells us that the enacted plan was drawn under a process that was not prioritizing compactness, was not prioritizing minimization of county splits, and instead seemed to pursue a partisan outcome."

When Chen tested the partisan outcomes of his 500 maps, most split a fifty-fifty state right down the middle—9 seats to the Republicans, 9 seats to the Democrats. Only 2 percent of the maps—10 out of 500—resulted in a 10–8 GOP split. Not a single random map gave Republicans 11 seats. None gave them 12. And certainly none resulted in a 13–5 split, which had been the result of the past three consecutive elections on the map selected by legislators.

Jacobson saw the power of those results and turned them into a chart. The 500 new maps drawn to adhere to strict neutral criteria were all clustered together. The actual plan sat way off on its own, like a distant planet. "You see the 500 black dots," Jacobson says, "then you see the actual plan, way out in nowhere land."

The victory in Pennsylvania showed every state a path forward. If the U.S. Supreme Court wouldn't hear partisan gerrymandering claims, state courts would. Jacobson, Jones and many of the same expert witnesses would team up again in North Carolina state court, and in September 2018, win new state legislative maps with the same strategy. Pennsylvania proved that courts didn't need an archive of salacious emails to strike down the maps; in the end, the maps themselves were smoking. And it wasn't one standard that proved that gerrymandering had occurred, it was all of them. It simply took brilliant legal and mathematical minds to connect the dots.

CHAPTER 8

Mathematicians Enlist for Duty

"I would like someday to live in a democracy."

Moon Duchin likes a challenge. When, as a freshman, she exhausted every math class in her Connecticut high school, the fourteen-year-old—who was given her name by parents "on the science-y fringes of the hippie classification"—began independent study with a Harvard professor.[1] Now the recipient of a Guggenheim fellowship, she teaches geometry at Tufts University and studies the nature of authority, expertise and proof as the director of its Science, Technology and Society program. Oh, and in her spare time, she dons a superhero cape and battles for democracy as co-chair of the Metric Geometry and Gerrymandering working group, which she founded after realizing that her work with complicated concepts like low-dimensional topology and nilpotent geometry had an unexpected real-world application: it might help strengthen the basic building blocks of democracy, our legislative and congressional districts.

Even this brilliant scholar was momentarily baffled when a cryptic email arrived in early 2018 from a law firm claiming to represent Pennsylvania governor Tom Wolf. Wolf wanted to hire Duchin to investigate a mystery. After the Pennsylvania Supreme Court declared the state's congressional map unconstitutional, the Republican-controlled legislature had first crack at drawing the new one. They produced a map that looked less obviously gerrymandered. It split only 15 counties, compared to 23 in the original, and just 17 municipalities rather than 66. Wolf, a Democrat, remained suspicious. Could a tidier-looking map be just as biased? Had Republicans complied with the court's demand for a free and equal electoral playing field, or did it still carry a silent but deadly stench of unfairness? Could Captain Geometry solve the case of the purloined maps? She wouldn't have much time. If the governor wanted to strike a deal with the legislature, he had only six days before the court simply imposed a new map of its own.

"The timeline wasn't fun," Duchin tells me, over lunch at a bustling Harvard Square cafe. Still, Duchin didn't even need that many days to unravel this enigma. She produced not one map, as the GOP legislators had, but 3 *billion* maps, all of which complied with the state constitution's redistricting criteria. They were also at least as compact in shape as the new Republican plan, and preserved at least as many intact counties. When Duchin compared the legislature's new map to her universe of possibilities, the number of maps that were *more* Republican-skewed was less than one in 2 million. The new map was an "extreme outlier," she concluded, and "extremely unlikely to have come about by chance." How unlikely? You'd have far better odds of winning an Olympic gold medal (one in 662,000), dating a supermodel (one in 880,000), dying from a flesh-eating bacteria (one in 1 million) or getting walloped by an asteroid or meteorite (1 in 1.6 million).

Here's the really amazing part. The legislature's new map *looked* prettier and more fairly drawn than the old one, but Duchin's study showed it was just as biased. Indeed, if you took all 3 billion of Duchin's neutral maps, plus the two drawn by the legislature, and arranged them based on the advantage they afforded the Republican Party, the most skewed map would be the 2011 plan which had been ruled unconstitutional by the state Supreme Court. The legislature's 2018 plan would come in second. That's second out of 3,000,000,002.

Duchin used several rigorous statistical methods and ran trillions of tests across billions of maps. All of them reached the same conclusion.[2] The new map appeared fairer at first glance—shapes were normalized and townships held together—but was nevertheless "carefully designed to minimize Democratic representation" even within its constraints. "The legislature was given a do-over," she tells me, "and came up with a new plan that was much, much more compact—and just as skewed." Caking concealer onto the map couldn't disguise its ugly intent.

Duchin had demonstrated something crucial, especially as the nation approaches a 2021 redistricting cycle that will be powered by data, algorithms and mapping technology that has become exponentially more advanced over the last decade: a district like Pennsylvania's 7th need not look as cartoonish as Donald Duck with his foot up Goofy's rear end to deliver the same swift, firm kick to democracy and fairness. The state Supreme Court had ruled that map out of bounds, in part, because of the way it looked. Pennsylvania Republicans had needed just two days to design something just as rigged—despite the fact that it passed an eye test, without obvious laugh lines or steakhouse parking lots stitching together nutty configurations. It took Duchin—a deeply accomplished mathematician who decided to put her own career on hold and dedicate her unique skills toward enhancing democracy—to see through the subterfuge.

"For me, it feels like dumb luck that I have skills and a background that are relevant here," she says. She did her dissertation on a "walking tour" Markov chain, fell into the redistricting world because of her expertise in geometry and compactness, and now has made a very compact full-circle return to Markov chains, using this complicated mathematics to demystify gerrymandering. She wears a bright red T-shirt that reveals a heart tattoo on her right forearm. It's not the symbol that's etched on so many other arms, however, but an *anatomical* heart: what it would look like if you took the body apart and studied it from the inside. This seems right. After all, her work reveals the wiring of redistricting, what makes it tick. And in Pennsylvania, she discovered a still-beating bias buried deep within.

The governor rejected the Republican legislature's new map, citing Duchin's neutral analysis. "It's still a gerrymander," Wolf said, and "clearly seeks to benefit one political party, which is the essence of why the court found the current map to be unconstitutional." The following week, the state Supreme Court enlisted a "special master"; he drew a map that recalibrated partisan balance. In November 2018, under fairer lines, Pennsylvania moved from electing a 13–5 Republican delegation to one evenly split at 9 seats apiece.

Implementing fairer electoral maps nationwide, however, will require training a small army of Moon Duchins: a new generation of citizen mathematicians who can undo a technological assault on democracy with superior skills of their own, with the storytelling skills to break it down clearly enough so that a non-mathematician can understand.

And so the next stage of the great redistricting arms race was on. Once again, it set citizens against partisans and politicians. Only this time, it was a group of math whizzes reporting for duty.

Jonathan Mattingly had never testified in federal court, had never been an expert witness, and had never mixed his fascinations with math and politics. But in October 2017, the Duke University mathematician sat anxiously in a federal courtroom in Greensboro, North Carolina, with nothing at stake except his beloved home state's representation in Congress. Mattingly expected to be the fourth or fifth expert called to the stand in Common Cause's challenge to the constitutionality of the state's congressional map, but just as he took in his surroundings and started to reflect upon how a nice mathematician like him had landed in a courtroom like this, an attorney grabbed his attention. "You're on, Mattingly," he told the startled professor. The three-judge panel had decided to fast-track this complicated case in just four days. Both sides, unexpectedly, would jump straight to their evidence. First, the judges wanted to dig into the math. "I testified for almost three hours," he says. "It was nerve-racking."

Mattingly is charming, blazered, with tousled hair that flops forward in front. He resembles a rakish Hugh Grant, or maybe a dashing British songwriter like Robyn Hitchcock in middle age. He's a native North Carolinian, however, born in Charlotte and educated at an elite science and math high school in Durham, which was then followed by degrees at Yale and Princeton, and finally a return trip to his home state, to Duke. Like many others, he was flummoxed when Republicans captured 9 of the state's 13 congressional seats in 2012 even though Democrats won the majority of statewide votes. More than half the votes; fewer than 31 percent of the seats. But Mattingly understood that we don't elect members of Congress by proportional representation, so he didn't think about it as a math problem until he listened to a public radio discussion that exposed gerrymandering as the culprit. The report noted that most Democrats won their seats with around 80 percent support, while most Republicans claimed victory in the low 60s. That seemed interesting but still anecdotal, perhaps having more to do with geography than nefarious maps.

"I know North Carolina. I grew up here. The shape of the state matters," he tells me. "It's a diverse state, it's a purple state, it has a lot of different areas." The experts on the radio insisted that the proper partisan breakdown should be 7–6, one way or the other. How did they know, Mattingly wondered. Where was the evidence that these districts had been cracked and packed to favor Republicans? Why would five, six or seven seats be the fair number of Democratic victories? "The scientist in my head kicked in. My mathematician alarm bells went off," he says. "I was curious. Could this just be where people live?" Could geometry and statistics produce an answer with some empirical force?

Mattingly has a restless mind. He's led secret lives pursuing applied mathematics topics that intrigued him, then would start to feel anxious because he hadn't proved a theorem for a while. That year, he had a summer student with an interest in politics and data, and thought maybe together they could figure it out.

Mattingly had an idea: they'd do some Markov chain Monte Carlo sampling. The only true way to evaluate fairness is to compare a map against other valid plans, so they would produce a grab bag of as many nonpartisan maps as they could and evaluate the state's congressional map against that suite of possibilities. It was a simple test. The computer produced 100 maps. Over 95 percent of the time, Democrats won between 6 and 9 seats. The most common outcome was either 7 or 8 Democratic wins. On the real map, Democrats won just 4 seats, a result that was an extreme outlier, not representative of the way people voted. Maps matter. Mattingly and his student proved it.

"I didn't change a single vote. I didn't block anyone from going to the polls. I didn't stuff any ballot boxes. The votes are all exactly the same. All I did was change how I drew the maps," he says. We're in his office on the Duke campus, cluttered with books and equations; the coffee mugs proclaim, simply, MATH. Changing the maps, however, changed absolutely everything. "And if I did that, I can go from nine Republicans elected, which would be the headline, 'Wave Republican Election,' right? Or it could go to nine Democratic seats, which would be 'Wave Democratic Election.' Without doing anything different."

A local NPR station showed some interest, but that was about it.[3] Mattingly got back to theorems, his doctoral students and other real work, though gerrymandering remained very much on his mind. His larger contribution to protecting North Carolina's democracy was still to come—as was the technology and computing power that would make his next set of maps so immediately revealing.

"I would like someday to live in a democracy," he cracks drily.

Gerrymandering might have still been a hobby for Mattingly in 2012, but other academics were beginning to understand that there was full-time work in using new technology and advanced computing power to help citizens and courts see through partisan gerrymanders and uncover the invisible intent lurking behind district lines. Two political scientists, Stanford's Jonathan Rodden and the University of Michigan's Jowei Chen, pioneered the modern era of simulated maps. They were considered the first to bring them into the courtroom, in 2014, when a federal court ruled in favor of Florida's League of Women Voters, finding that Republican consultants had conspired to run a secret, shadow redistricting effort that "made a mockery" of the state constitution. Rodden and Chen generated hundreds of possible maps, using neutral criteria, and concluded that the set selected by the GOP were extreme outliers, containing a level of partisan bias unlikely to be the result of mere happenstance. The judge ordered several congressional districts to be redrawn, but his ruling focused on evidence such as careless emails and memos that revealed the strategists' machinations more than on the maps themselves.

Rodden's office at Stanford is located high in the quiet hills above campus, inside a low-slung, tree-shaded building, and surrounded by the golf course Tiger Woods mastered as a three-time amateur champion. At a standing desk equipped with two giant monitors, Rodden has unraveled multiple plots against democracy, including the impact of voter ID laws on Michigan's college students and the likely result of Arizona criminalizing the act of mailing another person's ballot, which forces elderly Native Americans to travel upwards of an hour to the closest post office rather than allowing a trusted neighbor to drop it off.

When I visit, one stunning summer morning, Rodden is displaying a series of dot-density maps that show just how precisely Virginia lawmakers used race when drawing state legislative districts. "Zoom in on this," he says, pointing out a district line that runs directly along the border where the majority of black voters live. "That's how the line was drawn. The defense has to argue *that* has nothing to do with race." It couldn't be done with a straight face. It's as if Rodden has the invisible-ink light pen that reveals lawmakers' nefarious intent.

He displays another district on the screen, Virginia's 94th. "So this is the Virginia state house district that ended up being a tie," he says. Not only did the race end knotted at 11,608 votes apiece, but it ended up determining control of the House of Delegates. (When lots were drawn and the Republican candidate's name emerged, the GOP maintained control of the lower house 51–49. Had it gone the other way, the Democratic lieutenant governor would have settled any deadlocks.)

"See these red lines?" Rodden asks, pointing to small sections of the map that overlap two legislative districts. "These are voting tabulation districts. Normally, when you draw districts, you grab an entire VTD. That way, there's only one ballot. Everyone's voting in all the same elections, so there's no chance for a mistake. Split VTDs, and different precincts share the same voting place but, for example, a different down-ballot race for state house. That's complicated and introduces the chance that people vote in the wrong election. You might have to split one for population equality. But there's no reason to split"—Rodden moves the cursor along the line— "five VTDs in a row. It just . . . There's no reason to do it."

The story only gets wilder. A new affordable housing complex was built alongside Charles Street and Warwick Avenue in Newport News. Warwick Avenue divides two state house districts: on one side is the 93rd district, on the other side, the 94th. Most African American voters in Newport News live in the 93rd—but this housing complex sits in the 94th. More than two dozen voters—more than enough to swing the election and with it Virginia's lower house—were given the wrong ballot in error by poll workers.[4] "The election administrators must have known that they had been trying to stick all the apartment complexes in the 93rd. So they gave everybody that ballot. All these people voted in the wrong place, through no mistake of their own." It's outrageous on so many levels: a race that ended in a tie, with control of the House of Delegates at stake, was actually decided incorrectly—because legislators drew a surgical racial gerrymander that divided one voter tabulation center across two local legislative districts.

Rodden's work involves mapping the demography of districts. For example, he might compare an entire state voting file with the driver's license database, geo-code everyone down to the address level, and determine the impact of requiring various forms of voter ID district by district. "The level of fanciness that's required is not that high," he says. "It's not even computer science that's making the difference. It's the availability of data. It's an incredibly different world now than it used to be, because we have voter files. We have addresses. It doesn't even require a lot of coding."

Chen, meanwhile, has continued to perfect simulated district maps. He has become one of the most sought-after expert witnesses in the nation, with his exuberant energy, a Beatles-esque moptop and a perfect record of convincing judges that the fix is in. His work has been cited in victorious cases in North Carolina, Pennsylvania, Maryland, Wisconsin and multiple other localities. Chen, whose parents arrived in Chattanooga, Tennessee, from Taiwan in 1978, grew up fascinated by political geography. He watched religious white voters turn away from the Democrats as the South realigned with the Republican Party. He wrote his dissertation on the effects of political geography on redistricting.

"I studied political geography," he says, "but the way I studied it was by trying to separate out political geography from neutral redistricting factors, and learn more about racial gerrymandering, or partisan gerrymandering. And so it just became natural to want to ask as part of my research, well, what would districts in a state like Florida have looked like if they'd been drawn just purely according to nothing but nonpartisan traditional districting criteria? Just compactness, just following county boundaries." Time and again, the answer was simple. They'd have a completely different shape, and generate completely different electoral results.

Duke University's legendary basketball team attracts the nation's top freshman talent, then launches them into the NBA draft after a single sensational season. But even as stochastic dynamics and other advanced mathematics topics beckoned Jonathan Mattingly back toward theories and equations, he would not be a gerrymandering "one and done." Much like college hoops along North Carolina's Tobacco Road, Mattingly couldn't have ignored gerrymandering if he tried. Extreme maps had turned his state's politics toxic. A Republican supermajority in the state legislature, itself the result of extreme gerrymandering, made national headlines, among many examples, with its assault on the independence of the state university system, as well as with the infamous H.B.2 "bathroom bill," which required transgender individuals to use the bathroom of the gender they were assigned at birth.

Then, in 2016, a federal court struck down the state's congressional map as an unconstitutional racial gerrymander. Republicans made it clear that they did not intend the new districts to be any more competitive. How clear? Well, the legislature brazenly *demanded* that the maps deliver a 10–3 GOP edge. Why 10 Republicans and 3 Democrats? "I propose that we draw the maps to give a partisan advantage to 10 Republicans and 3 Democrats," testified Representative David Lewis, the GOP co-chair of the elections committee, "because I do not believe it's possible to draw a map with 11 Republicans and 2 Democrats."[5] They hired master Republican mapmaker Thomas Hofeller to make it so, cocksure in their own cleverness. They'd make the maps neater, but just as partisan. And they'd admit from the get-go that political partisanship, not race, motivated the maps. After all, while the federal courts looked disfavorably upon racial gerrymandering, the U.S. Supreme Court had never found a partisan gerrymander to be unconstitutional. Confession would set them free!

Mattingly, meanwhile, had a new colleague at Duke. After Republicans successfully pushed Tom Ross out of the presidency of the University of North Carolina system, the esteemed judge, scholar and public servant established an office at Duke. Painfully aware of and frightened by his state's about-face from bipartisanship, he was determined to study gerrymandering. He assembled a panel of respected jurists, most of them former justices on the state Supreme Court, equally split between Democrats and Republicans. He wanted them to simulate a redistricting commission and model what neutral maps and a nonpartisan process might resemble. They sat in a room, argued, explored possibilities and competing values, and finally reached consensus.

Mattingly, intrigued, now had three sets of maps to compare: the original 2011 congressional map thrown out as a racial gerrymander, the legislature's 2016 effort and now the set produced by the retired judges. He and his graduate students got to work. Once again using a Monte Carlo algorithm, they created 24,518 neutral maps from a probability distribution of all possible North Carolina redistricting plans. Then they used the actual voting data from the 2012 and 2016 elections to see whether the simulated districts produced the same results as the actual maps.

Spoiler alert: they didn't. The neutral maps produced at least one additional Democratic winner more than 99 percent of the time, using either the 2012 or 2016 results. "What we see," Mattingly says, "is that it wasn't accidental."

After he shared the results with Ross and others at Duke, it didn't take long for the legal team challenging the legislature's 2016 map as an unconstitutional partisan gerrymander to inquire about bringing Mattingly aboard as an expert witness. Which is how the "nice mathematician" found himself suddenly summoned to the stand that October morning in Greensboro, tasked with presenting the most important seminar of his career, with democracy in the balance.

This was a massive task. After all, it had only been two weeks since the U.S. Supreme Court heard oral arguments in *Gill v. Whitford*, the partisan gerrymandering case from Wisconsin that advanced a metric known as the efficiency gap. Chief Justice Roberts dumped so much cold water on the notion that it seemed like his own personal ice bucket challenge. While the Supreme Court's role as a political institution is undeniable, Roberts clearly wanted no part of determining an acceptable level of partisanship for every state legislative and congressional map. "We will have to decide in every case whether the Democrats win or the Republicans win," he said. "It's going to be a problem here across the board." How would the average citizen without an advanced math degree view those decisions, Roberts asked. The math might be complicated, but it's hardly nonsense. Roberts, presumably, with two degrees from Harvard, knows that. Some fun facts about the Markov chain Monte Carlo algorithm: It was developed as part of the Manhattan Project. The physicist Enrico Fermi dazzled friends and colleagues by using it to make lightning-fast predictions from a giant universe of possible outcomes. These days, it's used to make advances in drug development, weather forecasting, even artificial intelligence and machine learning. But for our purposes, think of the evidence Mattingly presented to the court like this. The professor stuffed a grab bag with 24,518 congressional maps, drawn randomly by this algorithm from the entire universe of possible configurations. Then, he explained to the court, he used the actual votes from North Carolina's 2012 and 2016 congressional races, precinct by precinct, to compare how many seats each party would have won on each of the maps. When Mattingly used the 2012 numbers, almost 80 percent of his ensemble of maps produced either 7 Republicans and 6 Democrats, or 7 Democrats and 6 Republicans. That's a far cry from the actual outcome that year: 9 Republicans and 4 Democrats, a distribution which occurred in only 89 of the 24,518 random maps—that's 0.36 percent. When Mattingly plugged the 2016 numbers into his maps, the actual outcome of 10 Republicans and 3 Democrats occurred on just 162 of the 24,518 maps—or 0.7 percent.

Then Mattingly took his analysis to a deeper level. He wanted to show that the legislators' map achieved its pro-GOP tilt by cracking and packing Democratic voters. So on each of those 24,518 maps, he organized the 13 districts according to the number of Democratic votes that were cast there in 2012 and 2016. When he plotted those results on a graph, both for 2012 and 2016, the distribution looked completely natural, a gradual slope from lowest to highest. The maps created by Ross's bipartisan panel of judges generated a similar neat line. The 2012 and 2016 maps? On those maps, a line charting the median Democratic vote takes on what Mattingly calls "the signature of gerrymandering": a dramatic, slashing S, with the three Democratic districts in the high 70 percents, then a sharp diagonal drop down below the 50 percent axis to the 10 Republican districts where Democrats stood little chance of victory. "What we see," he says, walking me through the charts in his Duke office, "is that it wasn't accidental. The most Democratic district is way up here—incredibly unusual." He points to the districts at the top of the S. "These have had Democrats packed into them." And then to the bottom of the curve. "And these have had Democrats that have been dispersed, so that they have less of an effect."

The court not only understood all this, it wholeheartedly endorsed his analysis, concluding that he "provided strong evidence that the General Assembly intended to subordinate the interests of non-Republican voters and entrench the Republican Party in power."[6] In a sober and deliberate 205-page decision, a bipartisan panel of three federal judges made history. For the first time ever, a federal court overturned a state's entire congressional map as an unconstitutional partisan gerrymander. The bulk of the decision explained how Mattingly's and Chen's analyses revealed partisan intent. It wasn't simply one silver-bullet theory: every single measure found that the legislature's map was an extreme outlier. The court did not have to accept any one standard. It could examine and accept guidance from them all.

"That was amazing," says Mattingly.

But while it was his work that made the decision possible, Mattingly was not the audience for this decision. The ruling had an audience of one: Chief Justice John Roberts. Any federal case involving congressional maps heads automatically to the Supreme Court on appeal. These judges wanted to send a clear message: Mr. Chief Justice, this isn't gobbledygook. Not to embrace this new math, they wrote, "would be to admit that the judiciary lacks the competence—or willingness—to keep pace with the technical advances that simultaneously facilitate such invidious partisanship and provide an opportunity to remedy it."[7]

Then this: "There is no constitutional basis for dismissing Plaintiffs claims as judicially unmanageable—not because they are irrelevant, unreliably, or incorrectly applied, but simply because they rely on new, sophisticated empirical methods that derive from academic research. The Constitution does not require the federal courts to act like Galileo's Inquisition and enjoin consideration of new academic theories, and the knowledge gained therefrom, simply because such theories provide a new understanding of how to give effect to our long-established governing principles. That is not what the founding generation did when it adopted a Constitution grounded in the then-untested political theories of Locke, Montesquieu and Rousseau. That is not what the Supreme Court did when it recognized that advances in our understanding of psychology had proven that separate could not be equal. And that is not what we do here."[8]

When the case returned to the Supreme Court in 2018, Roberts received a second chance to pass college statistics—and once again failed the challenge. But that means that gerrymandering litigation will move from the federal courts to state Supreme Courts, and it will give this "nice mathematician" even more opportunities to remake American politics. Mattingly seems more than eager for the opportunity. "I'm a citizen, too," he says.

Back in Cambridge, Moon Duchin imagines a throng of Jonathan Mattinglys. Just picture it: rakish intellectuals brushing the hair from their eyes and undoing the dastardly algorithms of extremism and division, and spinning that technology, in true superhero style, back toward truth and justice. She founded the Metric Geometry and Gerrymandering Working Group with the goal of gathering top minds in geometry, topology and computing to pursue cutting-edge research to address the nation's gerrymandering problem. "You're never going to remove all of the partisanship," she says. "But if we're successful, the boundaries of what people think they can get away with will narrow."

Duchin aims to build a robust mathematics of redistricting, and to build open-source tools for mapping that allow everyone to better understand districting and its political consequences. The group also runs a six-week Voting Rights Data Institute, more commonly referred to as the gerrymandering summer camp, where mathematicians and computer scientists can work together on projects and learn, potentially, how to become expert witnesses themselves. Duchin wants the group's work to evolve again in time for the 2021 redistricting cycle. If mathematicians have spent recent years uncovering mischief and elaborate conspiracies like an old-school Perry Mason or a newfangled investigator like Lisbeth Salander dropped into *House of Cards*, next time Duchin hopes that these algorithms and models might help start a conversation before a legislature approves a map. This next round of maps will be the first one in our history in which citizens and experts alike will be able to produce their own maps alongside the legislature. One of the things the MGGG is working on is building a program that would show legislators—and citizens—how different redistricting priorities create tradeoffs. What would it look like if a state wanted more competitive districts? Would more compact districts affect the partisan makeup of a delegation?

"There's just this giant research effort happening," she says. "The fundamental question for mathematicians here is, what does the world of possibilities look like, and how do you search and create it?" There are twenty-eight active projects coming out of the 2018 summer camp, with many more to follow. Students and scholars have written thousands of line of code for a Markov chain Monte Carlo algorithm capable of studying districting plans in all fifty states. Another group developed an app called Districtr, which allows anyone to make a map showing the communities of interest in their own district. Designers call it "civic engagement for citizens at all levels of technical expertise."

Meanwhile, Sam Wang's Princeton Gerrymandering Project has launched OpenPrecincts, a massive effort to build a central database of voting precincts across the country that make it possible to open the districting process to everyone and ensure that maps are fair. Eric McGhee and Nicholas Stephanopoulos (who created the efficiency gap metric), along with Ruth Greenwood, an attorney representing the Wisconsin citizens in *Gill v. Whitford*, launched PlanScore, which makes it possible for fair-minded legislators to check the partisanship, demographics and racial breakdown of maps in progress, and for voters to immediately assess the districts that politicians have drawn. Two top redistricting scholars, Michael McDonald of the University of Florida and Harvard's Micah Altman, won the 2018 Brown Democracy Medal for their Public Mapping Project and its open-source software, District Builder. Their project aims to even the playing field between people and partisans by giving everyone access to "transparent, accessible, and easy-to-use" online mapping tools. Ordinary citizens suddenly have access to the same information and tools that politicians have used to carve them up with such precision.

That will be the real redistricting revolution: when this technology is taken out of bunkers and back rooms and placed in the hands of everyone. When voters, not politicians, determine districts based on holding communities together, not cleaving them unrecognizable in the name of partisan gain. When citizens can debate what representation means—competitive districts? compact? statewide partisan symmetry?—and draw lines in the spirit of consensus and compromise that we want to see echoed in the politicians we elect to serve us.

At last, the revolution is well underway, and no one needs an advanced degree to join. In Pennsylvania, where it took John Kennedy, Moon Duchin, Jowei Chen and Wesley Pegden to unravel the most dramatic Republican advantage anywhere in the nation, a group called Draw The Lines PA is helping citizens stitch their communities back together again. Which is why Chris Satullo and Justin Villere are hosting happy hour at the Firehouse restaurant in Harrisburg on this Monday night in October. It's bar games for democracy, where the chicken tenders come wrapped in brown sugar and chili-encrusted bacon, and flash cards guide everyone through discussions about compactness, competitiveness and contiguity. Satullo has brought a jigsaw puzzle of the state's gerrymandered map, and within the shadow of the capitol where Republicans designed these impossible shapes, inside the second oldest firehouse still standing in the state, a young crowd endeavors to extinguish four-alarm unfairness. The challenge is not made any easier by wine.

Games and drinks raise awareness about gerrymandering, but giving citizens control of mapmaking software creates real change. After barnstorming hundreds of happy hours statewide (trendy mixologists at Philadelphia's Raw Sushi Bar even crafted a special Slay The Gerrymander cocktail starring tequila, sake and mint), Draw The Lines launched a mapmaking contest with $5,000 prizes for winners in several categories. The interest left even its organizers slack-jawed: More than 15,000 people signed up—senior citizens, law school classes, youth groups, even families—and worked on some 25,000 sets of maps. "You can see people working through the real, small, deep challenges of democracy," says David Thornburgh, the president and CEO of the nonpartisan civic group Committee on 70, which sponsored Draw The Lines.

When Thornburgh told legislators about the project, "there was a pat on the head," he tells me. "That's cute. A novelty item." Now they see the public fascination and engagement, and Thornburgh hopes they understand that it is not going away. "Their constituents now step forth in the grocery store and tell them, 'Here's my map,' or 'My kid drew a map that was more competitive than yours.'"

That's what it will take for citizens to win this unusual arms race against their own representatives. There is no such thing as the perfect map, no computer that can spit out ideal districts that offer fairness, competition and contiguity, while protecting communities and minority groups. "I don't think we should have the Gerry-o-tron 2020," Mattingly says, taking on a robot voice. "I'm Gerry 2020. Here's your map." The professor doesn't want an algorithm to determine everyone's maps. But when voters are included in a conversation about districting, when the technology is democratized, when the work of partisans can be checked by nonpartisan mathematicians, the playing field begins to even. Redistricting need not take place in the shadows, or be left in the hands of well-funded partisans armed with big data and the most sophisticated software. Gerrymandering, actual polls have shown, is less popular than even herpes or the detested nineties' rockers Nickelback.[9] Americans do not want politicians empowered to choose their own voters. Thanks to these crusading mathematicians, citizens can take that power back—just as long as one judge understands that this is not gobbledygook. Plenty of those citizens, however, aren't just standing around waiting.

CHAPTER 9

People Power

"It's like diving into *The Matrix*."

When President Lyndon Johnson signed the Voting Rights Act into law in July 1965, he proclaimed that "the right to vote is the basic right, without which all others are meaningless." Forty-four years later, the job of enforcing this landmark legislation fell to the nation's first African American attorney general, Eric Holder, who was just a teenager at the time but already on a path for law school, an earnest kid committed to a career that connected voting rights and civil rights. Holder became the nation's top lawyer fewer than three years after the Voting Rights Act glided through reauthorization for another twenty-five years, backed by a Republican president, George W. Bush, and supported overwhelmingly by both houses of Congress, including a unanimous U.S. Senate.

It was about to become much more controversial. In 2006, there was broad, bipartisan support for "preclearance," the Voting Rights Act's most critical enforcement tool. It essentially placed on probation parts, or all, of sixteen states with a history of deeply rooted discrimination. If those entities wanted to alter their electoral laws, they had to prove there would not be any discriminatory purpose or effect. Not long after Republicans swept a record number of state legislative chambers in 2010, however, more than two dozen new state laws and executive orders targeted early voting, voter registration efforts and additional photo ID requirements. And when Holder's Justice Department halted these voter suppression techniques under preclearance, citing discriminatory effects, a flurry of lawsuits resulted. It wasn't 1965 any longer, not even in Alabama or Texas, these suits charged; they asserted that, in theory at least, a new era of equality existed, and defended the rights of these entities to make their own election laws. The federal government no longer needed to monitor every move. In the forty-five years between 1965 and 2010, there were only eight challenges to Section 5 of the Voting Rights Act. Between 2010 and 2012 alone, there were nine.

Holder vigorously explained the theory behind Section 5 and defended its necessity. In a dramatic speech at the LBJ Library in Texas in late 2011, he stated his fear that some might "allow this time—our time—to be recorded in history as the age when the long-held belief that, in this country, every citizen has the chance—and the right—to help shape their government became a relic of our past." His efforts, Holder said, honored the generations that took extraordinary risks, willingly confronted hatred and ignorance, and stood before billy clubs, fire hoses and bullets to fight for the right to vote as the very lifeblood of democracy.

Imagine, then, his profound dismay when the Supreme Court, in a 2013 case from Alabama called *Shelby County v. Holder*, overturned Section 5 as "based on 40-year-old facts having no logical relationship to the present day," according to Chief Justice John Roberts, in a nation that "has changed." Holder had clerked with the NAACP's Legal Defense Fund as a law student and joined the Justice Department's public integrity division straight out of Columbia, working on voting rights issues. Now the Court had gutted a key enforcement mechanism that protected democracy, and did so in a case bearing Holder's name. "We only call it *Shelby County*," Holder cracks when we discuss the case, with a wincing half-smile.

The *Shelby County* decision unleashed a wave of new voter suppression techniques blessed by a majority of Supreme Court justices. Holder would leave office as a tireless opponent of gerrymandering, now certain that nothing other than collective faith in democracy was at stake. But this battle was not his alone. A citizen militia would need to stand up and defend the vote, understanding that it's the ongoing responsibility of us all to safeguard the rights we hold most dear.

When Holder vowed to make redistricting sexy, he probably didn't see this evening coming. It's a Monday evening in late July 2018, and Holder has been pinned in a Columbus, Ohio, kitchen by a wealthy workers' comp attorney with an unearthly pinkish-tan glow. The local lawyer, a big Democratic donor, stands between the former attorney general and a gazpacho fountain, wearing a partially unbuttoned blue gingham shirt and alligator loafers with no socks. He gestures with a giant glass of rosé, some of which spills onto Holder's non-alligator shoes, while he emphatically explains why he's *finished* donating to Ohio congressional candidates. His money will be given strategically, instead, to two otherwise anonymous down-ballot races, because the winners will hold a seat on Ohio's redistricting commission.

"I'll write a big check!" he tells Holder. "You know I'll write a big check!" he adds enthusiastically, pointing his glass toward his candidate of choice, Zach Space, the Democratic auditor nominee. "You wrote me a big check today!" Space says quickly and appreciatively, wearing the pinned-on permasmile of any politician at a party with their awkward new benefactor. But the congressional folks? Cut off! The lawyer told the party so today. "They called me and I said, 'I'm not giving you another dime.' It's gerrymandering! They get nothing ever again! I'm giving to the auditor and the secretary of state."

In Ohio, even the lawyers who look freshly delivered from the Yellow Pages' back cover are woke. Gerrymandering has turned this bellwether state's politics inside out, securing Republicans a 12–4 edge in Congress and supermajorities in both state legislative chambers. Exactly 7 of the

297 races for the lower house between 2014 and 2018 have been within 5 points; heroes and legends like LeBron James or Ohio State football coach Urban Meyer can bring championships back home, but even Ohio's most beloved figures would struggle to make those other 98 percent of the state's house districts even remotely competitive.

That's what brought Holder to this well-appointed home in his role as chairman of the National Democratic Redistricting Committee. He needs more donors and Democrats to connect the party's flailing fortunes in states like this to the outrageously tilted districts Republicans drew during the last mapmaking process. There are still plenty of Democrats in Ohio; they've simply been cracked, packed and stacked so they can't win many elections, ratfucked into oblivion by brilliant mapmakers and strategists who, unlike 2010's Democrats, understood that winning the contests for auditor and secretary of state brought the power to banish the other side to political Antarctica.

"This is about fairness. They're a minority power exercising supermajority power. That has to stop," Holder tells the assembled crowd. The living room is rapt and alive; the fancy hors d'oeuvres are wrapped in bacon; every book on display has something to do with the musical *Hamilton*. "If we have a fair fight, we will do just fine. But you have to forget this notion of down-ballot. And you can't just yell at the TV, at MSNBC or Colbert."

"We shoot the TV in Ohio," interrupts the lawyer from the kitchen.

Such was Eric Holder's 2018. The former attorney general could have cashed in countless billable hours. He could have made bank on his status as the first African American to hold the office, or his long friendship with Barack Obama. Instead, he spent the year in living rooms like this, across our most gerrymandered states, urging Democrats to refocus on state legislatures and redistricting, pushing voting rights and a democracy agenda into the headlines and trying to make the least sexy contests just a little hotter. Over many months, I followed Holder into black churches and universities, house parties, law offices, even YWCA conference rooms as he rallied support for judges in North Carolina and Wisconsin, these easily ignored races in Ohio, and even called rural Georgians from a nowheresville strip mall party headquarters next to the Licken' Chicken'.

All of it was unglamorous. Much of it was thankless. In late 2017, both Holder and I were asked to discuss redistricting for a private audience of Democratic U.S. senators. Senators shuffled in and out of the ornate caucus room off the chamber floor. It was early, the morning after election day, but Democrats were ebullient from big wins in Virginia. The general elation made it all the more shocking when Senate Minority Leader Charles Schumer peered down at Holder, glasses on the tip of his nose, and pinned the party's gerrymandering problem on race. The problem, Schumer fumed behind closed doors, was that civil rights groups and African American incumbents wouldn't surrender even a piece of their safe districts for the general good of the party. What, he demanded to know, with a condescending tone that made me shiver and a racial undercurrent that made much of the room cringe, was Holder doing about that? Was he having conversations with those groups?

The kernel of truth inside Schumer's otherwise off-base observation was decades old. During the 1990s redistricting cycle, Republicans and black Democrats joined forces as unusual, but understandable, bedfellows. Conservative white Democrats held a hammerlock on Southern politics; both Republicans and African Americans were underrepresented as a result. Blacks in North Carolina may have been reliable Democratic voters, but the state hadn't sent a person of color to Congress since 1900. By 1994, North Carolina had two African American representatives, from districts packed with black voters. That year, however, Republicans took Congress for the first time in five decades. The packed "majority-minority" seats also bleached the surrounding districts whiter and more conservative, tilting them red.

The black caucus understood the devil's bargain of cracking and packing and wished to be part of a Democratic majority, but they also harbored a natural distrust of white Democrats diluting their voice. Schumer's racially tinged outburst, however, was so disrespectful and condescending that I thought for sure the tension would escalate. But Holder quietly assured Schumer that he was in regular touch with civil rights groups. That's when Missouri senator Claire McCaskill jumped in with her awkward race-related plaint. Missouri's black members of Congress had such safe districts, she charged, that too many African Americans didn't bother to turn out to vote for white statewide candidates, like, for example, herself. Could Holder make that clear in his meetings as well? The former attorney general had grown accustomed to this treatment in brutal oversight hearings from House Republicans; he likely didn't expect it from his own side.

Holder, however, had quickly grasped how GOP gerrymandering caromed Democrats into the abyss, even if Schumer and McCaskill misunderstood the finer points. Not long after Barack Obama's reelection in 2012, Holder told me, he and the president were looking over the numbers. "We thought we had done well in terms of the raw vote, but it wasn't at all reflected in the number of representatives we had at both the state and federal level," Holder says. It's the day after the Columbus house party and we're in the parlor of a Cincinnati law office where he'll soon hold a lunch-time Q and A with young Democrats. "So what's going on? REDMAP had been a small part of my consciousness before the 2012 election. I'd heard the phrase, but it wasn't anything I had really focused on. Then we saw the election results." Democratic congressional candidates won 1.4 million more votes nationwide; Republicans held the House 234–201, thanks to a 56–24 edge from purple Pennsylvania (13–5), Ohio (12–4), Michigan (9–5), North Carolina (9–4), Virginia (8–3) and Wisconsin (5–3). If those fifty-fifty states had fifty-fifty delegations, the GOP edge would have been 218–217. It's easy to imagine a very different second Obama term, with a smaller and less influential Freedom Caucus, much more incentive for compromise, and without government shutdowns or four dozen votes to repeal Obamacare. Holder looks back on that election and realizes that Obama's legislative agenda curdled the very night he won reelection. "There's no question gerrymandering had an impact. I think it certainly shut down, in a substantial way, legislative avenues—which forced him to use executive power," Holder reflects. "He had an impactful second term, but he did not have the ability to make it a durable one. The use of executive power, as we've now seen, can be reversed relatively quickly."

When the U.S. Supreme Court hollowed the heart of the Voting Rights Act in 2013, in *Shelby County v. Holder*, and eliminated preclearance of new voting laws in states with a history of race-based discrimination at the polls, both newly gerrymandered legislatures and red states across the South and Southwest wasted no time passing new voter ID bills, closing precincts, curtailing early voting and more. "People had underestimated the importance of gerrymandering, the hollowing out of the Voting Rights Act," Holder says. "You had conceptually the notion that this was not a good thing. But then it became real."

Texas implemented its strict photo ID law fewer than twenty-four hours after the court's ruling. Alabama and Mississippi jumped at the opportunity to enforce voter ID laws that the Justice Department had previously blocked. Gerrymandered North Carolina, meanwhile, quickly went to work on H.B. 589, a package of voting restrictions that included a voter ID bill that carefully targeted African Americans, in addition to ending same-day registration, annual registration drives and most early voting. "These are civil rights issues," Holder tells me. It's just spreadsheets and data files instead of fire hoses and attack dogs. "We're not fighting George Wallace and Bull Connor. But there's a straight line between the civil rights movement and what we're fighting now."

Holder's a Democrat. At every stop we made, someone asked him if he would seek the presidency in 2020. But he insists that the NDRC is not "a partisan attempt at good government." The only way to "break this fever" of extremism in Washington and state capitals, he suggests, is by ensuring that neither party holds unilateral power over electoral maps. Neither Congress nor the Supreme Court seems likely to set fairness guidelines. Therefore, "you've got to elect Democrats, so that when the process happens again in 2021, you've got two parties at the table." Now, that's some nifty political jujitsu that might encourage, say, Republicans in Maryland, which is gerrymandered by the Democrats, to check for their wallet. Holder, however, pledges that he'll fight any effort by Democrats to gerrymander where his party has complete control. "If that was the game, I wouldn't put my name on it," he insists. "Barack wouldn't have put his name on it. It's going to be on us to be critical of Democrats who do that, and, frankly, stop it from happening."

In December 2018, Holder proved true to his word. New Jersey Democrats attempted to assure themselves unfettered power over the state's bipartisan redistricting commission, reworking the state constitution to give legislative leaders the right to select its members. Holder blasted this as unfair and a step backward, which added to pressure on the legislature to back down. It did.

It's easy to be cynical about a partisan effort that promises it will reform partisan behavior. Believe him or not, however, Holder has been remarkably consistent: he wants to undo REDMAP, not install BLUEMAP. He's convinced that Republican voters hate gerrymandering just as much as Democrats and independents do. Just look at Ohio, he says, where redistricting reform passed with more than 70 percent approval. Or Florida, where two Fair Districts amendments soared past 60 percent approval during the 2010 Tea Party wave. "Republicans, conservatives, independents, Democrats. The people get it," he says.

And it's the people who will have to fix it. Back in Columbus, Holder beseeches the room to become engaged citizens. "We have the capacity to create the change that we want," he says, highlighting the civil rights movement, women's rights and opposition to the Vietnam War as times when regular people "pushed, pushed, pushed" for change. "That's what we have to do again."

In North Carolina, simply pushing back has been an all-hands effort. REDMAP plus the *Shelby County* decision turned the clock back five decades in this otherwise progressive purple state, disrupting any arc toward progress and placing voting rights in the crosshairs. North Carolina became not only ground zero for partisan gerrymandering, but also a national test site for Republican efforts to entrench themselves in power by any means necessary, no matter the will of the people. Republican congressional maps were so antidemocratic that they made history with an unconstitutional two-fer: for the first time, a congressional map was overturned as a racial gerrymander and its replacement tossed out as an illegal partisan gerrymander. Then, after *Shelby* removed preclearance, the state legislature responsible for those monstrous maps gutted early voting, preregistration for teenagers and same-day voter registration, and also enacted one of the nation's toughest voter ID laws. A federal appeals court would overturn that law for "target[ing] African Americans with almost surgical precision." The legislature simply moved to enshrine it in the state constitution, then began canceling judicial primaries, changing the process for electing state Supreme Court justices and muting the new Democratic governor's voice on the state election board. If state legislatures are sometimes the laboratories of democracy, North Carolina's had become a meth lab.

Two individuals led the struggle for the vote: the Reverend William Barber, whose Moral Monday movement turned tens of thousands of everyday North Carolinians into fervent weekly protesters filling the state capitol, and Anita Earls, whose Southern Coalition for Social Justice won some of the most important legal battles against GOP gerrymandering and suppression shenanigans. Her state's sudden metamorphosis into Mississippi transformed Earls as well. After big wins against the state's bonkers congressional maps and the severe new voter ID requirements, Earls decided she wanted to stop challenging the laws and start ruling on them. Earls made the difficult decision to leave the nonprofit she founded and announced her candidacy for the state Supreme Court. She took on a Republican incumbent on a narrowly and deeply divided 4–3 court, a potential swing voice against a determined legislature that was doing all it could to prevent a changing state from having its voice heard. "North

Carolina is at a tipping point," Earls tells me. "That's why there's this fight to hold onto power."

It's a Southern Monday morning so steamy that when Eric Holder and Earls arrive for an event at a Charlotte law office, residents of the luxury condos on the upper floors of this swanky highrise are already bikini-clad and poolside. Holder's here to draw attention to the race. There isn't a more important election in the state this year. In a sign of its importance, Republicans have passed five laws changing the electoral rules, one of which will be deemed unconstitutional by the state Supreme Court. First, they eliminated judicial primaries, forcing all candidates into the November election. Republicans thought that would favor them, since the party planned to unite behind their incumbent and assumed more than one Democrat would covet the seat. The GOP legislature even mandated that Supreme Court candidates appear on the ballot alphabetically, but starting with the letter F—not missing any detail that would 'F' Earls over.

"Five separate laws trying to influence the outcome of an election," Earls says, with more sadness than anger. "We're not a democracy. The Republican Party has publicly and openly said that they think they should control the judiciary. They think the legislature should control the judiciary because they think if they write the laws, they should choose who interprets them. That's a complete reversal of the concept of balance of powers and checks and balances! It's an antidemocratic notion, and I just, at a very fundamental level, disagree with it."

Earls, the daughter of a mixed-race couple, has spent an extraordinary lifetime fighting for every voice to be heard. The family moved from Missouri—where interracial marriage remained illegal before the U.S. Supreme Court's decision in *Loving v. Virginia*—to Washington state in search of opportunity and understanding. But as an elementary school student, Earls felt the unwelcoming sting of garden hoses trained on her even in suburban Seattle. "Equal Justice Under Law," the words etched on the U.S. Supreme Court building, took on an especially powerful meaning. After excelling at Williams College and Yale Law School, she moved to

North Carolina so she could join Julius Chambers's firm and be mentored by one of the giants of civil rights law, the winner of landmark cases on voting rights, employment discrimination and school busing. Earls dreamed of furthering and deepening Chambers's legacy. Instead, she found herself saddened to be practicing at a time when conservative courts increasingly shut their doors and closed their ears to the claims of people in the communities she wanted to represent.

"When that monster of a suppression law was passed," she tells me—the 2013 bill that installed one of the strictest voter ID laws in the nation and eliminated the early voting days most likely to be used by minority voters, among other restrictions—"and there were young folks sitting in the gallery of the General Assembly with tape across their mouths protesting that law, and people being arrested and going to jail to stand up for the right to vote, I just said to myself, 'We're in an extraordinary period, and all of us owe it to each other to fight the hardest we can for our principles.' So that's why I thought it was important to run. I think that this is what these times demand of us."

On January 4, 2019, a victorious Earls took the oath as North Carolina's 100th state Supreme Court justice. Republicans had outsmarted themselves. A second Republican had joined the race, a constitutionalist disgusted by the legislature's unending chicanery. Legislators did all they could to knock him off the ballot or remove the party affiliation next to his name. They failed. The two Republicans split the vote, and Earls won with 49.5 percent. Days after her victory, Democrats took a page from Pennsylvania and filed a new anti-gerrymandering suit, this time alleging that the state legislative map violates the state constitution's guarantee of fair and equal elections. (When I went to the North Carolina general assembly's web page to read Section 6, which governs voting rights, I received a "page not found" error mesage, which could explain a lot.) This new case will begin with a three-judge panel and then likely land before Earls's court. One person, who stepped up to battle one specific injustice, just might have become the deciding voice.

Many hoped that Justice Anthony Kennedy would become that decisive voice in curbing partisan gerrymandering. So when the U.S. Supreme Court punted the Wisconsin case and Kennedy retired, it would have been easy for Ruth Greenwood, a Campaign Legal Center attorney representing the Wisconsin voters, to despair in this doubly discouraging moment. Greenwood will admit to feeling briefly frustrated, as well as misled and betrayed by Kennedy, who she'd believed really wanted to resolve this issue before retiring, rather than throwing up his hands and leaving it for a less friendly court. Then she got back to work.

The court's compromise, after all, at least kept their case alive. Often when a case fails on standing grounds, it gets dismissed altogether. The justices gave Greenwood's team another opportunity to make the case—but at the district level. That meant Greenwood needed to recruit dozens of additional plaintiffs, potentially as many as one for each of the 99 Wisconsin assembly districts. "It seemed daunting at first," she admits. Greenwood hit the road and discovered a woman who founded Supermarket Legends, a dynamic voter registration group that works for open, clean elections. She lived in a district packed with Democrats. "You could make her district 20 points less Democratic, and that would give Democrats an opportunity in the districts around her," Greenwood says. "All these people talk about this. They care about their district, but they also care about their region and their state. I just wish sometimes that I could have John Roberts with me to talk to these people and be like, 'We're not making this up. Here is this person. They are harmed.'"

Greenwood's drive for justice keeps her "strangely optimistic," even about the prospects of bringing Roberts around. "He wants to be a great American, right? Not just a great Republican?" I'm not sure whether she's trying to convince me or herself. "And to be a great American and a chief justice of a court that is going to have some respect, well, this is an issue where the people clearly are crying out for change."

Four days after the 2018 election, in which the Republican gerrymander provided red sandbags that held back a mighty blue Wisconsin wave, I joined Greenwood and all the new plaintiffs for a strategy session and meet-and-greet at the Madison home of lead plaintiff Bill Whitford. A light snow falls outside; Whitford lives so close to the waterfront you can feel the icy chill. A sign on his lawn proclaims that "science is real" and "kindness is everything." Inside, two framed drawings show how everyday folks can reach astonishing heights: a courthouse artist's sketch of Whitford at the U.S. Supreme Court, seated next to Arnold Schwarzenegger, hangs beside a drawing of purple trees, holiday lights and two smiling faces surrounded by hearts—the bright, cheerful work of a grandchild. If this case makes history, it will be due to the persistence and inventiveness of political scientists, lawyers and mathematicians, yes, but also to the determination of regular citizens like Whitford.

The case arose from a group that began meeting at a Milwaukee tea room called Watts, a regular gathering of Wisconsinites who revered their state's bipartisan tradition of open, clean government and bemoaned the extreme partisan politics and policy that emerged after Republicans took over state government in 2010, then redistricted themselves a decade-long upper hand. "It's been fun and it's been a good retirement activity," Whitford says. "Saving democracy." After Greenwood's summer-long recruitment efforts, there are twenty-seven plaintiffs here today from across Wisconsin. I meet Wendy Sue Johnson, who just lost a race for the 68th assembly district by 15 percentage points, and ask what it was like to run in one of these gerrymandered districts—and why she bothered. "Exhausting," she says. "Frustrating." But the high school social studies teacher and lifelong Eau Claire resident saw it as her duty. "We can't give up. We need to contest every election." She spent six months campaigning, and barely moved the needle despite the statewide blue wave. "It just proved our case is a solid," she said, shaking her head. Another plaintiff, Deborah Patel, lives in the wealthy suburbs of Milwaukee, and wears a gorgeous blue scarf and heavy turquoise jewelry. She decided to get involved in politics after the surprising 2016 election results led to a political awakening; she couldn't understand why her assembly district had such crazy lines or why her neighborhood had been carved out and tacked onto a conservative Republican district. "It's amazing that a wealthy white woman from River Hills is saying that her Fourteenth Amendment rights are being denied," she says with a laugh. "It seems a little odd. But they are."

Gerrymandering was also just a word from a long-ago civics class for Hans Breitenmoser, a dairy farmer and county supervisor who became so frustrated by the polarization in his state that he led a nonpartisan resolution on the Lincoln County board that called for fair maps and a nonpartisan commission to draw all state legislative and congressional districts. His hair is graying at the sides, and he wears a flannel shirt and jeans with a dark blue jacket zipped up halfway. "Right now, not to sound dramatic, but we are hanging onto our democracy by the skin of our teeth," he says.

Gerrymandering, meanwhile, has become such a hot topic in the state that Patel says her friends are actually jealous of her role in the case. "I had a late wake-up call," Patel says. "Now this is the little way that I can make a civic contribution and give back."

It's hardly necessary to be a former attorney general, to run for the state Supreme Court, or to join a gerrymandering case and take it all the way to the U.S. Supreme Court in order to make a major contribution to a better post-*Shelby County* world. Sometimes the work is as simple but crucial as helping someone like Crain Thomson. On Sunday mornings, Thomson has a home in his Virginia church choir. But when the rousing music quiets, home is once again the streets. Many years ago, Crain's state ID was stolen as he slept and he hasn't been able to get another, he told the *Washington Post*.[1] Turns out you need ID to get an ID. You also need a job to pay for the ID—a job you probably won't be able to get without the ID you don't have. Forget about a bank account in which to deposit the paycheck, or being able to drive a car to work, or everything else that an ID makes possible.

It's a huge problem: more than 11 percent of Americans don't have a state-issued identification card. That's 21 million eligible voters who lack the ID they need to make their voice matter.[2] Broken down by state, the numbers seem somehow more daunting. In Texas alone, 600,000 registered voters lack the ID they need to actually cast a ballot. In Georgia, it's a staggering 675,000 people. In Alabama or Virginia, more than 200,000 registered voters have this problem.

Voter registration remains relatively easy in most states. Just fill out the form. But having the right ID to actually cast your vote—well, that's a longer and more complicated process. Until a young African American activist stepped forward, no one was trying to do anything systematic to fix it.

Kat Calvin didn't understand all those connections or comprehend the vastness of those numbers when she crossed the desert back to Los Angeles, in tears, after spending election day 2016 in Las Vegas as an election protection volunteer. Hearing such stories for sixteen hours made it clear to this lawyer and tech entrepreneur that if Democrats wanted to win, they needed to defeat suppression efforts and mobilize people who *couldn't* vote. Instead, she watched in frustration as national Democrats focused post-2016 strategies on appeals to rural, working-class whites. She groaned louder as activists squandered precious time writing elaborate, handwritten postcards and mailing them into red-state special elections, as if a personal appeal from a blue-state grandmother might persuade a Trump voter to reconsider.

"Literally because it was common sense," Calvin replies when I ask how she got the idea for the group. "Nobody was working on anything practical. I like to look at a spreadsheet every night and see what my impact was. Also, nobody was talking about voter ID laws." After 2016, thirty-four states had some form of voter ID requirement, and the momentum seemed unstoppable. Voter ID might lose in the courts, but state legislatures just fixed the laws by making them *more* surgical and restrictive. Academic studies would demonstrate, compellingly, that voter ID created new barriers to voting in the name of solving a voter fraud "problem" that didn't actually exist. But Calvin watched the huge wave of ID laws and took note that no state ever repealed theirs or made helpful modifications.

"The solution was obvious," she said. "Just get them the ID." Obvious, sure. But not easy—and not inexpensive. Calvin launched Spread The Vote with a Georgia chapter and flew to Atlanta to run an inaugural ID drive. It failed miserably. Calvin was used to being named to *Fast Company* and *Forbes* lists of the most creative people in America, not to getting everything backward month after month. "We made the horrible mistake of setting up at grocery stores or knocking on people's doors and asking, 'Do you have ID?' People would literally run from us or slam their doors." It's easy to understand why: who in an at-risk community would admit to a stranger that they lacked proper ID, and risk getting caught in an immigration dragnet? The people Spread The Vote needed to reach most didn't trust that they were there to help. "That was bad," she says now. "We had to do everything wrong."

Calvin learned crucial lessons. Everything would be harder than she thought. Everything would take longer and cost a lot more money. If she wanted to reach people without IDs, she needed to partner with the organizations that were already serving them: senior centers, homeless shelters, Meals on Wheels, free clinics, food banks, county jails packed with people accused of misdemeanors who can't afford bail, anyone working with teenagers or on voter registration drives aimed at students who don't have a driver's license. "We go wherever they are," Calvin says.

Calvin spent eleven months on the road. She had no funding. She didn't pay herself for three months. She put everything from rent to Chipotle on her credit card. She slept on couches, and drove cross-country four times setting up offices in Florida, Tennessee, Texas, Georgia and Virginia. She eventually raised enough money to hire statewide directors. Mile by mile, she also realized that voting might not be the top priority of someone who lacks an ID—because if they don't have an ID to vote, they don't have it for anything else in their life. The free voter IDs offered by most states—if you can get to the specific office, on the specific day, during the specific hours, and they have the specific forms—don't make much of a difference if people can only use them to vote, then go back to being homeless the other 364 days of the year. "You cannot go to someone and say, 'I'm really sorry about that whole homelessness thing, but all I care about is if you can vote. So can I help you get this useless voter ID card?'"

An official state ID requires the same documentation as that "useless" state voter card, but cost money. Help someone get a state voter ID card and there's some small chance they'll use it to vote. Help them get an official ID and that might transform their life. Spread The Vote does it all: they work with state and federal bureaucracies to get new Social Security cards, birth certificates and other documents. They fill out the paperwork. They drive people to the government office, which might be several counties away. Most importantly, they pay for everything.

"It's extra money. But it's an ID you can use," says Calvin. "When you go into a shelter, you can tell them, 'I'm going to get you this ID that you haven't been able to get for years, that you could use to get a job, to get out of this place, to get housing. To get medical care for your kid. Then when the election comes around, can we come talk to you about voting? And do you mind if we register you to vote?' It changes the conversation."

The process usually takes three to four weeks, and has cost a minimum of $40 and as much as $600 per person. It takes a long time to generate the kind of numbers that will make a big impact. It's easier to impress funders with stories about registering hundreds of thousands of voters—without any idea whether those potential voters have the necessary ID—than it is to do the hard work, every day, across enough communities in enough states to make a difference. But just think about those 1.4 million Floridians with felony convictions who are now eligible to vote. Imagine how hard it will be to get them all registered. Then imagine the scene at the polls when someone arrives, anxious to cast that first ballot in years, and they're sent away because of a missing ID. "They're going to be rejected, or they're going to get a provisional ballot, and then they'll never vote again," says Calvin.

This problem, however, goes well beyond former felons and the homeless. First-time voters are just as unlikely to have the proper ID. Some of them don't live with their parents—who have the paperwork stashed away somewhere. Calvin spends much of her time in Texas, where thousands of students left important paperwork behind fleeing Hurricane Katrina or lost it in Hurricane Harvey. Other students think their school ID will work on election day. It won't. In Texas, legislators made certain that a gun permit qualifies at the polls but a student ID does not. Calvin spends a lot of time in Texas classrooms, teamed with organizations who get students registered and fired up to vote. When she asks these newly registered voters if they have official ID, less than a third usually raise their hands. "Every single one of them had just been registered by an organization, which is why we were in there with them," she says, a little fury in her voice. "If we weren't in there to collect the names of the kids who didn't have ID, all those kids would go to vote and get rejected." Calvin shakes her head in disgust. "It's insane, but voter registration organizations just don't think about it."

Calvin wants these electoral newbies to have an easy first experience voting, and empathizes with the thousands of students who don't have an ID simply because their high school eliminated driver's education and fewer of them get licenses. She's in it, though, for the cases where that ID might make the difference between life and death. Spread The Vote helped one homeless man whose ID was lost or stolen during a police raid at the shelter. Without the ID, he couldn't stay in the shelter any longer. He relocated to a park bench, promptly got arrested and was fined $600—and couldn't get his lost ID replaced until he paid the fine. Calvin wrote the check.

Big funders have stepped in with even bigger checks. Calvin has raised an additional $3 million ahead of 2020, more than four times the budget she had to spend during 2016. She hopes to help 10,000 people before the next election and expand into seven more states with the strictest voter ID laws, including North Carolina, Mississippi, Alabama, West Virginia and Louisiana. "Our work is far from done," Calvin says. "After we get through all the voter ID states, we're going to keep expanding. You can't vote, or even think about voting, when you don't have a place to sleep, a way to eat or a way to feed your children."

⬤

Cheryl Strickland had never been able to vote for a governor who looked like her. Excited to have her voice heard, Strickland arrived at her precinct in tiny Snellville, Georgia, at 6:15 in the morning, forty-five minutes before doors even opened. But when poll workers at Anniston Elementary finally allowed voters inside, something went wrong. The electronic system used to check voters in, called Express Polls, malfunctioned. Harried volunteers offered paper ballots to a growing and grumpy crowd. Strickland wasn't having it.[3]

Gwinnett County had become ground zero for controversial voter suppression schemes in the weeks before the state's gubernatorial election between Republican secretary of state Brian Kemp and Stacey Abrams, the Democratic state house minority leader attempting to make history as the nation's first female African American governor. As the longtime Republican stronghold, northeast of Atlanta, steadily diversified, something else grew—barriers to the ballot box that targeted communities of color.

Our elections are something of a small wonder, a one-day democracy pageant thrown by volunteers and low-level civic officials at libraries, schools and senior citizen centers nationwide, conducted on machinery that often predates the VCR. But in 2018, as voter suppression looked less like an accident and more like a strategy, the difference between cluelessness and willfulness looked different across partisan lines. Trust that voting officials actually served the best interests of voters? How 2016.

Especially in Gwinnett County. Voters like Strickland would have been hopelessly naive to believe in a democracy fairy who watched benevolently over a fair and nonpartisan vote. After all, in late October 2018, several lawsuits, including one filed by the ACLU that described the county as a "constitutional train wreck," challenged the way officials struck minority voters from the rolls if their registrations were not an exact match with their driver's license or Social Security card. Say a middle initial was missing. Or perhaps it was listed as the letter A on the voter form but written out as Alejandro on a license. You were likely to be knocked off the rolls in Gwinnett County. Officials there also took every opportunity to reject absentee ballots, setting votes aside for something as minor as a missing birthdate or a signature that a voting official decided did not match a sometimes decades-old registration. Again, voters of color were disproportionately affected: a startling number of rejections, well over half, happened to be voters of color.

Strickland, herself African American and nobody's fool, turned down the paper ballot. She stayed put until the machines worked. "If I have to wait here until 8 o'clock at night, I will," she said.

This was not the only snafu in Snellville, or, of course, across America. If you wanted to report a problem at your local polling place, you called the national Election Protection hotline at 866-OUR-VOTE. The person answering the phone would be an election lawyer, backed by a national, nonpartisan coalition of civil rights and good-government organizations. The phone rang on the ninth floor of a nondescript office building on K Street in Washington, DC. K Street is our capital's swampiest swamp, home to all varieties of influence-peddling and former politicians cashing in connections and reputations on behalf of the wealthiest and most powerful. But on this one day, in a handful of rooms stretching across two floors, the righteous-minded remembered why they loved law and public service and signed up for 5 a.m. shifts taking phone calls from places like Gwinnett County. It's where I wanted to be on election day.

Surrounded by half-eaten bagels, bowls of leftover Halloween candy and enough Starbucks cups to caffeinate *The Walking Dead*, lawyers who might bill four figures for an hour's work got busy guaranteeing their fellow citizens' most basic rights for nothing. Jammed twenty to a row, elbow to elbow at makeshift tables, their usual Capitol or White House view reduced to the bowed head of a volunteer across the table, they formed a wall protecting the vote. There was no shortage of work. Before the end of the day, they'd answer more than 31,700 calls and some 1,700 texts, and file multiple lawsuits.

It's a massive effort, coordinated by the Lawyers' Committee for Civil Rights, led by the trailblazing attorney Kristen Clarke. It becomes more expansive and impressive every two years, even though Clarke wishes dearly that none of it was necessary. "It feels like we've turned the clock back to the Jim Crow era," she tells me. "Some of the tactics that we're seeing—like the ones in North Dakota where even those Native Americans who are working hard to overcome the barriers placed in front of them are still being rejected because their street address on the ID doesn't match information in the state's 911 database? I mean, these are election officials who are resorting to any tactic and using any justification imaginable to lock people of color, in particular, out of the ballot box."

Every one of those stories gets collected here. Twenty-five states have made their voting laws tougher and more restrictive since 2010. That includes six of the ten states with the largest populations of African American voters. Spend an election day here and you see the magnitude of these laws and the brute force they exert. The story of any democracy is who gets to vote and who has barriers placed before their participation. From this vantage point, watching the calls roll in about polling places that have been changed, precincts that have run out of ballots, voting centers that simply didn't bother to open, it becomes clear that voter suppression is the story of the 2018 midterms—and that there are two ways for our democracy to go. There's the road of greater participation, and the one where some people struggle fiercely to have their voice heard at all.

Down the road from Strickland's precinct, at Snellville's Anderson–Livesy Elementary, poll workers remembered to set up machines but actually forgot the power cords. The machines lasted all of forty-five minutes under battery power. In Detroit, election officials lost the machines themselves. Voters in many Chicago precincts were handed a one-page ballot; trouble is, the entire ballot was two pages long. A white poll worker in

Houston, Texas, questioned the residency of a black voter and demanded that she fill out an additional residency verification form. When the long-time resident resisted, the official put her hands in the woman's face and screamed, "Maybe if I'd worn my blackface makeup today you could comprehend what I'm saying to you."[4] Other polling officials were simply ignorant of the law. In Mebane, North Carolina, a precinct plagued by broken machines and long lines, officials actually told voters that if they left the line, they'd also give up their right to vote.

"It's like diving into *The Matrix*," Scott McBroom tells me. He's a corporate lawyer who usually spends his days working on contracts. But every election day since 2004, he has answered calls here. It's as educational for him as it is for the anxious callers. A handwritten sign behind him reminds everyone of the deadlines for voters who cast a provisional ballot in Texas, Georgia or North Carolina to produce identification. "You learn how many voting problems there are," he says. "And there are just so many. They sit you in front of a screen with a picture of the fifty states, and someone calls in with a question about absentee voting in Oregon, or they just moved to Louisiana and don't have the right ID, or maybe they've been stopped from walking into the booth to help their grandma vote in Idaho."

McBroom's first call of the day came from a man in Texas whose driver's license had expired a week earlier. Would he be able to vote? Regardless of what he'd been told at the polls, turns out he could—Texas accepts a license as voter ID as long as it did not expire more than four years before the election. The relieved voter hustles back to the polls, knowing the law, and with a number to call for immediate legal help if he meets any continued trouble. Next to McBroom, another lawyer handles a similar case from Texas, where a voter with a military ID—accepted under the state's stringent requirements—has been denied permission to cast his ballot. He too is armed with the law and told to call right back if the poll worker gives him any additional problems. Across the table, lawyers research voter ID requirements in Atlanta's Gwinnett County and assure a Virginia voter that their ID will work. "As long as you haven't moved you're fine." A Texas polling place is forty-five minutes late to open. A Georgia voter never received an absentee ballot. Polls aren't open as expected across Maricopa County in Arizona.

If a lawyer can't resolve the problem on the phone, or if a local election official remains unmoved, the lawyer raises a hand. A captain rushes over for more information, and decides whether to elevate the concern to one of several litigation nerve centers two floors above this room. "This is easy enough work on our end," Katherine Clemons, one of the legal captains, tells me, "but it can be really complicated and scary for voters. It shouldn't be that way. Maybe they're told they have to cast a provisional ballot. People don't know what to do. We're here to help."

Meanwhile, several floors below, a giant social media hub isn't waiting for calls to come in, but is instead aggressively mining Twitter and Facebook. Two giant computer screens hang above eleven young staffers, each with a TweetDeck loaded with preprogrammed columns: voting lines, broken machines, intimidation. They see any tweet nationwide with those words, and more. There are columns in Spanish, monitoring *"no puede votar,"* *"problemas para votar,"* and *"quiero votar."* A young volunteer builds a Twitter list of secretaries of state, beginning, naturally, with Kansas's notorious Kris Kobach. "We did a version of this in 2016 and realized we needed to escalate our efforts," says Jesse Littlewood of Common Cause, "both with more people active on social media and knowing what we know now about social media misinformation in the 2016 elections. We wanted to make sure we were more prepared." Whenever they see a complaint about not being allowed to vote, confusion at a precinct, malfunctioning machines or polls that have not yet opened, someone immediately responds with the 1-866-OUR-VOTE number and encourages them to call. The goal is to be the first Twitter response; in case the post goes viral, they want the good information to be high atop any feed.

"If there are five or six or a hundred viral threads today about voting issues or voter suppression, we want to make sure one of the top replies is 'Your vote counts. Stay in line. Ask for provisional ballots,'" says Jack

Mumby, a T-shirt-and-goateed volunteer with intense brown eyes and an ear for how Twitter talk intersects with political communication, who runs the social media team. "Sometimes when things go sideways at the polls, people get discouraged and they get out of line. We want to avoid that."

They've spent weeks studying the phrases people are most likely to use if they encounter trouble at the polls. "Someone's going to say, 'I couldn't vote,' or, 'They made me vote provisional,'" Mumby says, both hands wrapped around his coffee. "It's a lot of work to get our searches set up in the nonpolitical voice of how actual people actually talk." But Twitter can also be the first line of communication. If they notice something unfolding here, Mumby runs it into the adjoining "state lines" room, a giant conference room fueled by mini-donuts and giant boxes of Goldfish crackers. "Who's got Florida?" he roars in at one point. "Report of an eighty-year-old man with a rifle near a polling place." "Who's got Kansas?" he calls at another. "Update from Dodge City," where multiple precincts had been surprisingly shuttered in the runup to election day.

They're also searching for trouble. A #VoteWeds meme has been circulating, thrust forward by unidentified bots. That meme has a cousin, "Election Day is November 7," when it's actually November 6. Whenever they see false and confusing news—"Polls close in Maryland at 7," when really it's 8 p.m.—they push back with the accurate information. They also have hotlines open with Twitter and Facebook so that if people are spreading intentional disinformation—"Police are at the polls checking citizenship papers," say—they can flag it for removal as a terms-of-service violation.

The most sophisticated techniques are led by Trevor Davis, an expert on digital disinformation who has methodically tracked down the owners, accounts and funders behind networked propaganda campaigns. Davis runs his own firm, CounterAttack, and got involved after an alarmed media consultant asked him to dig into suspicious Twitter behavior in Ohio in 2016. Davis peeled back the layers and discovered an entire network of pro-Sanders "Bernie Bros" who, weeks before, presented as anti-Catalan secessionists in Europe. They'd purged tweets but Davis found their trail anyway, then built his own software to identify propaganda networks. Bots and phony accounts leave quiet tells and digital fingerprints. Davis looks at how long an account has been active, for accounts with a sharp dropoff in shares which suggests their posts are being pushed to an audience that doesn't exist, for the same link being retweeted with constant subtle variations in text. There's money to be made, clicks and advertising to be driven, by spreading sexy false stories. And sometimes foreign governments and other nefarious operators are behind the lies. Davis loads up a sample story to show me how it works, this one a trending piece from a conspiracy site which targets California senator Dianne Feinstein as an operative behind election interference. Its social media pushers include accounts that have deleted more than 14,000 tweets, changed their language four times, and changed the home city in their biography on a half-dozen occasions.

"Accounts do that because they're being repurposed," he said, "and knowing that history and looking at that history can show what is potentially state-sponsored and what is a commercial network." An established Facebook or Twitter account with followers and history has real value. It has accumulated trust according to the platform's algorithm, as well. Such accounts are sold across the dark web and on openly Russian-affiliated sites like buyaccs.com. "If I register an account in November 2018 and start tweeting 'Black Panthers at the polls,' it's a little suspicious. I could set up a Twitter account today and tweet 'Democrats vote on Thursday.' Who cares? It takes time and money to build an audience. It is hard. It's not cheap. It's not instant. And pulling the plug on the individuals and institutions behind that is the objective. We don't want to go after it on the account level. We want to unplug it on the network level, and to do so based on evidence."

As we talk, Davis notices a suspicious bot network pushing out the alarmist Department of Justice voter fraud page about federal personnel at the polls, and heads off to take a deeper look at their traffic stats. The Election Protection team has never had such superior technical power. They need it against suppression this determined. "I'm also so encouraged by the level of energy that we're seeing," says Kristen Clarke. "Our democracy ends up in a far worse place if we don't keep fighting."

People power alone will not safeguard voting rights. The aggressive national measures that once protected the notion of one person, one vote have disappeared. We should be ready for more gerrymandering, more voter purges, more disenfranchisement. We should not expect the courts to help us. And it would be folly to expect a fairy-tale vision of democracy in a nation where the powerful and privileged have eagerly excluded women, blacks and other minorities, whether based on property, a poll tax or, now, a voter ID. However, in a post-*Shelby* world, this citizen vigilance might be the best weapon we have. Fortunately, and unfortunately, we're getting quite good at it. It would be better, still, for citizens eager to defend democracy to seek public office. Luckily, that's underway as well.

CHAPTER 10

Punching Up Down-Ballot

"If Trump can be president, why can't I run for city council?"

I t's a gorgeous June evening in 2018 in Washington, DC. As the sun streaks red against the U.S. Capitol, two would-be presidents play cornhole on a Chinatown rooftop. It's easy to imagine senators Cory Booker and Kirsten Gillibrand competing twelve months from now on debate stages across Iowa and chasing each other across snowy New Hampshire. But tonight they are tossing beanbags before a cheering young crowd fueled by a pale rosé and piles of guacamole. It's a celebratory fundraiser for Run for Something, the brainchild of Millennial activists Amanda Litman and Ross Morales Rocketto, which is teaching hundreds of first-time Millennial candidates how to get elected to state legislatures, county commissions, school boards and judgeships. Most of them are women or candidates of color; many of them are running in places like Montana, Oklahoma and Arkansas, states in which Democrats have either surrendered or gone plain extinct.

Neither Booker nor Gillibrand wants to lose. The New Jersey senator, stylish in a dark suit and white shirt, his tie long removed, eyes the raised platform with the same focus he'll bring to Brett Kavanaugh's confirmation hearings three months from now. Gillibrand, every bit his sartorial equal in a sleeveless, flowery sundress, sheds her shoes and even a leg brace to get more power behind her underhand toss. She steps back and sends a low, arching beanbag skittering toward the hole. It crashes against the platform and slides dramatically inside. She dances in delight, painful leg or not, then promptly mocks Booker on Twitter. He takes defeat in stride; after all, his line for selfies is longer. Booker snaps them all himself, a master of the right distance and angle in this Instagram-age campaign skill, a veritable Annie Leibowitz of the iPhone. "We're here because people facing incredible odds and insurmountable obstacles kept fighting and kept resisting," Booker tells me, "and figured out what they could do to make a difference. Democracy is really built not from the top down, but from the bottom up."

And we're here because Litman turned anguish into action, channeling her devastation after working seven-day weeks to elect Hillary Clinton toward helping others determined to go from spectator to participant, but lacking any clue where to begin. "I'm not going to sugarcoat this," Litman tells me a few days later when we meet in New York for lunch. "Running for office is fucking hard." But as Litman took stock while the pain of a bitter defeat slowly dulled, she realized that what progressive politics needed most was a rebuilt pipeline of young candidates at the state and local level. Republican focus down-ballot had provided the GOP not just complete control of Washington, but a modern record number of governors and 70 percent of all state legislative chambers. That had handed them control of decennial redistricting, which allowed them to draw themselves friendly maps that both entrenched their power and discouraged Democrats from running. "When I talk to old white male donors, they say, 'I've thought about running for Congress,'" she says, rolling her eyes. "I'm like, 'Of course you have.' You know who hasn't? The young Latina who should."

Litman quickly conquered the highest summits of electoral politics. She held a historic title: Hillary's email director. No, not those emails. Litman directed all the campaign's email fundraising efforts and communications. She raised $330 million—that's almost a third of a billion dollars—one small donation at a time. She managed a staff of nineteen, and she'd just turned twenty-six. It was exhausting and exhilarating and totally life-consuming. The campaign haunted her dreams, and destroyed her health: kidney infections, an everpresent migraine hum. She'd wake most nights in a cold sweat and reach for her phone to track fundraising numbers, or to nervously check for an overnight news alert that had arrived while she dared close her eyes. Did I mention that she loved it? The rest of America couldn't bear "Fight Song" one more damn time, but the campaign theme became Litman's unapologetic anthem. "I miss my home / But there's a fire burning in my bones," she'd sing, atop her desk, top of her lungs, on debate nights. It was everything she'd dreamt about, ever since *The West Wing* turned her into such a politics-obsessed teenage nerd that she cut class to trail Clinton, Barack Obama and John Edwards across Virginia during the 2008 Democratic primary. Now she was this young, and this close to the White House. "I believed that if we won it would be such a fuck-you to every guy who ever told me I was too ambitious, too loud, too brash, too much. It was personal to me," she says.

Election night was crushing. Behind closed doors at New York's Javits Center, campaign officials assured everyone that everything would turn out fine, even as Florida and North Carolina went into the red column. The Midwestern firewall just had to hold. As Clinton's top aides tried to keep the troops fired up, dismaying results from Wisconsin started crawling behind them on a bank of TVs. That's when people started to cry. Litman stayed there until 4 a.m., two hours after Clinton dialed President-elect Trump and conceded. Someone had to keep the website updated. In the cab home to Brooklyn, sobbing, shaking, she asked the driver to pull over so she could throw up. The next day, she sat in the third row for Clinton's concession speech, eyes red, barely having slept at all, wearing a campaign sweatshirt she wouldn't remove. Then everyone went to the bar next door and ate french fries. "I remember making jokes like, 'Now that none of us are working for the federal government, are we smoking weed again?'," she tells me. "At least we'll be high while we mourn. What do you do?"

Then a Facebook message arrived from a college classmate she hadn't heard from for years, now a teacher in Chicago. "She was pissed," Litman says. "She says, 'If Trump can be president, why can't I run for city council?'" The city council and state legislature, together, had decimated public education budgets. The woman wanted to get off the couch and do something. It was a good question. Litman had just helped guide a presidential campaign—and didn't know where to send a friend who wanted to fight back. "Why don't I have an answer to that?" she wondered. "Why have we not created a solution to this?"

If her old friend wanted to march for change, then run for office, thousands of other people would have the same desire. They also wouldn't know the first steps, and probably wouldn't have a Facebook friend with Hillary's number in her contacts. Litman emailed dozens of former colleagues. Should she build this? Help people step up onto the all-important bottom rungs of politics? Was it a dumb idea? It was too obvious, right; someone else must already be doing it? A friend connected her to Rocketto, a young progressive strategist who had started organizing and running campaigns in college, who was toying with a similar idea. They were unemployed and depressed, but they possessed stellar digital skills and could raise buckets of money. They built a website. A designer friend provided the polish. Litman's dad, a lawyer, filed the nonprofit paperwork. They launched on inauguration day, and a pal leaked the advance story to *Politico's* "Playbook." Litman imagined a slow trickle of interest. Instead, it was a deluge: 1,000 people contacted them in the first week.

When we met in early summer of 2018, that number had soared to 18,000. Run for Something had trained, endorsed and helped seed the campaigns of hundreds of hopeful Democrats. Warren, Booker and Gillibrand, the three most prominent presidential hopefuls in the U.S. Senate, were suddenly alongside them. "There was no infrastructure for this kind of candidate recruitment. None. There was nobody doing it. If we're able to do this right," Litman says, eyes aglow, "it's sort of a shadow national party with a very explicit focus. Could be cool!"

Could be transformative. Two years after the most devastating night of Litman's life, election night 2018 looked completely different thanks to Run for Something and related efforts by dynamic young activists, almost all women, some completely new to politics, who upended their lives and left high-paying jobs to rebuild the progressive bench from the ground up. More than 200 Run for Something candidates won state legislative seats, some capturing red-state seats that had been in Republican hands for longer than the young candidates had been alive. That's 10 percent of all 2018 Democratic state house gains, all for just $2.1 million, and not much more than the average budget for one U.S. House race.

While Run for Something helped funnel enthusiastic candidates into electoral politics, groups like Flippable, Sister District and Forward Majority provided a different approach. They focused their efforts on reclaiming the state legislative chambers most crucial for the 2021 redistricting. They targeted blue and purple states which had been under complete GOP control since 2010, such as Michigan, Pennsylvania, Florida, Virginia and North Carolina; red states with changing demographics, like Texas and Arizona; and competitive states including Washington and Colorado, where a small number of Democratic gains would be enough to create a blue trifecta.

There are 7,383 state legislative seats nationwide. Each group had a related but distinct approach. Run for Something allowed people to support a big pipeline of new candidates who might win, might lose, but would definitely help change the face of the party. Flippable used intensive data analysis to uncover the precise districts within target states that Democrats had the best potential to actually win. Forward Majority took that a step further: if Democrats needed to win 12 seats to take control of a chamber, for example, they'd likely need to run candidates in at least twice that many districts to claim enough victories and take full advantage of a wave, so they scoured for the third- and fourth-tier possibilities. Live in a blue state and want to work on a meaningful campaign? Sister District will connect you with local volunteers elsewhere and put you to work.

"It can be like, 'Cool, what's your flavor?'" says Catherine Vaughan, the CEO and cofounder of Flippable. "We can have a constellation of organizations. I was talking with Amanda once and told her I love her Twitter presence. She's so good at being irreverent, authoritative, fun and sassy. And she's like, 'You guys are nerds! Own it!'"

Together, they channeled dollars and volunteers toward these small local races with massive national impact. Republican strategists and donors had long ago unlocked the importance of these elections and built the party's national power one state legislative chamber at a time. Democrats ceded this field and understood the impact of redistricting too late, not until they looked back at the 2012 and 2016 elections and asked why they kept losing ground even when they won more votes. Republicans captured more than 700 state legislative seats in the 2010 Tea Party wave, then locked in those gains with redistricting, tilting the playing field an even rubier red. In all, Republicans gained more than 1,000 state legislative seats during the Obama years, and used those majorities to enact measures making it more difficult to register to vote or cast a ballot in twenty-five states, further disadvantaging Democrats and consolidating GOP power.

"If you want to make a difference, do the homework and find the most effective way to do it," says Vaughan, who founded Flippable while still in her twenties after working to provide effective health care in Rwanda and Ethiopia, then leaving a high-powered San Francisco consultant job to move in with a host family in Columbus, Ohio, and coordinate volunteers for the Hillary campaign. "Spend your dollars and spend your time on the most important thing. I just wanted to help create tools that would help people get it."

Redistricting wiped away competitive seats even in closely contested states. Strong Democratic candidates had little incentive to seek offices they were certain to lose; donors, likewise, didn't want to squander money on hopeless causes. "Democrats had an entire cycle of losing," says Vicky Hausman, the cofounder of Forward Majority. "So you see less money, less talent, and this perpetual shrinking sense of opportunity and what might be possible. Which makes sense! If you don't have a lot of money or talent, you see a constrained view. You protect what you have, or pile onto the most winnable races. The essential work is to expand the field and go into some of the tougher races."

That's why these new groups were so important. Democrats contested more than 5,300 of the 6,066 state legislative seats up for election in 2018, the highest percentage in more than a decade. In one year, they won back almost 450 of the seats that had washed away over the previous decade. This did not happen top-down, as part of some mandate from Washington. It came bottom-up, as Run for Something, Sister District and Forward Majority delivered energy, candidates and strategic smarts to races that the party ignored. They channeled the frustrations and passions of a nationwide resistance into the local races that mattered most. These groups didn't just help flip chambers; they flipped the entire script. They won majorities in the Colorado and New York senate, and eroded GOP majorities in Pennsylvania and Arizona. They cracked a Republican supermajority in North Carolina and significantly improved their party's position in Florida, Michigan and Texas, gaining important yardage with one election to go before the next redistricting.

"We're just citizens who have been activated. If our majority—our three-million-person majority—was engaged in state politics, everything is different," says Rita Bosworth, the cofounder of Sister District, which started with a Facebook conversation and now has 30,000 nationwide volunteers organized through sixty-five active teams on the ground. They focused on thirty-two legislative elections—and won sixteen of them—in nine states where Democrats might flip a chamber or make inroads into gerrymandered GOP majorities. "It's been a wake-up call. People who care, but weren't as engaged, who didn't think they needed to be a part of tending to democracy, now understand this is something we all have to do for the rest of our lives. We have to be watchful—or else what's happening now happens."

Bosworth's epiphany arrived during the 2016 election, as the San Francisco public defender watched two Democrats, California attorney general Kamala Harris and congresswoman Loretta Sanchez, devour more than $20 million campaigning against each other for a U.S. Senate seat certain to stay in the party's hands. She thought about all those squandered dollars and how many state legislative races it could win, had those dollars been channeled into tighter, local races where they'd make more impact.

Her three cofounders—political director Gabrielle Goldstein, partnerships and engagement director Lala Wu and programs and communication director Lyzz Schwegler—came together largely through a secret Facebook group of liberal lawyers established after the 2016 election. Frustrated when that group led to more discussion than action, Bosworth and Goldstein went their own way and laid out their idea on a simple Squarespace website. Emails started rolling in from across the country. By spring, Bosworth, Goldstein and Wu had abandoned successful law careers to save democracy full-time. "This organization is bathrobe to business casual in ten minutes," cracks Wu.

We're in New Orleans for the Netroots Nation activist convention, and Goldstein knows the secret sentence that gains us access to a private, absinthe/vampire speakeasy high above Bourbon Street. The hostess leads us through one bar, down a long corridor and up a long spiral staircase, and unlocks a mystical lounge with wild goth decor, purple couches and Bauhaus on the jukebox. Quickly, a round of Broken Mirror cocktails appears before us: absinthe, lime and simple syrup, topped with chartreuse. It's Goldstein's first time in New Orleans and she's immediately uncovered the coolest place in town. Similarly, all four founders were completely new to politics, but, as determined, never-stop-working lawyers, they networked and asked questions and just kept going. "We're truly a little extreme," admits Wu.

"We're also trained to look at where the gaps are, what has been over-looked, where could we have an outsized impact," says Goldstein, whose legal practice focused on bioethics, a topic in which she's also earning her doctorate at Berkeley during her spare time. "It became clear really fast that state leg"—it's a soft g in their lingo, like "ledge"—"was critically over-looked," as far as redistricting but also "in terms of a policy pipeline and the leadership pipeline."

"Our model seems so obvious to us," says Schwegler. "Focus on state leg. We'll organize people, we'll get them to work on these races, and then we'll do all these field operations. It seems so logical that it's taken us a long time to really understand that no one else is doing this."

Back in Columbus, Vaughan found herself coming to a similar conclu-sion. She took a leave from McKinsey and Co. and left San Francisco to work for the Hillary campaign and months on a host family's sofa. When the campaign ended with whiskey and tears, Vaughan planned to head back to consulting and the Bay Area. Over farewell margaritas, the team tried to unpack what had gone wrong and what might come next. The conversation turned to gerrymandering. Ohio is enough of a competitive, bellwether state that they'd all put their lives on hold, thinking the state's electoral votes could decide the presidential election. But Republicans still held a two-to-one edge in the state legislature. They'd all gotten to know state house candidates from rallies and events, who were running underfunded races in hopeless districts, with odds so less than zero that Bret Easton Ellis and Elvis Costello would sympathize.

Vaughan had spent several years working with the Gates Foundation and others on health problems in east Africa that were completely prevent-able if the right resources landed in the right places. "I've spent several years of my career focused on how to get rich people to donate to more data-driven and effective organizations. How do you use data? How do you think strategically?" We're in Flippable's tiny office space under the Manhattan

Bridge, appropriately maximized to do the most with a little. People in politics are really good at understanding who has power and how to build a web of relationships, Vaughan says, but less skilled at building and judging effective organizations. "How do you help them see that maybe the way they're giving their money could be optimized? That's a lot of what we're trying to do here."

Forward Majority's Hausman had a similar background; as a partner at the global strategy firm Dalberg, where she led the Americas team and the global health practice, she worked on bringing business-school analysis and smart-data analytics to philanthropy. Rural governments in sub-Saharan Africa lacked the money they needed, for example, to buy and deliver bed nets to citizens before the rainy, mosquito season. "There are these unsexy barriers that really impact people's lives," she tells me. "My frame of reference was a foreign assistance system that's big and bureaucratic. We can't fix the whole thing, but we can use business strategy and analytics on specific problems that are fixable." Turned out, one of those problems was democracy right here at home. "I never thought about state legislatures before," she says. Perhaps there was a disruptive approach to solving that problem as well.

Friends connected her with David Cohen, one of Barack Obama's very first staffers in 2007, who had watched the *New York Times* needle tip toward doom on election night and in a fever dream out of *Jerry Maguire* spent sleepless nights working on a mission statement and a business plan to fight back in states where demoralized Democrats were stuck on permanent defense. "You have these weakened state caucuses struggling with how to be successful with limited resources," he says. "You've got folks who have really not taken a strategic view of how to approach winning a chamber. Did they work hard, raise money, do good work? I don't know. But if we judge on outcomes—which we should do every once in a while in politics—it's not good. I wanted to build a national group solely focused on outcomes, on winning races, and to do so independently of whatever local politics or issues stood in the way."

Virginia, which holds its state elections in odd-numbered years, provided the first testing ground in 2017. Democrats carried Virginia's electoral votes in 2008, 2012 and 2016, and held both U.S. Senate seats. But Republicans controlled the wildly gerrymandered state assembly with a 66–34 advantage, as well as the state senate. All 100 assembly seats would be contested in 2017, offering these groups a chance to prove their strategies and survive the "Hunger Games" gauntlet of national funders. Democrats required 17 victories to flip the chamber, and earn a seat at the table for the next round of redistricting. They had energy and momentum on their side—and exactly 17 districts carried by Hillary Clinton the year before that seemed like natural targets. Democratic caucus leaders, however, said they only had the resources to mount a challenge in 8 to 10 districts. Democrats could run the table and still end the night with Republicans in charge. Someone had to take on the tougher battles.

Forward Majority left the low-hanging fruit for the party to win, and used their data analysis to uncover opportunities to expand the map. "We went into districts where Republicans had been in office for decades. We took out the house whip, Jackson Miller; he had been in office since 2006. Everyone said it was a safe seat. We took out a guy named John O'Bannon, he had been in office since 2001 and hadn't seen a challenger in eight years," says Forward Majority's Cohen. "People like this, according to the conventional wisdom, were unbeatable. We showed that when Democrats try, they can win."

Indeed, but narrowly. Every dollar mattered. Debra Rodman defeated O'Bannon with 51 percent. In the 40th district, Democratic challenger Dante Tanner ousted incumbent Timothy Hugo with 50.1 percent. Forward Majority worked in 16 races and won 12, half of them nail-biters taken by challengers with between 50.1 and 53 percent of the vote. Forward Majority partnered with leading academic experts on political persuasion and put every campaign technique through careful testing. They determined that these Virginia voters wanted information without spin, so they sent direct mail that presented the Democratic case as a voting guide. That tactic moved the needle in their direction by 1.2 percentage points. They tried something called "social pressure messaging." Whether or not an individual voted is on public record, which enabled Forward Majority to calculate voter turnout grades for people based on the percentage of elections they participated in; they then developed a Facebook ad that compared a voter's grade to other people in their zip code. When they tested this strategy, however, it had zero effect on Facebook itself, so they married Facebook profiles to cell phones and tried it via text message. *That* worked, driving turnout by half a point. "You would never run a serious congressional campaign without doing this," says Cohen. "This is known best practice. The problem at the state legislative level is so often, we just don't do this. We think that, I don't know, coattails or something will carry state leg to victory. It doesn't. You have to actually run a campaign."

Run for Something helped elect Danica Roem, who became the state's first transgender legislator, knocking off the conservative who proposed the state's "bathroom bill." That wasn't what she talked about door to door, however: she won with an unrelenting focus on fixing local highways and easing Virginia's commuting woes. Sister District, which contributed to 15 key Democratic victories, discovered underfunded state parties, county parties that were no longer functional and a dire need for volunteers, leadership and organizing. "We wouldn't exist if the Democratic National Committee had been doing their job all these years," Goldstein says. "If you're running in Virginia's 12th, you don't have the capacity to organize thousands of volunteers, nor the access to them. Have you ever been inside a state leg campaign office? It's literally three people. They're young, they're underpaid, they're overworked." Sure, winning campaigns need cutting-edge digital strategies backed by analytics. They also need coffee, bottled water and printer toner. "We asked the campaigns to give us Amazon wishlists. People who were looking to give money could actually donate real things to real campaigns. It's a totally different model of electoral engagement."

Flippable's Vaughan says that Virginia taught her the importance of going for the "full flip." Democrats won 14 seats; control of the legislature came down to the tie in the 94th district, and the unlucky draw that gave the victory to the Republican candidate. All the activists wished they'd picked one more district or worked that much harder. But while the blue wave fell just short, politicians got plenty wet. Virginia's legislature, which had long resisted expanding Medicaid to the 400,000 state residents who fell into the coverage gap, reversed course.

"Elections have consequences," Danica Roem tells me, "and you had nineteen Republicans who flipped their Medicaid votes from last year because of what they saw." Both sides negotiated a deal they could live with: Democrats won the additional coverage, Republicans won work requirements. "We had to compromise. That's what it took to bring them on board. But I'm not going to let the perfect be the enemy of the good. This is a very good thing we got done." None of it happens—and all those people go uninsured—without the newcomers' postcards, door-knocking, printer paper, digital strategies and campaign advice.

In Washington state, Flippable and Sister District helped win a 2017 special state senate election that tipped the balance of power from 25–24 Republican to 25–24 Democratic. That one victory created a blue trifecta. The first thing Democrats did was pass a comprehensive set of electoral reforms, including automatic voter registration, same-day registration, preregistration of sixteen- and seventeen-year-olds, and a state voting rights act. "It's the foundation of democracy itself, and I think we achieved the best suite of voting rights in the country," Washington governor Jay Inslee tells me. "After five years of being in the desert, we had something called the Wishing and Hoping caucus," says senate majority leader Sharon Nelson. "We had this package ready; protecting voting rights and countering what has been happening nationally was our top priority. But it took that twenty-fifth vote to make it happen." In New York state, three Run for Something challengers primaried and defeated state senators who ran as Democrats but caucused with Republicans. New York's Democrats and Republicans had happily conspired for years to maintain the state's anti-quated election laws: New York not only lacked any early voting at all, it also held state and federal primaries on different days and required anyone who wanted to change parties in order to vote in a primary to file the paperwork a full year in advance. Three weeks after the Run for Something coalition flipped the chamber, hyper-restrictive New York became a national model for fair and open elections. Suddenly New York achieved nine days of early voting, automatic voter registration and even preregistration of sixteen- and seventeen-year-olds.

●

At Forward Majority headquarters, in a small office high above Manhattan's Fifth Avenue wallpapered in swing-state legislative maps, David Cohen and Ben Wexler-Waite are walking me through their Pennsylvania model. This is one of the most gerrymandered state houses in the nation, consistently electing forty more Republicans than Democrats even in years when Democrats win more votes. But Cohen believes they can put the chamber in play with careful data analysis. They have the 203 districts divided into seven tiers: very likely flip, likely flip, wave target, strong district performance, aggressive target, longshot, and hopeless. Tiers one through three are districts where Hillary Clinton or an index of candidates they called "mixed Democratic performance" topped 50 percent. There are 22 of those. They need just 20 seats for the full flip, and have identified 45 targets within the first five tiers. But the state Democratic caucus? They lack the resources to contest even the 22 winnable districts in the top three tiers. "Good Lord," says Cohen. Democratic caucus officials, naturally, get very excited when they learn that Forward Majority plans to invest in their races. "They'll say, 'Great, you should do these top-tier races with us!'" Cohen shakes his head. He's not interested in winning the six easiest seats. That's not enough to win control. They want to play in enough seats so they're at the crest of any wave. They want to put Republicans on the defensive and force them to spend money in districts that have been safe as houses.

Their spreadsheet includes a stunning level of detail on every district. How much money the last challenger spent. How Hillary Clinton performed. Five cycles of election results up and down the ballot. The percentage of college-educated women. The racial demographics. The best Democratic performance there to date. "Here's a good district to look at," Cohen says. "It's a Republican-held seat. Hillary's performance in this district was 62.9. Okay? Holy shit, this is a good district. Best Democratic [state house] performance was only 48. So they didn't win. But what were the expenditures? Wow, the Democrat was outspent $400,000 to $28,000. No one has taken a serious run at this district in recent memory." On the list it goes.

Run for Something's Litman takes a different approach. She's not thinking about what it costs or what wins or which killer text alert will increase turnout by 0.2 percent. A relentless focus on specific winnable districts, she suggests, reinforces the Democrats' vicious cycle of avoiding whole swaths of the country. She's after candidates rooted in a community who are committed to getting out there and talking to people. She calls it her "fuck yeah" test. "When I talk about them to someone, do I get visibly hyped," she says. "Are they excited? Are they pumped? One hundred percent of our candidates pass that test." It's not that she believes voters need to be inspired by every candidate. "That's a false thing we've expected, that Obama has done." But are these candidates people you hear speak and want making decisions on your behalf? "I trust you. I like you. You have this district's best interest at heart. Fuck yeah." In Florida, twenty-four state legislators with A or A− ratings from the National Rifle Association lacked challengers in the days after the Parkland High School massacre. Run for Something spent $100,000 on events, TV and print ads, and a digital campaign to recruit candidates. "We were the only people pushing these districts," Litman says. "Those incumbents should have to tell voters, 'Yeah,

I'm with the NRA.' Why should the Democratic Party get to decide those districts aren't winnable and this isn't an argument worth having?" Fuck yeah, indeed.

"Barbara Bessette, a substance abuse counselor running for state house in Montana. Native American. A competitive barrel racer in her spare time. Fuck yeah. Lina Hidalgo in Texas, running for county executive in Harris County. If she wins, she'll be one of the most powerful women in Texas. First-generation American, family from Colombia, Harvard Kennedy School graduate. Sharp as hell. Could win! Fuck yeah. Anna Eskamani in Florida, running outside Orlando, former Planned Parenthood staffer. She'll flip the seat. She'll be governor of Florida one day. Sara Innamorato, who took down the dynastic Pittsburgh power family. Hell, yes."

Run for Something said "fuck, yeah" and celebrated 221 victories in its first two years. They helped flip seats in 20 states; 55 percent of their endorsements were for women, and half were for people of color, which means they could change the look and feel of our politics for decades to come. Bessette, by the way, is now Representative Barbara Bessette. Lina Hidalgo is now Judge Hidalgo and runs Harris County, Texas, population 4,653,000, at age twenty-seven. Anna Eskamani, the daughter of Iranian immigrants, represents Disney World. "The first group that endorsed me," she told me, "was Run for Something."

In Pennsylvania, Democrats flipped 4 state senate seats; the biggest upset was landed by Katie Muth, an athletic trainer and part-time anatomy teacher who knocked on more than 40,000 doors and knocked out a Republican who had won his previous two reelection campaigns by 18,000 and 22,000 votes. "Flippable gave me my first big check," she tells me. "They gave me five grand and I about fell off my chair." Democratic Party organizations at the state and national level, she says, favored male candidates who looked better on paper but wouldn't do the hard work of fundraising and door-knocking. Flippable invested in a young woman. "You know what women do?" she says. "They put their heads down, they listen and learn, and they get the fuck out there and work."

Run for Something and Forward Majority also worked on behalf of Sydney Batch's campaign for the North Carolina state assembly. Batch managed an upset victory despite a breast cancer diagnosis during the campaign. Then, in May 2019, as she recovered from a mastectomy, GOP lawmakers tried to use her absence to override a veto of a "born alive" abortion prohibition. Batch left her sickbed and prevented that from happening. "I was hoping to take three weeks off to recover, but unfortunately I did not have that ability," Batch told *Talking Points Memo*. "When I realized that Monday, [Republicans were] planning to hold the vote it was worth physical sacrifice and pain to come in to vote."[1]

Forward Majority, meanwhile, helped Democratic candidates flip 43 seats—all in states won by Trump in 2016. They dared play in Texas and Arizona and broke new ground. Texas saw the biggest Democratic gains in any state under Republican trifecta control. In Arizona, Democrats would have shattered a GOP trifecta few people thought beatable had 267 votes gone the other way across just a handful of districts. "We helped put state legislative chambers in contention for Democrats—in some instances, for the first time in decades," says Hausman. But as she always knew, it is a long-term project to rebuild in states decimated after the national party slumbered through 2010. So it may be a bigger deal that across Forward Majority's six target states, Democrats had 31 "close losses," where the candidate won more than 48 percent of the vote. "Defending seats that were close wins, and winning those that were close losses is the essential path to victory in 2020," she tells me. And now that the U.S. Supreme Court has ruled that federal courts can't determine the constitutionality of partisan gerrymandering claims, Democrats either win back chambers in these states in 2020 or face another decade in the wilderness.

Back on that Washington, DC, rooftop, a third U.S. senator and potential Democratic nominee, Elizabeth Warren, slides out of the Run for Something bash before the cornhole battle commences. "This is the future," she tells me quietly, holding her arms open wide before the room. "The crucial act of citizenship now is engagement." Indeed, if the forty-sixth president of the United States was pitching beanbags that night (or sneaking out early), it hardly seems a stretch to suggest that the forty-ninth or fiftieth might have been there as well, along with future senators and governors and state representatives, all inspired to run, and shown how to do it, by a new generation of activists who reinvented the party where it had been neglected by their elders—down ballot, where it matters most.

Even more representative elections, however, will be possible when we update the very way in which we vote. That battle has also been engaged.

CHAPTER 11

Maine's Ranked Choice

"The people can't be stopped."

This rainy autumn Monday is the very reason why cozy brewpubs exist. Chill hip-hop plays inside Foulmouthed Brewery in South Portland, a repurposed auto mechanic's shop in a once-grimy waterfront neighborhood in the shadow of the Casco Bay Bridge. A slatted wooden canopy overhangs the bar, but otherwise the vibe is minimalist Scandinavian cool: white walls, white subway tiles behind the bar that make vintage taps look majestic, artsy posters above each one that describes the offering. Even their take on poutine is crafted: Maine potatoes, house-smoked pork gravy, local cheese curls.

Tonight's crowd, a politically minded assemblage of locals and beer nerds as eager to discuss Putin as poutine, faces an awesome challenge: taste a flight of one-of-a-kind brews and rank their favorites. Will it be the Rhubarb de Garde, "a strong amber French-style Farmhouse aged on rhubarb for a tart, earthy punch"? Maybe the Gruity Pebbles, with "wood sorrel, arena berries and cherries," that tastes like "Juicy Juice and booze." Or perhaps The Brat, a German-style session ale with a "noble hop finish."

It's not just a drinking game with fancy artisan IPAs, but a dress rehearsal for election day. In 2018, Maine became the first state in the nation to embrace ranked choice voting for congressional elections and other local and federal offices. Now the hippest League of Women Voters in the nation is using beer—along with pizza, ice cream, coffee and most anything else ingestible and legal—to help voters understand how the new system works, but also how natural and fun it is to rank favorites.

Maine adopted ranked choice through a statewide ballot initiative in 2016. There were so many reasons behind this reform that you'd need a ranked ballot to sort them all. An old-fashioned New England independent streak has long coursed through this state's politics, just as wild as the local blueberries that infuse Foulmouthed's bourbon barrel ale. Mainers regularly send independents to the U.S. Senate; they produce larger-than-party statesmen and women like Margaret Chase Smith, George Mitchell and William Cohen; and they have a proud tradition of third-, fourth- and fifth-party candidates seeking the governor's office.

Crowded ballots, however, complicate politics. Too many Maine campaigns turned into debates over which candidate was spoiling the race for someone else. Voters struggled between choosing the candidate they liked best or the one they thought stood the best chance against the person they liked least. In nine of the previous eleven races for governor, dating back to the early 1970s, the winner took office with a plurality, not a majority, meaning that more than half of all voters preferred someone else. When Paul LePage, a Tea Party bully with a posterior fixation, became governor in 2010, telling the NAACP to "kiss his butt" and boasting that he'd "give it to people without Vaseline," the most popular bumper sticker in the state proclaimed "62.4." It was a cheeky reminder that only 37.6 percent of Maine voters backed such nasty, lubeless politics.

Ranked choice removes all that messy strategic calculus. It's extraordinarily popular and common worldwide, and 2018 was the year it exploded in the U.S.: San Francisco used ranked choice to elect its first African American woman mayor, Memphis rejected an effort by politicians to rescind it, and Santa Fe used it for the first time. Voters had approved it ten years earlier in a charter commission reform package, but it took FairVote's

Maria Perez to threaten lawsuits and otherwise cajole the city council to implement it. "I am an insanely optimistic person, and that's what drives me to push beyond probably where most people would give up," Perez says.

Voters list their favorites in order. The election mimics an instant run-off: if no one has a majority after the first round, the last-place candidate is eliminated and his or her supporters are reallocated to whoever those voters picked second. If Florida voters had used ranked choice during the 2000 presidential campaign, for example, Ralph Nader voters could have listed Al Gore as their second choice without helping elect George W. Bush instead. "You never have to choose between the lesser of two evils when there's another candidate you like better," Jill Ward, the president of the Maine League of Women Voters, tells the Foulmouthed crowd.[1] These instant run-off rounds continue until someone reaches 50 percent. That means the winner is always the candidate with the widest support, and it's more difficult for someone with a passionate but small base to sneak through in a multi-candidate field.

Even after several drinks, everyone's got the process down. "Fortunately, with this election, there are no bad candidates—that's not always true with politics," Ward says with a laugh as the drinkers begin to winnow down the field. The oddball Rhubarb and Juicy Juice-flavored brews have passionate supporters, but ranked choice forces a genuine consensus, and in the end, a traditional golden IPA named Presidential Tapes emerges as the winner.

But while voters grasp ranked choice instinctively, Maine's politicians did not allow this bold experiment in democracy to happen without a fight. The story of ranked choice voting here is one of citizens determined to protect what they love about their state's politics—lots of choices, quirky independents, brave Democrats and Republicans unafraid to buck knee-jerk partisanship—and match it to an electoral system that guards against winners that most people don't really want.

Citizens demanded a more civil and majoritarian politics and sought to use their state as a laboratory of democracy. An insular state power structure, terrified of change, attempted to sabotage the reform at every turn. The legislature conspired to have ranked choice undermined by the judiciary, then gutted the initiative well after midnight in a special session they hoped few were watching. There were plenty of eyes, however, and they got right back to work. Reformers started collecting signatures for another petition drive, this one a People's Veto to rebuke the legislature, refusing to surrender to long odds, intransigent politicians or the brutal Maine winter.

"I have never found another case in the country where the people initiate a law, they pass it, the legislature repeals it, the people put it on the ballot again, pass it again, and go through all that we went through," says Kyle Bailey, campaign manager for the Committee for Ranked Choice Voting. "People felt the urgency. When you're kicked, you can get back up, fight even harder, and channel that anger and frustration into positive action. We started what we thought was a campaign, and it became a movement."

Paul LePage and Donald Trump could not have had more different childhoods. Trump grew up in New York, the son of a multimillionaire developer who gifted him some $413 million over his life. LePage's story could have been penned by Dickens. The second oldest of eighteen kids, he still carries the half-dollar coin his father tried to buy his silence with after he beat the then eleven-year-old so badly he ended up in the hospital. He never went home again, choosing the freezing streets of Lewiston, Maine, over another night under an abusive father's roof. "I lived on the streets, I lived in hallways, garages," he remembered in an early campaign video. "For a couple years, I lived anywheres and everywheres."[2] Eventually two families helped raise him, a local college allowed him to take his entrance exams in French, and he worked his way up through Maine's paper industry and became mayor of Waterville in 2003.

Their political styles, however, practically make them siblings—and LePage mastered the art of the squeal back when Trump's tweets merely pushed his branded keychains and bland inspiring quotes. LePage compared the IRS to the Nazis' secret police, and boasted that he wanted to tell President Obama to "go to hell." He argued that Maine's opioid crisis had been inflamed by "black and Hispanic people from Waterbury, [Connecticut,] the Bronx and Brooklyn" who "come to Maine and sell their poison," then "impregnate a young white girl before they leave."[3] When a state representative suggested that rant was unacceptably racist, LePage challenged the lawmaker to a duel and said he'd shoot him right between the eyes. "I've spent my life helping black people and you little son-of-a-bitch, socialist cocksucker," LePage seethed in a voicemail which he challenged the Democrat to make public because "I am after you."[4]

That's a touch more rough-and-tumble than Margaret Chase Smith, whose biggest controversy came when she opposed an Air Force reserve promotion for actor Jimmy Stewart—"a fine fellow and she admires his acting ability," an Associated Press report indicated—because the genial star of *Mr. Smith Goes to Washington* simply "hasn't been turning out for training the way he should."

LePage first captured the governor's office in an epic five-way 2010 election. The firebrand led polls throughout the contest, but struggled to break the high 30s against two main challengers: Democratic nominee and house Speaker Libby Mitchell and independent Eliot Cutler, a longtime aide to Maine's esteemed U.S. senator Edmund Muskie. LePage owned the conservative base, but polls throughout October showed Cutler and Mitchell dividing Democrats and independents almost equally. Mainers who recoiled at LePage could only track the polls and back whichever opponent appeared to be running strongest; in the final days, the anti-LePage forces broke toward Cutler, but it still wasn't enough. Cutler finished with 36 percent, just under 10,000 votes short of victory, as Mitchell faded to third with 19 percent. In a "first past the post" system, it didn't matter that fewer than four in ten Maine voters wanted their state led by LePage, or that a *Bangor Daily News* poll showed that the majority of Mitchell voters would have picked Cutler second. That small plurality turned the extreme choice of a fired-up base into everyone's governor.

LePage's pugnacious and vulgar style did not budge throughout his first term, and neither did the opinion of most voters. His approval ratings remained mired in the mid-30s throughout most of his first term. But when he had to face voters in 2014, LePage could take comfort once more from a crowded field. Cutler returned for a second independent bid, while Democrats nominated Mike Michaud, a popular six-term congressman. This time, Cutler faced the spoiler question from the day he announced. Republicans even ran ads supporting his candidacy throughout the summer, hoping to keep anti-LePage independents from drifting toward Michaud.

From June through October, polls showed that either Michaud or Cutler would crush LePage in a two-way race. But in this three-way election, as November neared, Cutler remained a distant third, polling in the mid-teens. His supporters, including independent U.S. senator Angus King, peeled away. In a bizarre late October news conference, Cutler admitted he was a "realist" and a "long shot," and freed his supporters to back Michaud if "compelled by their fears or by their conscience." Yet he defiantly remained in the race, insisting that he would not let polls "drown out the voices of thousands of Mainers who believe that standing for principles, ideals and ideas makes you an American, not a spoiler." He collected 51,000 votes on election day, while LePage won reelection by fewer than 29,000.

That election day, volunteers also collected almost 40,000 signatures for a ballot proposition to establish ranked choice voting.

Paul LePage did not bring about Maine's ranked choice voting experiment all by himself. Indeed, Kyle Bailey, the League of Women Voters and many other good-government reformers endeavor to steer the story away from the governor. Several legislators introduced a ranked choice bill as far back as 2001, before LePage even became Waterville's mayor. State representative Diane Russell, a Democrat from Portland, introduced similar bills every two years beginning in 2009, but couldn't get them out of committee.

"Everyone thinks I invented this because I hate Paul LePage. I didn't even know who Paul LePage was," says Russell, a red-headed spitfire who is so energetic she hardly needs the coffee and scone we meet for in Portland's Munjoy Hill neighborhood. "I'm a systems person. If I see a flaw in the system that's going to take us down the wrong road, but you can divert that system or put a new mechanism in and make things run smoother, why wouldn't you do that?"

The Maine chapter of the League of Women Voters endorsed ranked choice in 2011, after gathering a study group and researching the issue for three years. An independent state senator, Dick Woodbury, managed to get a ranked choice bill to a full vote in 2013, but it fell in both the house and the senate. Russell did help push ranked choice into Portland's new city charter; the state's largest city began electing its mayor using that system in 2011, and fifteen candidates jumped into the race.

While those statewide legislative efforts failed, the elections won by LePage showed Maine voters how broken the state's electoral system had become and crystallized the advantages of ranked choice. Mainers value common sense, after all. No one liked voting for the lesser of two evils when they preferred another candidate. No one liked to worry that a vote for their preferred candidate would be wasted. Most people longed for campaigns to become civil again, for issues to matter. Most people wanted a level playing field, and for voters to get a Republican if they wanted a Republican, a Democrat if they wanted a Democrat, or an independent if that candidate had the most support. Yet Bailey, Woodbury and Cara McCormick, another Cutler staffer, found themselves reliving *Groundhog Day,* working on a second gubernatorial race that had become entirely about vote splitting and the spoiler effect.

"We never even got a chance to talk about education or health care," says Bailey. We're in a South Portland Starbucks, and with his shaved head, no-nonsense demeanor and faint Southern accent, Bailey resembles the tough-minded Hollywood football coach or army sergeant ultimately revealed to have a heart of gold. "All those things that should matter most in our elections—values, vision, policy, ideas—kept taking a back seat to what the polls say, who's the spoiler, and voting strategically. That dominated the conversation." As election day approached, they had an idea: they'd run an initiative for ranked choice. But they had to move fast. They needed 61,000 signatures to get an initiative on the next ballot, and Maine's population is so rural and dispersed that any successful campaign needs to collect at least half of those names on election day. They'd have to start the process right away. Quietly, they cut and pasted the language from the League of Women Voters working group and sent it to the secretary of state's office, not even knowing if it would be approved in time to get petitions printed before election day, let alone get volunteers organized and trained to staff precincts statewide. But ten days out, around the time Cutler gave that confusing press conference, they got the OK.

"It's Monday the week before election day, and Dick calls me, all innocent. 'I'm in the neighborhood. Can I stop by?'" remembers Diane Russell, who felt certain it was too late to mount a signature drive in the remaining eight days. "'We've got the petitions.' I looked at him and said, 'I just need a minute.'" Then everyone got to work. Some 200 volunteers signed on through a Facebook call to action. Russell built a spreadsheet to coordinate key locations. Woodbury started driving the petitions to all the small towns around the state. "People driving in snowstorms," Bailey recalls. "We didn't have any money. Didn't have a bank account. It was kind of a hope, a dream and a prayer."

Then, on election day, something unusual happened. Voters who tended not to make eye contact with signature collectors, who usually power-walked past the table and back to their warm cars, actually waited in line to sign a petition for ranked choice voting. They wanted a process fix. On one day, having had barely a week to organize, they gathered 38,000 signatures. Politicians should talk to everyone and not just a narrow ideological base? *That's common sense*, voters would say when the signature collectors explained what they were doing. If my first choice can't win, my vote counts for my second choice, so the winner has a majority? Sign me up! Then they'd ask, why aren't we doing that already? "We knew we were onto something," Bailey says. The new group, the Committee for Ranked Choice Voting, aimed for the 2016 ballot. They wanted time to collect the remaining 23,000 signatures needed and to come before voters in a high-turnout presidential election year. But they also wanted more time to do voter education.

Volunteers started knocking on doors, set up shop at fairs and festivals, wrote letters to the editor. No one knew what kind of resources the campaign would have, so the reformers needed to be stealthy and strategic. "Instead of trying to be on the front page of the newspaper, let's just try to be on page six every day or every week," says Bailey. Local papers published 500 letters to the editor backing ranked choice. There were 40 ranked choice beer elections, 150 house parties, even contests for ranked choice flowerbeds. The League of Women Voters explained the process in senior centers, libraries and schools. Wherever Mainers gathered in the community, someone was there to explain ranked choice voting. Most importantly, they didn't talk about Paul LePage at all. Everything remained scrupulously nonpartisan. After all, the last six Maine governors who took office with a mere plurality included two Republicans, two Democrats and two independents. "This was about people voting for what they want, leveling the playing field and getting rid of strategic voting," says Bailey. It worked. On election night 2016, Maine became the first state in the nation to adopt ranked choice. The referendum earned the second highest vote total in Maine history. It won towns that went big for Donald Trump and ones that turned out for Hillary Clinton. Organizers celebrated a huge victory for government by the people. "I thought we were there," says Woodbury.

Only McCormick saw what was coming next. Ranked choice became law on January 7, 2017. A new legislature was sworn in. McCormick had a sudden realization: "Oh my God," she told the *Boston Globe*. "They're going to try to repeal our law."[5]

●

Here's where a story of dedicated and freezing grass-roots petitioners battling for a twenty-first-century political reform collides with a nineteenth-century armed insurrection. Our classic image of a modern electoral dispute comes from the 2000 Florida recount. Who could forget that balding election official with the magnifying glass giving himself bug eyes trying to determine the intent behind a hanging chad? But in 1879, a three-way race for governor in Maine ended in near civil war.

Republican Daniel Davis won the most votes, but fell 0.3 percentage points short of a majority, throwing the election into Maine's legislature. Governor Alonzo Garcelon, a Democrat, finished third but fought desperately to hang onto power. Garcelon and the Democrats teamed with the Greenbacks, an anti-gold standard party, and falsely alleged voter fraud by Republican legislative candidates. Conspiring with the election board, Garcelon invalidated enough Republican votes on fraudulent technicalities to tip both chambers of the legislature to a fusion coalition of Democrats and Greenbacks. Republicans turned to the courts and won key victories. Garcelon, however, ignored the rulings and continued to seat legislators who would help keep him in office. That's when things nearly turned violent. Tensions escalated to such a pitch that Republicans, led by U.S. Senator James Blaine, gathered armed forces across from the state capitol. Garcelon's troops took up positions to defend the building. Gettysburg hero General Joshua Chamberlin somehow managed to de-escalate a dangerous situation and restore the rule of law. Chamberlin arrived in Augusta and took command of the state militia and local police forces. He faced death threats, loaded weapons and a citizenry ready to wage bloody battle against neighbors, but, over twelve anxious days, convinced Garcelon and the fusionists to stand down, recognize the state court's decision and ratify Davis's election. The next legislature, eager to ensure peaceful transitions of power and prevent Mainers from taking up weapons against one another, amended the state constitution to allow elections for governor to be decided by plurality.[6]

Nearly 140 years later, Mainers were arguing once again about the meaning of plurality. Republicans in the Maine senate asked the state Supreme Court for a "solemn occasion"—a nonbinding decision on whether a law passed constitutional muster. Justices delivered a split verdict: they analyzed the phrase "a plurality of all votes" and decided that meant ranked choice would be acceptable in statewide party primaries and federal elections, but not state elections. That would require a constitutional amendment. A stalemated legislature didn't know what to do next. "That gave the whole thing a bloody nose," Maine secretary of state Matt Dunlap tells me. "There weren't enough votes to repeal it, or to amend the constitution. You're stuck in limbo. I got a bit alarmed. Of course, I was accused of trying to undermine the whole thing because I wasn't out there cheerleading for it. My job isn't to cheerlead. It's to implement it, and I had to be honest about what it would take. A lot of people didn't want to hear that."

Reformers expected some opposition, but also imagined that politicians would be afraid to undo a law passed by the people. The obvious solution would have been a bill to amend the constitution. Instead politicians of all sides began to advance repeal. A half-dozen different bills emerged. The regular session came and went. An October special session was ultimately required, and, in the dead of night, after hearing testimony from outraged citizens for hours, the legislature undid not only ranked choice but three other citizen-led initiatives that would legalize marijuana, increase taxes on the wealthy to fund education, and expand Medicaid. Bailey, McCormick and Woodbury watched from the balcony, seething, as the legislature gutted ranked choice with a poison pill: they delayed implementation until 2021, and required passage of a constitutional amendment by then.

It was death by political impossibility. "We weren't going to let them get away with it," McCormick says. They had one shot left, but it required a second petition drive. "You don't have time to grieve," says Bailey. "We had to turn right around and run another campaign." They would attempt a People's Veto of the legislature while mounting a multipronged legal strategy to force implementation in time for primaries in June 2018. The clock was ticking.

⬤

Ninety days. More than 80,000 signatures. A higher bar than the previous drive, and in much less time. Winter in Maine. Reformers were desperate to collect signatures on election day, but first Dunlap, as secretary of state, had to approve the People's Veto language. It took until the very last minute: 4:30 p.m. the day before. Once again, a volunteer army had be mobilized, petitions had to be printed and distributed. Pens froze in the cold. Names were collected on ski slopes and outside holiday services. "Over the Christmas holiday, every day I'd wake up and look at the thermometer and think, 'Those poor guys are out there,'" Dunlap told me. And all that work merely forced another election—a second statewide referendum on ranked choice, to be held on primary day in June. That's right: the first statewide use of ranked choice would come on the very same day that voters decided whether or not to keep it. Give it a test drive and decide if you want to take it home.

The League of Women Voters went into overdrive. "It became really clear to us that there was a need to educate people who didn't like it," says Anna Keller, the executive director of Maine Citizens for Clean Elections. The campaign's office is located in downtown Portland, and decorated with homemade signs, afghans and flags demanding "Make Government Accountable to the People, Not Special Interest Groups" and "Proud Home of Clean Elections." "The people who were going to vote against it still needed to know how to use it. We were able to reach out to those people. The campaign, coming out of the legislative session, was feeling fiery. 'The politicians are terrible! The rule of the people has been overwritten!'

That's how you get people fired up to vote—but it also burns some bridges along the way."

At the same time as Bailey, McCormick and the Committee were rallying turnout for the People's Veto, they were defending the use of ranked choice voting for the June primaries in court. Reformers sued Dunlap to hurry implementation. Then, when the legislature cut funding for implementation, Dunlap became a hero, finding money in his own budget to hire a private courier system to collect results town by town (to satisfy an arcane state election provision) when the legislature wouldn't fund it and the state police would have cost too much. LePage slammed ranked choice as "the most horrific thing in the world" and threatened not to certify the results. But candidates behaved exactly as reformers hoped they would: on the Democratic side, campaigns were so civil and high-minded that two hopefuls for governor actually cross-endorsed each other as second choice. And voters—whether because they enjoyed the primary experience or because they wanted to stand up to a legislature that had overturned the will of the people—reinstated ranked choice by an even bigger margin than it gained the first time around.

"People told me that they felt like their vote actually counted," said Sarah Rawlings, the advocacy and organizing director for Maine Citizens for Clean Elections and the senior project manager for ranked choice education. "'I felt like I actually was expressing my voice. I did more research. This was easy. This was empowering. I got to choose who I really wanted without risking helping someone I can't really tolerate.' Those reactions were really validating to hear."

In November, ranked choice delivered exactly what it promised: a multi-candidate election with no spoilers, and liberation from strategic voting. In Maine's 2nd congressional district, incumbent U.S. Representative Bruce Poliquin battled a Democrat, Jared Golden, and two independents. Poliquin led by 1,910 votes on election night—but failed to break 50 percent, having earned 46.4 percent of the first-round vote. That placed second-choice votes in play. When both of the independents (winners of

23,000 first-round votes) were eliminated, votes broke toward Golden and he was declared the winner, 50.53 percent to 49.47. The system voters demanded through two petition drives and two statewide ballot questions, beating back defenders of the old way at every turn, produced an election that gave voters more voice, more choice and a representative with true majority support.

"The people are sovereign. The people are more powerful. Even when it seems like the deck is stacked and the odds are against you," Bailey says. "At the end of the day, the people are more powerful than any governor, any secretary of state, any attorney general, any state legislature. The people have the power; they just have to choose to exercise it. When we do choose to exercise democracy, the people can't be stopped." That powerful message has also been learned by a new generation of voting rights warriors.

● CHAPTER 12

Youth Saves the Day

"If they don't want you voting, that means we have to."

In 1960, four African American students from North Carolina A & T State University took a seat at the downtown Woolworth's whites-only lunch counter and politely ordered a cup of coffee. It took almost six months for the coffee to arrive, but every day they waited bent the moral arc toward equality. The Greensboro Four's courageous protest inspired sit-ins at bus stations, restaurants, beaches and hotels across North Carolina and the South, anywhere blacks and whites lived under different sets of rules, and many did not end until the 1964 Civil Rights Act finally mandated desegregation of public accommodations. Today, that Woolworth's is an international civil rights museum, a piece of that lunch counter resides in the Smithsonian, and the closest intersection, Sycamore Street, has been renamed February One Place in the students' honor.

A mere 1.3 miles away, a straight shot down Market Street, the largest historically black college in the United States has an invisible line running through it, a modern-day version of separate but equal. Now a new generation—here in Greensboro and on campuses nationwide—has picked up the same old fight for fairness. The barriers are subtler, easier to justify and disguise, but every bit as consequential. Yet once again, students are ready for the fight.

Turn left from Market onto Laurel Street and it dead-ends at a tree-lined walkway of the North Carolina A & T campus, a popular path from the engineering school to the student center. This is also the precise dividing line between the 6th and 13th congressional districts. The library, student center, business school and six of the school's thirteen dorms are located in the 6th district, represented by conservative Matt Walker. The cafeteria, art gallery and the seven remaining dorms sit in the 13th, represented by conservative Ted Budd. No "whites only" sign need hang in Greensboro. This district line cracks the majority-minority city so precisely that it dilutes the African American vote and practically ensures that Greensboro will continue to be represented by two conservative white men for years to come.

"The line is too specific, it's too effective," senior Braxton Brewington tells me on a gorgeous fall afternoon as we walk the boundary. The irony isn't lost on anyone here. The state's white power structure found a new way to keep control of this city where history has been defined by explicit racial bias, and then ran the new dividing line, quietly, straight through the intellectual center of African American life here.

"The idea that the lawmakers in North Carolina saw fit to suppress my vote and the voting strength of my peers because we attend this wonderful university is baffling," Brewington said on the courthouse steps, as he supported Common Cause and the League of Women Voters in a lawsuit against this transparent gerrymander. "The right to vote should be easy, accessible; it should present multiple opportunities for itself, not create restrictions and constraint. This is not only an unconstitutional gerrymander but an attack on our campus." In 2018, it would not be the only one.

●

The J. Wayne Reitz Union is the heartbeat of the University of Florida, a sweeping, sunlit student center that could easily be mistaken for a college town resort. Across six floors and 350,000 square feet there are enough restaurants to have breakfast, lunch and dinner someplace different all week. Student entrepreneurs sell jewelry, clothing and even virtual reality games in a startup incubator called the Gator Hatchery. There's an entire campus of "leisure studies" offering non-credit guitar, dance and tennis lessons. Epic games of capture the flag have been played as part of Gator Nights, which also hosts big-name comedians and bands. There's a bowling alley, snooker tables, a hotel and, yes, even a twenty-four-hour study center, in case that's the kind of college experience you're into.

But until this year, there was one thing the 55,000 students and 5,300 staff members could not do in the Reitz Union: vote. Taking part in Florida's fourteen days of early voting required a thirty-two-minute walk or an hour-long bus ride to the office of the supervisor of elections. Almost 70 percent of Gainesville's voting-age population is affiliated with the university. But none of the three early voting centers were convenient to campus.

This frustrated Megan Newsome, an astrophysics major, who didn't need to consult Kepler's Second Law or the Harmony of the Spheres to figure out what to do. She added a self-taught minor in voting and democracy and launched a Vote Everywhere branch on campus, registering more than 3,000 voters. But what good is registering if you can't get to the polls? So she organized a shuttle service and started providing Ubers and van rides. "So many students who used the shuttle thanked me and said, 'We would not have been able to vote if not for this,'" Newsome tells me. She has an easy smile, red hair well past her shoulders and a steely determination to help students make their voices heard. But after Newsome's team made the last trip of the day, they heard the opposite lament: students who still hadn't voted told them they now had no idea how they would make it to the polls. "That's when I was, like, that is not acceptable," says Newsome. "I can't just sit there and be OK with that." Government-owned community centers were on the list of acceptable locations approved by the state legislature. The county election board had power to name an additional location. Why not right in the middle of the busiest place where most people in Gainesville lived, worked or studied?

Newsome had such political skills that she talked the university into paying for the shuttles. Officials in Gainesville and Tallahassee proved harder to sway. Students first requested that the local supervisor of elections designate the Reitz Union as one of the city's three early voting locations. Ken Detzner, Florida's secretary of state, shut that down. When Florida expanded early voting in 2014—in response to long lines and overwhelmed precincts during the 2012 election, which resulted from cutbacks in early voting (a Brennan Center study suggested that some 200,000 voters gave up and went home[1])—the legislature approved a long list of potential sites, including city halls, libraries, fairgrounds, civic centers, community buildings, stadiums and senior centers. Detzner interpreted that list narrowly. It didn't include colleges, so a college site—even a college stadium or community center—wasn't allowed. It was a no for the Reitz Union, and a no for any site on any campus statewide. The Gainesville mayor and city council passed a resolution backing the students. But when Newsome pushed the city attorney, Nicole Shalley, and the election board to use their discretion and name the Reitz Union as the county's additional location, Shalley refused, then stopped returning emails and phone calls.

"I kept thinking that this was such an obvious thing that everyone would be on the same side," Newsome tells me. "Every time we encountered opposition, someone would tell me I should've expected that. You know what? I didn't. I still had a lot of hope and faith." That faith, and her search for a bipartisan solution, brought Newsome to the office of Gainesville state senator Chuck Clemons, whom she asked for help in updating the law to allow early voting to take place on college campuses. Clemons offered the back of his hand. If voting isn't convenient, he told Newsome, students would simply have to work harder to have their voices heard. After the shuttles, the work to get the university to help pay for them and the determination that drove her campus's turnout numbers far above the national average for college campuses, Newsome couldn't believe what she was hearing. "It was, 'Voting should be so important to you that you'd want to walk thirty minutes to get there. It's an honor!'" Newsome agreed with him. "That's why we've been doing that," she told the senator, reminding him of the long walks and the dedication behind the shuttle service. "We're asking: can we please not do this anymore?" It was the national debate over voting encapsulated in one casual exchange: Is voting so sacred that people ought to be willing to overcome any barrier or inconvenience to cast their vote? Or is it such a fundamental right that it ought to be made as easy as possible?

"Every time I got a no, or got brushed off, it motivated me further. It was really just like, 'What are these people so scared of?'" she says. "If they don't want you voting, that means we have to." Newsome wanted to let legislators know that students cared and were watching. She wrote an op-ed for the Gainesville newspaper asking that the law be updated to make voting easier for the state's 800,000 college students. "The change is minor in detail, massive in effect, and common-sense in nature," she wrote. "Allow public colleges and universities to be early voting locations."[2]

Turns out her audience was larger and more influential than she expected. Her piece caught the attention of Guy Cecil, a University of Florida alum, a longtime Hillary Clinton strategist and the chairman of Priorities USA, a Super PAC that directs the spending of hundreds of millions of dollars. After the 2016 election, Cecil concluded that Democrats had been outfoxed on redistricting and voting rights. He believed that focusing on individual elections didn't make a lot of sense when big structural issues needed to be addressed. Cecil looked at where Republican officials allowed early voting, where they consolidated precincts, where fewer machines were sent, and connected the dots. Many states, including Michigan, New Hampshire, Texas and Wisconsin, had made it harder for students to vote at their college address. "Look, if there were two cases of this, you could say, 'Okay, this is not some grand strategy,'" Cecil tells me over coffee in Washington. "But this is everywhere there are Republicans in power. It's either the most remarkable coincidence in the history of coincidence, or it's a systematic effort to depress the vote. I'm going to go with the latter." And he had the brilliant voting rights attorney Marc Elias by his side, eager to battle these imbalances in court.

Together with the League of Women Voters, Newsome and Cecil alleged that Detzner's narrow interpretation of the state's early voting statute created an "unacceptable impediment" to voter participation, creating "obstacles that only exist on campus" for "students who are often casting their very first vote." They pointed out that the statute plainly allows stadiums and community centers as early voting sites, and that Detzner himself, encouraging the 2014 expansion, recognized that the state needed to be flexible and responsive to many different communities. So why exclude college campuses? The only explanation, they argued, was an effort to "particularly burden young voters animated by a belief that doing so will assist in gaining or maintaining a partisan political advantage." That violated not only the students' First Amendment rights but also the equal protection clause of the Fourteenth Amendment, and the Twenty-Sixth Amendment, which gave eighteen-year-olds the vote.

An outraged U.S. district judge agreed, finding that Detzner's interpretation of the law "imposes significant burdens" on students and "reveals a stark pattern of discrimination." "This is not a mere inconvenience," wrote Judge Mark Walker, but "lopsidedly impacts Florida's youngest voters," and only Florida's youngest voters, without any compelling government interest. "Its target audience is unambiguous," he wrote, and the state's defense "reeks of pretense."[3] Newsome marveled over "how stern it was," feeling comforted that justice would prevail and "that there was a legal ruling with all the things that I had been thinking about so long."

Her relief turned to jubilation in late October, when Sabrina Ochoa, a twenty-year-old psychology major, bought an iced pumpkin latte in the Reitz Union and then became the first University of Florida student to cast an early vote on campus, right there in the Reitz Union. "Kind of surreal," Ochoa said. "I woke up this morning and didn't think I was going to make history."[4] In the first two days alone, more than 1,000 students voted early in Reitz, part of an amazing national statistic: early voting among citizens aged eighteen to twenty-nine surged by 188 percent from the 2014 midterms.[5]

⬤

That surge needed to overcome a mighty seawall. In Texas, where a stringent voter ID requirement accepts a concealed handgun permit but not a college ID, the barrier felt especially steep. Students exercised pressure, backed up by the threat of litigation, and won important victories. Texas State University students won two extra days of early voting as well as two additional voting locations after lines backed up for hours during the limited time the campus's one polling place was open.

Two hours west, in Waller County, five students at another historically black university, Prairie View A & M, sued county officials for failing to provide reasonable access to an early voting site either on campus or anywhere in Prairie View. Under the plan approved by Waller County officials, there were no early voting sites in Prairie View during the first week of early voting. One campus site was authorized for three weekdays in late October, and was open for a total of twenty-seven hours. There were no weekend or evening hours. In Waller, meanwhile, a town half the size of Prairie View, majority white whereas Prairie View is majority black, authorities opened two early voting sites during the first week for a total of seventy-three hours, including evenings and weekends. There's significant racial tension in these towns. If the names sound familiar, it might be because Sandra Bland, an alumna of Prairie View A & M heading back to campus for a new job, died mysteriously in the Waller County jail after being arrested on a traffic violation. Officials called it a suicide.

"I don't want this to be the reason, but it looks like we're PVAMU in a predominantly white area, and they don't really want us to vote," Damon Johnson, one of the five student plaintiffs, told the *New York Times*.[6] The suit pointed to decades of "restrictive or unnecessary voter registration and property requirements; baseless selective prosecutions and voter challenges; and, more recently, needless reductions in access to early voting and polling locations" that make registering to vote and casting a ballot "unduly burdensome, if not impossible" for African American students. Simply filing the lawsuit generated results: the county expanded the available early voting hours on campus and added a weekend day at an off-campus location.

Student activism also defeated parts of Iowa's stringent new voter ID provisions and restrictions on early and absentee voting. Iowa's secretary of state, Paul Pate, a Republican, pushed back against Donald Trump when the president-elect falsely alleged that 3 to 5 million people had voted illegally in 2016. "I certainly don't see that in Iowa," Pate said. The state legislature, however, baldly admitting that voter ID and election integrity was necessary for "a whole lot of issues that we care about, abortion, gay marriage, a whole lot of social issues,"[7] made it dramatically harder to cast an absentee ballot—requiring an application several months before the election and an unscientific and arbitrary signature verification, among other provisions—and created a burdensome ID procedure.

They should have tightened their own procedures instead. Officials matched Taylor Blair's registration to someone else, and mailed that person Blair's card. Ultimately, the Iowa State student and vice president of the Young Democrats was only allowed to cast a provisional ballot after he swore an affidavit. Blair sued, alleging that the new requirements were the "culmination of the efforts of Republican officeholders to undermine the right to vote and make voting more burdensome for partisan advantage," and that the GOP had specifically targeted voting methods used by Democrats, Latinos, African Americans, young people and the elderly. An Iowa judge rejected the state's arguments in a July 2018 decision that added additional days of early voting, called the state's own voter ID education materials misleading and "an inaccurate depiction of current Iowa law," and described the absentee ballot provisions as an "additional and unnecessary obstacle in the way of exercising the right to vote." The court described voting as a fundamental Iowan right and declared that "the legislature is not entitled to a limitless ability to regulate fundamental rights."[8]

Yet Republican legislatures nationwide have adopted measures similar to this unscientific and ineffective "signature match" program. This twenty-one-year-old industrial design student's lawsuit not only helped tens of thousands of Iowans cast early ballots, but delivered a legal body blow to a duplicitous "fraud-fighting" plan that only makes it more difficult for eligible voters to cast their ballots.

College Democrats from blood rivals Michigan State and the University of Michigan, meanwhile, partnered on a lawsuit that could expand the scope of the Twenty-Sixth Amendment—which gave eighteen-year-olds the right to vote, and helped Megan Newsome bring early voting to Florida universities—by using it as a weapon against suppression tactics that target young people. While Florida and Texas authorities piled creative new barriers between college students and the ballot box, Michigan had the widest participation gap between the total population of 18- to 24-year-olds and those who actually voted. One law helps explain what has been called a nearly insurmountable barrier between young people and the right to vote: Rogers' Law, so named after the state senator turned congressman who wrote it in 1999, in part to aid his own ascent to Washington.[9]

Rogers' Law sounds simple enough: it requires that a citizen vote where their driver's license says they permanently reside. First-time voters in Michigan must also appear to vote in person, meaning that students who register by mail or as part of an on-campus registration drive can't vote by absentee ballot. The real-world effect of this pair of laws makes it extremely difficult for college students to vote. Student addresses change every year, and getting a new license is both expensive and requires an afternoon at the DMV. Many young people who remain on their parents' health care plans or car insurance policies don't want to complicate matters with a different address. A student from Traverse City or Muskegon, for example, attending the University of Michigan in Ann Arbor, either runs that daunting obstacle course or faces a seven-hour round trip home to vote on a Tuesday when classes are in session.

The state legislature's nonpartisan policy analysts understood what the impact would be. "Critics of the bill have concerns that the legislation will discourage voting and decrease participation, particularly among college students," wrote the House Fiscal Agency. "Indeed, some people suspect this is the intent of the bill." It worked as imagined. Before the passage of Rogers' Law, participation among Michigan's 18- to 24-year-olds surpassed the national average. Afterward, it plummeted, and by 2016 it had become the worst in the nation. Almost 65 percent of all Michigan citizens voted that year, but just 37.8 percent of young people.[10] Registration, right at the national average, was not the problem. Turnout was. All that worked out well for Mike Rogers, however. He ran for the congressional seat in Lansing, home to Michigan State and more than 50,000 students, in 2000, the year his restrictions went into effect. The new provisions created so many challenged registrations and such chaos at precincts near Michigan State that the phones went down. Mike Rogers? He won his seat by 111 votes.

The margin in New Hampshire's 2016 U.S. Senate race was just slightly larger—Democrat Maggie Hassan defeated Republican incumbent Kelly Ayotte by 1,017 votes—but the impact was the same. In a state where close elections are as common as moose warning signs, Republicans doubled down on suppressing the college vote. Donald Trump and Kris Kobach established the narrative, wrongly alleging that a bus caravan of Massachusetts Democrats voted fraudulently in the Granite State. It turns out that three people were charged with double-voting in New Hampshire and Massachusetts; all of them backed Trump twice. Regardless, Republicans established a "voter fraud czar" charged with digging into the residency of election day registrants, and even authorized state law enforcement to show up at private homes to double-check the residency papers of voters.

Just in case those intimidation measures were insufficient, the next two measures were surgically designed to chill the votes of the state's 90,000 college students. Senate Bill 3 required voters who registered within thirty days of an election to prove that they are "domiciled" where they seek to vote or face thousands of dollars in fines, even for improperly completed paperwork. Then House Bill 1264 tightened eligibility again: voting in a state election would launch a sixty-day countdown for people to get a state license and register their car, if they had one. In other words, college students faced an expensive and anti-democratic choice: pay several hundred dollars to vote where they spent at least nine months of the year, or lose the right to vote in New Hampshire.

"It's literally a poll tax," says Garrett Muscatel, a twenty-year-old Dartmouth College junior, as we chat in the campus's Baker-Berry Library on a chilly late October morning days before the election. "It's even more ridiculous because the nearest DMV is forty minutes away. Students have to drive forty minutes, pay a huge fee for the driver's license, then drive back. These bills are designed to make sure that no matter how enthusiastic students are, they won't be able to have their voices heard."

It's already snowing in New Hampshire, and to Muscatel, a California native, this is a reminder of the winter day when he first encountered snow on a campus tour and decided right then that New Hampshire was the place for him. He worked on Hassan's campaign, and felt personally insulted when Republicans alleged that the victory he had worked so hard for was fraudulently won. After the two suppression measures passed the state legislature, he became a plaintiff in a lawsuit challenging the residency requirements, and helped convince Dartmouth's Office of Residential Life to set up a table at the polls to verify students' residency. And then he launched his own campaign for the state house from Hanover.

Steps away, in the library lobby, twenty-two-year-old Emma Baker staffed a NextGen America table and coordinated campus volunteers on a "dormstorming" effort armed with voting brochures and baskets of Halloween candy. "It was me and every mom at the CVS this morning," she says with a laugh. NextGen, founded by billionaire environmental activist Tom Steyer, aims to register hundreds of thousands of young voters in swing states, Millennials who already skew progressive. Registering them, delivering them to the polls, not only helps tip the balance of power in closely divided states but also develops a liberal infrastructure to counter well-funded conservative efforts. Those efforts have been effective on campuses like Dartmouth, where student publications funded by national conservatives trained the young Laura Ingraham, Dinesh D'Souza and others in the ways of cutthroat parry and thrust.

Baker has her entire get-out-the-vote effort organized on a Google spreadsheet, complete with number of beds, door-knocking goals and volunteer shifts, matched up with color-coded files for every dorm on campus. Ever since classes began, they've been sitting at tables or going door to door, even wandering campus with clipboards, all to encourage students to sign postcards pledging to vote. Now they're determined to get them to the polls, even down to arranging transportation. "College students are as affected by what comes out of the legislature as anybody else," she tells me, mentioning student loans, health care and minimum wage bills as just three examples. "They've targeted college students. But we're all about making voting as easy as possible."

A seventy-minute drive away, across Tunney Mountain, past sugar barns and maple farms, Vanessa Calabrese and Rowan Cummings are tabling for NextGen inside Plymouth State's student center, the Pawsway, covered with signs proclaiming "Consent Is Sexy" and advertising Green Week with virgin pot brownies. Steyer has not skimped on the swag: free "Vote" baseball caps, T-shirts, water bottles that read "resist, win, repeat," even frisbees. There's a life-size cutout of Michelle Obama and a student in an inflatable T-Rex costume urging students to "make voter suppression extinct." Next to them, less flamboyant College Democrats try to attract passers-by with a sad display of Kit-Kats and an invitation to see Colorado governor John Hickenlooper speak on campus the next day; after two hours, however, the Hickenlooper sign-up sheet remains blank, while the Steyer gear and Dunkin' Donuts at the NextGen table vanish. Just under 4,000 students attend Plymouth State, and over the last eight weeks, tables, dormstorming and the occasional dinosaur stunt have generated 1,811 pledges to vote. On this morning, they're reminding students that they'll need ID and proof of domicile to cast their ballot, and trying to clarify rampant misinformation. "A lot of people were definitely confused," Cummings tells me. "It's voter suppression—with some loopholes."

Ten days later, legislators paid the price. Democrats flipped both New Hampshire's state house and senate. One of the victorious Democrats will be the youngest legislator in the house, Garrett Muscatel. He will head to the state capitol determined to protect voting rights, in between working on a political science degree.

"It's a lot harder to strip people of the right to vote when they're literally in the room voting on the bill with you," Muscatel says. "I hope I can make a difference that way, or maybe even sway some minds just by showing people that college students exist."

 **CONCLUSION**

Democracy won big on election night 2018. Yet even as champagne flowed at the Voters Not Politicians victory party in Detroit, as returning citizens in Florida rejoiced and imagined registering to vote once again, and as whooping Reclaim Idaho volunteers poured into the streets of Sandpoint to commemorate Medicaid expansion by posing with their iconic RV, activists celebrated with the same nervous feeling. *How will the politicians try and steal this victory?* They were right to be concerned.

Reclaim Idaho's Luke Mayville, the American history scholar, remembered the words of Frederick Douglass: "Power concedes nothing without a demand." Never did. Never will. "The limits of tyrants are prescribed by the endurance of those whom they oppress." These battles weren't over yet. If citizens wanted to prevail in this battle for democracy, even this moment of victory was an invitation to work harder still. So you expanded Medicare in a red state? Fight on. Defeated gerrymandering and deep-pocketed special interests? Keep going. Halted a presidential voter fraud commission in its tracks? Don't stop now. Won the largest expansion of voting rights since the Nineteenth Amendment finally allowed women's suffrage? Your determined adversaries aren't discouraged. They're testing your commitment to the combat ahead.

Sometimes—as Mayville and Volz would quickly learn—power concedes nothing even *with* a demand. Even if that demand comes from a supermajority of citizens.

"It's not about politics, it's about how you continue to overcome," Neil Volz, deputy director of the campaign that restored voting rights for Floridians with felony convictions, told Maryam Saleh of the *Intercept*.

These resounding nationwide victories for better elections, fairer maps and voting rights for all won in the courts and at the ballot box. Citizens earned decisive victories in states so many different shades of red, purple and blue to make a dizzying Pantone display. The campaigns were scrupulously nonpartisan, and fought by volunteers who believed that, standing together, they could fix something broken and restore liberty and justice for all. Ordinary Americans came together to rejuvenate a democracy that partisans are all too eager to corrode, and that the U.S. Supreme Court remains sadly uneager to defend.

But this determination—and even their overwhelming victories— would not sway the forces of suppression to change their ways. Instead, those lawmakers turbocharged their efforts and shifted the battlefield, far from citizens and back to their own turf: the back rooms and cozy corridors of the very unrepresentative legislatures these citizens had battled so hard to democratize. Extraordinary citizen efforts, meet your old friend politics-as-usual.

Idaho lawmakers took it on themselves to add strenuous work requirements and other restrictions onto the Medicaid expansion that more than 60 percent of state voters demanded. Mayville had imagined that would happen, but even he couldn't have predicted that the legislature would go for the kill-shot: a well-funded effort to destroy Reclaim Idaho's key organizational tool—the ballot initiative—and crush this movement just as citizens began to feel their collective power. Idaho's legislature voted to impede the ability of citizens to force initiatives, requiring signatures of 10 percent of registered voters in 32 of the state's 35 senate districts (up from 6 percent in 18 districts), and whacking the time allowed to collect signatures from eighteen months down to six.

When the governor vetoed those changes, which would have made Idaho one of the toughest states in the nation to put an initiative on the ballot, legislators promptly introduced four new bills, some even *more* radical. "A number of legislators actually said, 'The voters didn't know what they were doing,'" Mayville told me, shock and disgust in his usually measured voice. "They can get away with this in a one-party supermajority state because they don't have to face all the voters, just a tiny slice of the Republican primary electorate." Mayville estimates that's somewhere between 5 and 15 percent of all Idahoans. "They've given up and turned on democracy. You hear this idea that 'We're not a democracy, we're a republic,' as if that's a rationale for rendering popular votes illegitimate."

Citizens unrigged the system at the ballot box. Politicians tried to knot it back up again. It's almost as if it were a national plan: Arkansas, Idaho, Florida, North Dakota, South Dakota and Utah enacted new restrictions on ballot initiatives. According to the Ballot Initiative Strategy Center, in the first half of 2019, legislators in sixteen states introduced more than 120 bills aimed at making it harder for citizens to go around unrepresentative legislatures and put policies directly to the people.[1] "This is a way to make sure that there is absolutely no way that anyone can do something that Republican lawmakers don't already approve," Florida state senator Oscar Braynon, a Democrat, told the Associated Press.[2]

Even if that included 64 *percent* of all voters. In Florida, those five million Democrats, Republicans and independents who stood together to end the unfair and antidemocratic practice of felon disenfranchisement—and restored the voting rights of more than 1.4 million neighbors who'd served their time and earned back every privilege of citizenship—had that will unwound by 89 Republican legislators. In two party-line votes, the 67 house Republicans and 22 senate Republicans added new barriers that would require citizens with felony convictions to pay all associated fines, fees and restitution before they can vote. Insulated from voters, they had no need to listen to them. And so they did not. The legislature retroactively altered the amendment and stripped Floridians of voting rights if those fees remain unpaid, even if they were not part of the original sentence. This now requires the most vulnerable and impoverished Floridians to generate hundreds of millions of dollars, collectively, to become citizens again.

Expert estimates on how many people will be trapped by these new requirements vary widely, anywhere from 600,000 people all the way to 1.1 million. But behind those figures are devastated individuals like Coral Nichols, a Republican who runs a prison diversion nonprofit and pays the state $100 a month restitution after finishing her sentence for grand theft. Trouble is, she owes $190,000 in fees. "Heartbreak after hope," she told the *Christian Science Monitor*.[3] Nichols estimates she might get to vote in Florida if she manages to live to the age of 188.

"This is a poll tax," the Reverend Jesse Jackson told me. "Those who want to keep African Americans away from the polls haven't given up since the ratification of the Fifteenth Amendment in 1870." Jackson rattled off an unseemly roll call: gerrymandering, voter ID laws, purges of voting rolls, strategic precinct closures in black neighborhoods. Sometimes it's high-tech, surgical and almost invisible. Other times it's blatant, such as "providing fewer machines, resulting in longer lines at our polling places," all to discourage voting. "Now that a pro-democracy movement is advancing a powerful set of electoral reforms, it's the poll tax again."

And so Jackson fights on, as does Volz, optimistic but with eyes ever searching for the next pothole. Jackson has seen the arc of moral justice bend toward justice and detour back to discrimination over seven long decades. Volz says he remains excited about what Floridians won, rather than bitter over what was taken away. "Where other people see obstacles, we see opportunity," he says.[4] "That is part of the heartbeat of this entire movement. It took us ten years to get to last November, and we're in this for the long haul." Meanwhile, several prosecutors in Florida's largest counties got to work on a solution of their own: finding a way to convert fines and fees into community service or other sanctions. "We should not be an obstacle for a person who has the right to vote," Miami Dade County state attorney Katherine Fernandez-Rundle told WLRN-TV.[5] Fernandez-Rundle told the TV station that her office has the ability to alter older cases as well as future ones.

That same entrepreneurial spirit is alive within Andrew Gillum, who fell 32,500 votes short of becoming the state's governor in 2018 then got right back to work registering voters—no matter how hard the legislature made it. He founded a new group called Forward Florida with the goal of registering 1 million new voters before the 2020 elections. "Democracy in Florida is under absolute and complete attack," he told me. "Oppression and disenfranchisement are a system. We have to fight back against it, in spite of all of the obstacles. We have to keep doing the difficult work of democracy. There is no alternative."

Here's the good news: tens of thousands of Idahoans now have health insurance which they didn't have before Reclaim Idaho's fight. That number may be smaller than originally hoped, but it's still a huge victory in a state where any challenge to Republican lawmakers seemed impossible. Michigan still has to determine how its independent redistricting commission will be funded, but no matter what, citizens will draw the maps in 2021. Fewer Floridians with felony convictions will be able to vote in 2019 and 2020 than imagined, but anywhere from 300,000 to 650,000 citizens have won back their civil rights and civic voice. Remember, as does Volz, the two steps forward before the half-step back.

Voting rights activists won a powerful reminder as well: our current fight against voter ID, gerrymandering and voter suppression is actually the latest chapter in a struggle over the vote that's as old as the nation itself. While we might like to imagine that our nation's story is one of ever-expanding suffrage, with courts protecting and defending this fundamental freedom, it has never been as simple as that. The struggle did not end with the passage of the Fourteenth Amendment, or the Voting Rights Act or, certainly, with the resounding passage of all these democracy reforms on election day 2018. This is no time to celebrate or rest. The work will only get more difficult. Opponents grow more defiant, not discouraged. Sadly, they include political leaders all too willing to turn democracy itself into a political issue.

When Mitch McConnell responded to the bold, nonpartisan democracy reforms introduced in the House of Representatives in January 2019 as a "power grab" and "simply a naked attempt to change the rules of American politics to benefit one party," it was an early sign of how ugly this battle would remain. Yet there's no getting around the uncomfortable truth: McConnell was describing the actions of one side. His own.

We're on our way to learning the answer to an existential question: What happens to a representative democracy when one party is no longer committed to the foundational notion everyone must be represented, equally?

Lawmakers have two choices: they can make voting harder, or they can make it easier. McConnell's party has gerrymandered, purged rolls and enacted ever-more-precise anti-voter laws. They've made fraudulent claims of voter fraud under a fig leaf of "electoral integrity," while their words and deeds strip bare the real goal: a whiter, more rural, and ultimately smaller electorate that they believe will allow them to continue to win elections even as the nation becomes something else entirely. When citizens fought back in 2018 via the ballot initiative, they took that right away. When Democrats attempted to use the political process to ensure an equal playing field for both parties, the Senate majority leader accused *them* of playing politics.

It's a nifty rhetorical trick, but exceptionally dangerous. It traps democracy itself, our most fundamental rights and values, in the polarized hell that is red versus blue.

Democracy, after all, isn't some rarified idea. It's how a diverse and often disagreeing nation finds a way to live together and solve problems.

Without the vote, democracy doesn't exist, and neither does the rule of law. No one wins everything every time. But elections provide the opportunity to persuade one another, discuss our differences and then come together again with the understanding that the side with the most votes won. When the rules are rigged, when the side with the most votes *loses*, voters, understandably, lose confidence in the legitimacy of the results and in the system itself.

The consequences could be frightful. It's easy to imagine entire sections of the nation living in a "democracy desert," with a state government that places ever more determined and sturdy barriers between citizens and the ballot box, locking in an enduring and even anti-majoritarian one-party rule that seeks to prevent growing populations from assuming power. Coastal states, meanwhile, will continue to experiment with making voting easier. Our democracy is atrophying and growing all at once, depending on the state one calls home. All Americans should find this immoral and unacceptable, but even those who would enact or justify these tactics must understand that it is historically unsustainable.

Fundamental democratic rights should not vary across the fifty states, let alone across county lines. But hyperlocal suppression efforts are expanding at those levels, and politicians have found the language and mastered the tools to make them look race-blind while targeting communities of color nevertheless. It's not overstatement to suggest that if current trends continue through the 2021 redistricting cycle, many U.S. states might not resemble anything close to a democracy at all.

This isn't some apocalyptic vision. It's a project that's well underway. Throughout 2019, some states moved to protect and expand the franchise. Delaware and New York established early voting. New Mexico passed automatic voter registration (AVR) and same-day registration. Hawaii instituted AVR and pre-registration for sixteen- and seventeen-year-olds. Washington state adopted a Native Americans Voting Rights Act. Eighteen states and the District of Columbia have now enacted or implemented AVR since 2016 alone. When New Jersey's Democratic legislature attempted to rig the state's redistricting procedure in December 2018 to their own benefit, they were shamed and halted in their tracks almost immediately by the loud protests of activists, Eric Holder, and even the state's Democratic governor.

In a healthy democracy, driving up participation would be a bipartisan goal. Oregon led the way with AVR in 2015, and the program has been a huge success, passed by Democrats but benefiting everyone. According to a Center for American Progress study, AVR helped add 272,000 people to the rolls in 2016, 116,000 of whom were considered unlikely to sign up otherwise.[6] Some 40,000 cast ballots in 2016, catapulting Oregon to the highest voter turnout growth in the nation—and *Republicans* to more seats in the state legislature, even as studies showed that the new voters were more diverse than the previous electorate.

Red states, however, have chosen a different strategy. Republican legislatures moved to curtail ballot initiatives in Ohio, Florida, Michigan, Missouri and North Dakota, and worked to undermine those passed by voters in Utah and Idaho. Republicans in Missouri launched a stealth attack on the "Clean Missouri" amendments that mandated a new nonpartisan legislative mapmaking process and an end to special-interest donations over $5.

Parking became the new battlefield in Florida, where legislators undermined the legal victory for early voting on campus with a sneaky provision that allows local election officials to disallow it if there are not adequate spots for cars. Parking is always at a premium on college campuses, which often require a parking permit—but most of the people voting, being at the college already, would arrive at the polls on foot.

Texas lawmakers voted to make it a felony for anyone to cast an ineligible ballot, even by accident, and subject anyone who puts the wrong zip code or other incorrect information on a voting application to criminal charges and jail time. Arizona sought to restrict the ability of citizens to vote early. Tennessee, meanwhile, sought to make it harder for activist groups to conduct voter registration drives by requiring expensive new training and fines for submitting incomplete applications.

Democracy has always been a battle, with every precarious advance threatened by politicians eager to retain power by rigging the rules. This feels less like a battle, however, and more like a permanent state of war, with one side willing to bust every norm and American ideal in the service of installing an enduring form of minority rule.

Hope must not be lost. After all, no one is fooled. The crowd that won't let go of "voter fraud" claims now bring to mind the classic *Saturday Night Live* sketch starring Chevy Chase as a killer land shark who knocked on apartment doors pretending to deliver flowers or a candygram. "Candygram, my foot!" the resident would respond. "You're that clever shark and you know it." Now, accusations of voter fraud get the same dismissive response, and the citizens and legal teams leading the fight back have a well-worn playbook filled with victorious strategies.

Let's return to Texas, where lawmakers, who apparently missed the humiliating defeat endured by Kris Kobach in Kansas several months earlier, attempted a galling assault on voting rights. In January 2019, mere weeks after his appointment as Texas's secretary of state, David Whitley questioned the citizenship status of almost 98,000 registered voters and claimed that 58,000 of them had cast at least one ballot since 1996. He demanded that county officials strike them from the rolls unless each appeared at their registrar's office with proof of citizenship within thirty days. Then he sent the list to the state attorney general for potential prosecutions. The president, exhibiting little knowledge about the facts that led to the demise of his voter fraud coalition, jumped in on Twitter: "These numbers are just the tip of the iceberg. All over the country, especially in California, voter fraud is rampant. Must be stopped!"[7]

Trouble is, there were about 98,000 problems with this list. Apologies to Jay-Z, but citizenship wasn't one. Whitley's spokesman told the *New York Times* that the study's methodology contained "very little, if any" room for error—except many people on the list had registered to vote at their *naturalization ceremonies*. The secretary of state's office said they simply didn't check that. Others registered when they applied for a driver's license, which also requires proof of citizenship. Only as county officials investigated did they discover that the state's eye-popping claim was pumped up by thousands of duplicate names, and many thousands more who had become citizens over the nearly quarter-century since 1996.

The local election boards received their lists on a Monday. By Tuesday, the charges had fallen apart. The largest list of names, some 30,000 potential noncitizen voters, went to Harris County, which includes Houston. "We are not willing to include at this point that we know of anybody on this list who is not a United States citizen," Douglas Ray, a special assistant attorney for Harris County, told the *New York Times*. By February, a federal judge halted the review of names, decrying the entire process as a "mess" that unfairly targeted naturalized citizens and a "solution looking for a problem."[8] Three separate lawsuits argued that its real purpose was a "witch hunt" determined to frighten Hispanics and other minorities away from voting. In April, Whitley settled those lawsuits by rescinding the advisory, ending the voter roll purge and agreeing that the state would cover $450,000 in legal fees. In May, he resigned.

Smart idea: unlike Kobach, he surrendered his losing battle before a federal judge ordered him back to school for remedial legal education.

Why do Republicans willingly choose this path over and over again? After all, a political party confident that its ideas have broad support and will prevail in a fair election shouldn't have to place obstacles between the people and the ballot box. It wouldn't gerrymander with such ferocity or concoct voter suppression schemes with such surgical precision. This is how you rig democracy, not how you resuscitate it. It's the sort of constitutional hardball that corrodes the legitimacy of elections and institutions. It's desperate, power mad and almost impossible to stop. Republicans could reach out, broaden their base and help fix our democracy while something meaningful remains to repair. Or, terrified of their base and willing to bring our entire system crashing down over anti-majoritarian loopholes that allow them to retain power, they could abandon any pretense of a commitment to democracy at all.

My quest to understand the GOP's suppression strategy brought me one summer's day to visit with three Washington wise men—conservatives, institutionalists, now institutions and lifers themselves—each opposed to Trumpism in a distinct way. The morning began at the center of Washington's permanent government-in-exile: breakfast at the Four Seasons, where the frittata arrives with peas and truffles and the lemon ricotta French toast has been enjoyed by lawyers, lobbyists and presidential golf buddies since the Carter administration.

Speaker Pelosi can be spotted here many mornings, perhaps at the regular table of longtime DC fixer Vernon Jordan. When Ivanka Trump wanted to meet the Washingtonians who really get things done, the GOP's Georgetown doyennes brought her here to mingle table by table with CEOs, corporate philanthropists, hedge fund gajillionaires and layers of the Obama state department and speechwriting teams. Everyone here speaks a common language; the First Daughter and DC's wealth-and-power set bonded over a shared real estate broker. This is my first time dining here, but before I can say a word the hostess greets me with, "Good morning, let me bring you to Mr. Will's table." There, tucked into the *New York Times*, is the thinker and columnist who has defined conservatism for five decades.

I want to talk to George Will because most Republicans in Congress and the conservative media establishment have marched onward in their red Team GOP uniform and equated party membership with party loyalty—no matter the leader, no matter the policies, no matter the cost to democratic norms. Not Will. When it became clear that Trump would be the GOP nominee and the establishment began to line up behind him, Will left the Republican Party rather than pay fealty. After a live, spittle-flecked argument with a furious Bill O'Reilly, Will and Fox News parted ways. "It's their toy," he shrugged. "What really drove O'Reilly mad was when I laughed at him." He's described Trump as a "sad, embarrassing wreck of a man," an "almost inexpressibly sad specimen," and "as bewildered as a kindergartener at a seminar on string theory." He's scoffed at the GOP voter fraud theories and supported reinstating felon voting rights in Florida. "I just don't like the idea of unending punishments. You commit a crime, you do the time. Start over," he tells me. "There's also something very unpleasant about politicians trying to pick their voters. We're supposed to persuade the electorate, not shape it with statutes." Will even urged fellow conservatives to vote against Republicans in November 2018, disgusted with Republican leaders like House Speaker Paul Ryan, who "sold his soul for a tax cut," shocking friends and politicos who never imagined they'd see the day Will called for Democrats to run both chambers of Congress.

"Have you ever read Arthur Koestler's novel *Darkness at Noon*?" Will inquires, when I ask why it seemed that leaving the party was so easy for him, while the leaders he once admired and even called friends have rationalized away the toxins within the GOP. In the novel, about 1930s Stalinist purges, Gletkin's identity and his membership in the party are one and the same. "A political party isn't a home," he says. "If you're a healthy person, one's identity isn't all wrapped up with it. The normalization of Trump is complete. So it's not my party anymore. I wasn't in despair. Parties are useful as long as they're useful. The Republican Party isn't useful anymore. Gone. Not a big deal."

Will orders three poached eggs, runny in a cup, with a toasted English muffin, and explains there was no real way to see this ugliness coming. "I don't know how," he says. "The whole thing was facially implausible. The bad news is that Republicans are afraid. The power of his tweets with 50 percent of the base. The good news is they despise him. They know that he's breathtakingly stupid, completely uninformed. All the adjectives."

It's a powerful metaphor: too many conservatives emulating the wrong characters from *Darkness at Noon*. Even behind closed doors, Will suggests, his former allies have fallen sway to strongman syndrome. "They are susceptible to the nationalism," he tells me. "Conservatives, for decades, believed in congressional supremacy and were suspicious of executive power. It's progressivism that always understood that it was an emancipated president running roughshod over the separation of powers that brought Wilson, Roosevelt, Lyndon Johnson. But then Republicans had their own heady experience with Ronald Reagan. And they fell in love with the presidency."

Republican senators abandon their principles for tax cuts and federal judges, Will says. The American people seem embarrassed by the sordid spectacle, but our politics has never been a high-minded, thoughtful exercise, he suggests. "We know it's going to pass. It doesn't mean things will get better," Will says, "but it'll get different." When I suggest it may not end well, Will counters with a simple, "But it will end. Everything does." Mark Twain and the novelist William Dean Howells once walked into a morning rainstorm, Will recounts, and Howells asked, "Do you think it will stop?" Twain replied, "It always has." A Republican insider walks past our table as we finish breakfast. "Good to see you," he tells Will. "Keep up the good fight, will you?" Will looks the courtly man straight in the eye. "I'm having no effect," he replies. As the man walks back to his own power breakfast, I politely suggest that can't entirely be true. "What's the evidence?" Will asks flatly. "I see no evidence that anyone is hungry for the truth."

Breakfast with George Will sent me back to *Darkness at Noon*, where this passage stopped me cold. "The best of them kept silent in order to do a last service to the Party. They were too deeply entangled in their own past, caught in the web they had spun themselves, according to the laws of their own twisted ethics and twisted logic; they were all guilty, although not of those deeds of which they accused themselves. There was no way back for them."

While Will insisted to me that "Trumpism without Trump won't exist," it wasn't entirely convincing. After all, so much of the norm-busting and constitutional hardball that abetted Trump's rise preceded his slow descent down that Trump Tower elevator in June 2015. Trump didn't draw the districts that put the House Freedom Caucus in charge, design the voter ID bills that kept minorities from the ballot box, or hold open a Supreme Court seat until his side won a presidential election. I wanted to talk to someone who'd done a more rigorous reappraisal of his own side's complicity, someone who'd come to understand that his party's role in stoking racial animus, relying on Fox News fact-free zones, and blocking voting rights had helped bring this Frankenstein's monster to life. I approached Bill Kristol as he was signing wooden eggs after delivering a speech to the influential "Politics and Eggs" membership in Manchester, NH.

When we finally sat down for coffee in Washington several months later, the veteran conservative thinker—a former chief of staff to Vice President Dan Quayle, an intellectual architect of the Iraq War, and a close adviser to the John McCain and Mitt Romney campaigns—told me that autographing eggs for the Chamber of Commerce crowd wasn't the strangest thing he'd done that winter. Turns out that the *Weekly Standard*, the conservative magazine Kristol founded after Bill Clinton ousted the first George Bush from the White House, holds an annual cruise; retirees, cable news green room groupies, and anyone who likes to catch some sun while hearing dark projections about entitlement reform can island-hop with their favorite conservative pundits. Kristol and the magazine had been Trump apostates from the beginning, so he was surprised when vacationeers—presumably the magazine's most dedicated readers—suggested it might be time to lay off the president.

"Just the degree of tribalism and team spirit and excusing things that I wouldn't have said people would have excused," he recalls, shaking his head. "I would have thought a lot of these people are like me. But people wanted to be defensive of the president and to stick to the team. I was amazed ordinary citizens"—and here Kristol is essentially describing negative partisanship, the notion that voters stick with their side because they're united in hatred of the other side—"have this much of that. Ordinary citizens! Not insiders. I mean, what do they care? It is an identity thing, right?"

Perhaps Kristol's biggest shock, however, arrived when his real fellow travelers, elite Republican donors and members of Congress, fell in line.

It's one thing, he muses, to rationalize backing Trump over Hillary Clinton because of judicial appointments and the courts. But rationalizing "good people" on both sides of a white supremacist rally in Charlottesville in exchange for a tax cut? The corruption and incompetence involving Trump family members and cabinet secretaries? Payoffs to porn stars? Footsie with Putin at Helsinki? A befuddled Kristol took to Twitter: "The GOP tax bill's bringing out my inner socialist. The sex scandals are bringing out my inner feminist. Donald Trump and Roy Moore are bringing out my inner liberal. WHAT IS HAPPENING?"

"The Republican party has been bad," Kristol tells me, but he's especially disappointed by members of the caucus who oppose Trump in private, then defend what he sees as indefensible. "The congressional side has been especially weak. A lot of people have accommodated this rather than confronting it." Then, he says, the talk from his friends and allies turned from acceptance to actual support, even praise that more was getting done than they'd ever hoped. Kristol shakes his head. "It's like we're looking at two different countries."

Kristol is not claiming ignorance of these forces. He says he battled the nativist, racist and know-nothing wings, and credits the *Weekly Standard* for pushing back hard against the influence of Pat Buchanan and Ron Paul. Kristol appeared on Brit Hume's Fox News show and the respectable Sunday-morning talkfests, and didn't pay much attention to the anti-climate change science and kooky conspiracy theories, or to the seedy underbelly of bullying and race-baiting that played out in prime time. Republican governors elected in 2010 and 2014, he argued, seemed to be doing serious, thoughtful work. And then the thing shoved under the bed devoured the respectable set. "I just figured it would be kept in check, and that was kind of what we do in big political parties," he says. "Then it kind of exploded, obviously."

He's thought deeply about it since, and he doesn't sound like a man looking to whitewash the same-old policies back onto the Grand Old Party.

Kristol launched an organization called Defending Democracy Together, attempting to unite Republicans and conservatives around the once uncontroversial notions of defending our institutions and upholding the rule of law, but also working toward more welcoming immigration policies and countering misconceptions about immigrants, particularly Hispanics.

"Someone said racism and bigotry is always the recessive gene in conservatism. There's some truth to that. But it was a recessive gene. It was kept under check, so to speak. And you can't change human nature, so you're not really going to get rid of all this stuff . . . then one day you wake up and the part you were just putting up with is now running everything."

But Kristol's a happier warrior than that, with a long view of history. He remembers how the ugliness of George Wallace and the Nixon era didn't disappear—perhaps it was just swept under the bed—but still the national political conversation moved on to foreign policy and Reaganomics, topics less central to race-related identity politics. And outside of Washington and luxury cruises sponsored by policy journals, Kristol's not convinced that our national divisions run as deep as they did in the 1960s, let alone the 1860s. He points to the almost immediate national embrace of same-sex marriage. "Maybe this can go away faster than we think. There's much less polarization on some issues than ten years ago." Even so, he worries about damage to vital institutions, and frets about the stability of a two-party system which, he suggests, has served the nation well for centuries. It would be catastrophic, he says, for one of these parties to become the voice of European-style nationalist populism. He stays inside the tent, for now, to fight those forces. and, he chuckles, because the Democrats wouldn't listen to him anyway. But he's also optimistic that Americans, including everyday Republicans, are better than this president and the party's current leadership and weak-kneed elected officials.

"Things that can do a lot of damage are not necessarily the same things that can create a new order. I am very dubious of a new Trumpian order coming," he says. "You read about these older periods, there can be ten- or twenty-year stretches like this and then it fades. People die off and new people come in. History suggests in the American case, except for the Civil War, that it usually doesn't end too badly."

⬤

Except, hours later and five blocks away, in the grand study of the American Enterprise Institute, Norm Ornstein sets the scene for armed insurrection about five sentences after we settle into the oversized antique chairs. It's not entirely certain what's more shocking: that we're having this conversation in the ornate reading room of a venerable conservative think tank, or that this veteran, rumpled eminence makes such simple, horrifying sense.

Ornstein says he's haunted by the notion that if a legal noose or impeachment were to tighten around Trump, he would pardon himself and everyone around him and then "take to Fox and Twitter and say, 'This is a coup. The deep state and Hillary Clinton are stealing the election I won. Take to the streets and bring back our democracy.' They go out with assault weapons. There will be violence and he'll declare martial law. There would be deep divisions in the National Guard and all that, but that would be disastrous."

Ornstein is an unlikely father of the #resistance, a Minnesota-born political scientist who quickly became one of the capital's most respected and studiously nonpartisan experts on Congress and how it should work. His parents knew to name him after what he would spend his life's work defending: the norms that allow complicated institutions to function, a civic religion of good government, mutual respect, and patriotism above partisanship. Though aligned with a free-market think tank, Ornstein kept his politics to himself, worked with John McCain on campaign finance reform, joined the boards of PBS and the Capitol Historic Society and even formed a comic partnership with Al Franken. AEI, he's certain, has lost money and donors by continuing to serve as his intellectual home.

In 2012, Ornstein and his longtime colleague Thomas Mann published a masterful book, *It's Even Worse Than It Looks*, which upended

Washington's prevailing wisdom. Congress was broken, these lifelong nonpartisans charged. Republican extremists and obstructionists, holding the institution hostage to their anti-government ideology, had undermined democracy itself. The media, accustomed to quoting and blaming both sides equally, wasn't equipped to tell the truth. The capital gasped. No one blamed both sides in polite company. "There's still this deep, deep fear here of being labeled as biased," he says. Trump's autocratic tendencies and ineptitude might have pushed Ornstein over the edge, but his election was a symptom of the problem, not its cause.

"Over many years, Republicans have adopted strategies that have trivialized and delegitimized government. They were willing to play to a nativist element," he says. "They tried to use, rather than stand up to, the apocalyptic visions of some cable television, talk radio and media outlets on the right." That broken system, Ornstein suggests, made it possible for someone "unhinged" to capitalize on it and walk away with the White House. He's not as sanguine as Kristol that this fever will break anytime soon.

For one, there's the structure of Washington: DC partisans don't turn on their own team. "It's not quite cultlike," Ornstein says, "but it's close. The equivalent of Beltway excommunication." Shunned by friends. Lucrative doors slammed shut on the K Street lobbying corridor. "Certain clients won't want any part of you. Fox News and talk radio might turn and go on the assault." Then there's the new structure of the party. "Republicans have moved away from the old merit-based system and made sure all those judges are going to be right where they want them to be, in terms of ideology," Ornstein says, and when he looks down the line at the next generation of state legislators, he worries that they make today's Freedom Caucus look agreeable by comparison. Finally, there's the structure of the U.S. Senate. By 2040, Ornstein says, half of the country will live in eight states. Seventy percent will live in fifteen states. They'll have thirty senators. The remaining sliver of the nation, more rural and conservative, will have seventy. "The illegitimacy of a minority basically taking from a powerless majority is going be an explosive atmosphere," he says.

Ornstein has spent decades counseling leaders to behave with wisdom, thoughtfulness and restraint. Now the institutions are ablaze. He fears that no one can extinguish these passions, even if they want to. "One reason why I have such antipathy toward McConnell," he says, "is that once you start breaking norms and make it clear that good behavior on the other side isn't going to be matched on yours, then they're just saps. The only way out is to bust further norms."

Ornstein's catharsis: frustrated tweets. This careful nonpartisan now drags the chief justice of the Supreme Court ("dishonest, hypocritical, partisan"), the attorney general ("Worst. Attorney. General. Ever."), former Wisconsin governor Scott Walker ("My God, he is so awful") and, of course, Trump ("Our president is a moron"). "If you believe that we're at an existential moment, you have to express it, and you have to be clear and blunt," he says. There's comfort in that, and Ornstein finds solace in watching the newly woke battle for democracy. Still, he sees a painful road ahead. He once believed that our political process produced leaders and that Americans could solve their biggest problems together. He once called senators like Susan Collins and even McConnell friends. They don't talk anymore.

"It's going to be tough. You have malign forces in the parties and a system tilted toward the big money," he says. "It can only be the grassroots efforts that will make a difference."

Sometimes, however, that difference arrives as a total surprise, and one brave action shields democracy from another domestic threat. And sometimes the smoking-gun evidence that might save democracy sits on a box-style bookshelf of a Raleigh, North Carolina, retirement community. That's where Stephanie Hofeller found a plastic bag containing eighteen thumb drives in October 2018, three months after the death of her father, Thomas Hofeller, the visionary Republican mapmaker we've come across throughout this story of suppression. Stephanie hadn't seen her father in four years. They'd become estranged after decades of a close relationship;[9]

Stephanie worked with her father at the Republican National Committee and helped him code voter rolls during the 2000s, all the while holding long debates about the ethics of his work drawing maps to benefit the GOP.

"He told me everything," Hofeller told me. "I was there as his daughter and in many cases his apprentice." On several occasions, Hofeller says, she thought she might be able to convince him that his mapmaking was doing damage to both his party and the nation. "Every time the Republican monolith took a turn to the right, I objected. I'd ask him, 'Are you watching this? Are you sure you're on the right team?' He'd just fall back on, 'Yeah, but the Democrats.' " Hofeller, his daughter told me, felt regularly betrayed by Republican leaders dating back to the early 1980s, when they dangled a top position at the Census Bureau in front of him, only to pull it away at the last moment. The RNC would wait until the last minute to renew his consulting contracts, causing Hofeller no end of financial angst. They even refused him a coveted parking permit at RNC headquarters. The man who drew the perfect lines had the most winding and indirect path to his office.

When Stephanie Hofeller visited her mother in Raleigh that fall and they began sorting through what few possessions remained, her eye was caught by her childhood jewelry box, which was prominently displayed on the bookcase in her father's bedroom, alongside the flag that draped his coffin and a photo of his parents. She opened it, and her breath caught when she realized that, despite years of difficulty and differences, the box remained exactly as it was when she had entrusted it to him. She took it as a sign. "I thought there was a chance that there might have been something specifically for me," she said in a spring 2019 deposition, "as in a note or a message of some sort that I would find."[10] That's when she saw the plastic bag filled with tiny thumb drives. Most were unlabeled, though one carried the tag "NC Data." She brought the bag back to her hotel and began to examine the 75,000 files saved on the eighteen drives. Her father had saved family photos, including early pictures of Stephanie's children, even one of her first musical compositions. She also recognized thousands of work-related documents: maps, population data, voter files, spreadsheets, emails. Even stricken with cancer, Thomas Hofeller worked until the end. And this man who preached security throughout his life, who taught legislators how to avoid creating any electronic record that might lead to "legal hell," left behind a trail of breadcrumbs.

"He wanted me to find them," she told me. "He knew full well that I would come to help my mother. All he had to do was throw them away."

Stephanie Hofeller had a more immediate concern than her father's papers. A Raleigh lawyer, whom Hofeller believed might be working with her father's former colleagues and political allies, was looking to declare her mother legally incompetent. Hofeller believed they really wanted to secure access to her father's files. The lawyer had convinced a court to appoint a temporary guardian. Not knowing who to trust, she made a phone call that would transform a case pending in the U.S. Supreme Court, and reveal the hidden link between the addition of a citizenship question to the census and the next round of redistricting that will begin in 2021. The phone call she made was to Common Cause, the nonpartisan group fighting to declare the North Carolina legislative maps her father helped draw an unconstitutional partisan gerrymander. Hofeller hoped they might provide her with an honest recommendation about a local lawyer she could trust. Only toward the end of the call, almost as an aside, did Hofeller mention her treasure trove of documents—uncertain whether they were worth mentioning, believing that most of the litigation to which they were relevant had been completed. "I was expecting those hard drives to be inflammatory," she said. "I had no idea that it was that immediate and that huge—that it would be that obvious."

Here's how huge: the files revealed Hofeller's final project, a sophisticated plan to hold back the changing face of Texas, Arizona, Georgia, Florida and many other competitive states with growing immigrant populations. These files are the Pentagon Papers of the citizenship question fight. They reveal the official lies and the level of corruption, all in vivid black and white. Thomas Hofeller examined what might happen if state legislatures redistricted not by the long-standing practice of total population but counted only the citizen voting age population (CVAP) instead. The sponsor of his research was a conservative donor eager to advance litigation and legislation to make this change. Hofeller's conclusion: drawing legislative districts based on CVAP "would be advantageous to Republicans and non-Hispanic whites" because it would dilute the votes of Texas's growing Latino population.

Why? Drawing districts based on total population counts everyone: voters and nonvoters, citizens and noncitizens, adults and children. It's based on the foundational theory, at the heart of the Constitution, that a representative's job is to represent all the people, not just adult voters.

Take a state like Texas, with a growing immigrant population, especially in the big cities. Subtract, for example, noncitizen Latinos and their children, and you end up with larger, and fewer, Democratic districts.

While it sounds nerdy and technical, this subtle shift has the potential to remake political power for decades to come, and potentially roll back two decades of demographic change across the South and Southwest. The key to the entire strategy? Gathering citizenship data, district by district, during the next census. "Without a question on citizenship being included on the 2020 Decennial Census questionnaire," Hofeller noted in one memo, "the use of citizen voting age population is functionally unworkable."[11]

The Trump administration claimed its reason for adding the question to the census was to better enforce the Voting Rights Act. The Hofeller files revealed this cynical power grab to overrepresent whiter, older and more rural areas at the expense of the cities and suburbs where most Americans actually live. They make clear that a shift to a citizen, voting-age population would dilute the votes of Latinos and enhance the power of whites and Republicans. Nevertheless, whether partisanship or race were at the heart of Hofeller's motivation, the results are the same: An expansion of the influence of white voters and Republican voters at the expense of communities of color. And an America that is increasingly anti-majoritarian, governed by unaccountable legislators from districts carefully drawn to protect them from voters. They revealed communications between Hofeller and Census

Bureau officials that went back years, showing how Department of Justice officials cut and pasted sections from Hofeller's memos into their request for the Department of Commerce to include the question for the first time since 1950.

Chief Justice John Roberts ultimately rejected the citizenship question because the Trump administration lied about its history. "Altogether, the evidence tells a story that does not match the explanation the Secretary gave for his decision," Roberts concluded. "We are presented, in other words, with an explanation for agency action that is incongruent with what the record reveals about the agency's priorities and decision-making process."

"That's a doozy, right?" Stephanie Hofeller says. "I have liberated those hard drives. I think that they needed to do what they are meant to do." But the fun was just beginning.

That same day, Roberts also issued his decision in two partisan gerrymandering cases, ruling the topic nonjusticiable, suggesting that legislatures, ballot initiatives or state courts were more appropriate venues than federal courts for challenges on the issue. The Common Cause case—about to be argued by Daniel Jacobson and Stanton Jones of Arnold & Porter, the attorneys who helped win Pennsylvania's new congressional map—had already been filed in North Carolina state Supreme Court, and benefited from the once-secret files. Also: that crucial victory by Anita Earls in the November 2018 state Supreme Court race solidified a majority likely to protect voting rights.

Hofeller's papers demonstrated two things, Jacobson said. First, it appeared that the North Carolina GOP had lied to a federal court. Looking to avoid new state legislative elections for as long as possible after an earlier map was ruled a racial gerrymander, they told the court in July 2017 that they had not yet started drawing new maps, even though Hofeller had actually already finished them. Second, while those politicians insisted that Hofeller had no racial data on the new districts, he did—and had ranked every district on his screen from most black to least. In September 2018, the court invalidated the state legislative maps and ordered that new ones be drawn within two weeks. In full public view, with absolute transparency. Without using any political data.

It's impossible to overestimate the impact of Stephanie Hofeller's individual action. Her profile in courage could change the course of democracy in North Carolina and many other states as well. And yes, it was courageous: She knew that once she came forward with these documents, Republicans and the media would recirculate stories about the estrangement between her and her father, which began when Thomas Hofeller demanded that Stephanie leave a marriage that involved domestic violence or else he would work to separate her from her children. He followed up on that threat, and, as she knew they would, North Carolina Republicans included every detail they could squeeze into a court filing smearing her.

But Stephanie Hofeller is certain her father left these documents behind on purpose. She'll always wonder why. Sometimes she thinks he was making an unconscious choice to come clean. Other times she posits that he wanted to even the score with Republican leaders who "never made him feel important when he was alive." She says that Hofeller had particular disregard for North Carolina lawmakers, on the grounds that they were greedy and motivated far too obviously by race and the desire to maintain white political control.

"If I was writing this as fiction," Hofeller tells me, "I'd think that I had to dial this back so my characters could be believable."

John F. Kennedy launched his presidential campaign more than six decades ago with a book called *Profiles in Courage*, a study of eight United States senators who displayed extraordinary integrity, largely during the years before the Civil War. They defended small-d democratic ideals at the most demanding times, even maintaining principled stands in opposition to their own party, no matter the personal or electoral cost. It's those characters, unfortunately, who would be unbelievable in Washington or our state capitals today. Such wisdom and leadership is in short supply, in either party, in the legislature or in the Supreme Court, at this time of crisis. The nation is at a crossroads. What happens next will determine whether we can maintain this ever-delicate multiracial democracy that recognizes the equality of all citizens—whether we are a nation for all, or for a shrinking few.

We know that our democracy is broken. More than that, we know that our democracy has been broken, actively and intentionally, by partisans who put their narrow ideological interests above all else, who chose to aggressively suppress and ignore the will of the people rather than committing themselves to listen to and represent all the citizens of a vibrant and ever-changing nation. This danger predates the election of any president, and will not disappear with a different one. There's no guaranteed stopping point for this divisiveness and erosion of rights. Our civic institutions and civic spirit could well suffocate from these toxins; there is no natural or man-made law that says that any democracy, even this grand American experiment, must last forever. Think that it can't happen here? It most certainly can. Democracy requires tending and defending, sometimes against long odds, and, yes, sometimes against our own leaders who would rig the system to benefit their side.

This is no time for pessimism, despair or mourning our powerlessness. We must elevate unrigging the system above the parochial interests of partisan politics. We must build a reform movement and structures of change that are capable of withstanding polarized elections, prejudice and fear, and politicians who would exploit those differences and anxieties for their own gain.

The exciting news is that something has been lit within the American people. Citizens who never before joined a protest took to the streets, circulated petitions, stepped forward to run for office, launched new organizations or joined movements that reimagined what democracy might mean.

They dreamed a different future. They ignored those who said the work would be too hard, scorned their efforts as irrelevant or warned that the odds of victory seemed far too uncertain for such a heavy lift. Then they devoted long hours to making their ideals come to life, whether that meant driving thousands of miles in a green RV, knocking on hundreds of thousands of doors, dedicating years to pro bono lawsuits, or braving frigid winters to fight for structural reform. They created nonpartisan movements in a deeply polarized era. Then they came together by the thousands and made those dreams real at the ballot box, winning resounding majorities of their fellow citizens, inspiring Americans in red states, in blue states, in every state, who still believe that all political power is inherent in the people, that all legitimate authority depends on the consent of the governed, that representative democracy must represent us all, equally.

Yes, the threats to democracy are growing. Yet those dangers have rallied, even reawakened, everyday Americans who still believe in these ideals to organize and fight for them anew. None of these fights will be easy. Powerful forces stand in the way and write the rules. Not every battle will be won, and some victories will be eroded. Hard work is no guarantee of success. But democracy has never progressed along an obvious continuum or straight line. Not now, not ever. Powerful ruling elites, wealthy and white, have rigged the game to protect their influence since the beginning of American democracy. We are engaged in a battle for power and control as ancient as our republic itself.

Nevertheless, this will be the defining battle of our times. The lesson of Katie Fahey, Desmond Meade, Luke Mayville, Stephanie Hofeller—let alone the tens of thousands of volunteers whose names we don't know— is that all of us have it within us to create great change. We do not need superheroes or the perfect presidential candidate to save us. We can, we must, find the courage to step forward and be the solutions ourselves. Voters Not Politicians, Reclaim Idaho, the Florida Rights Restoration Coalition prove that when we build coalitions, creatively harness our abilities and stand together for equality, we win. Let us find hope in the energy and devotion of our fellow citizens. Let us commit, all of us, to building a nation in which every voice is heard and carries the same weight. Let us move into the battles ahead bravely and unafraid, with open eyes but also open hearts, understanding the challenges but also the stakes, confident that with hard work and constant dedication, the country we want to live in lies within our grasp.

● *ACKNOWLEDGMENTS*

This book began with a quest for hope. I discovered it somewhere between Pocatello and Idaho Falls, riding shotgun in a rickety green RV, embedded with Reclaim Idaho's democracy warriors. They renewed my faith that a handful of organized, passionate citizens could bring about great change. Thank you to Luke and Elena Mayville, and Garrett and Emily Strizich, for letting me climb aboard.

Many inspiring activists allowed me to knock doors and register voters alongside them. *Unrigged* belongs to you. My thanks to Desmond Meade and Neil Volz, Florida's forces of nature. The dynamic Blair Bowie welcomed me at the Alabama Voting Rights Project, and trained me as a canvasser alongside John Paul Taylor, Ellen Bottecher and Sean Champagne. What an honor to work with you, steps from Montgomery's Dexter Avenue King Memorial Baptist Church. My days alongside dragon-slayers Katie Fahey, Jamie Lyons Eddy, Nancy Wang and the indefatigable Voters Not Politicians team in Michigan supercharged my optimism.

Wesley Pegden, Moon Duchin, Jowei Chen, Jonathan Rodden and Jonathan Mattingly patiently explained their genius-level, democracy-saving mathematics to a reporter still traumatized by high school calculus. Tara

Benally spent hours as my guide driving across San Juan County. Catherine Kanter and her Better Boundaries team opened their doors down the home stretch of a tight Utah ballot initiative battle that they needed every minute to win. Mimi McKenzie, Benjamin Geffen, Michael Churchill, Jennifer Clarke and the high-powered crusaders at the Public Interest Law Center, as well as Daniel Jacobson and Stanton Jones of Arnold & Porter, relived their Pennsylvania triumph and let me drink from a Donald Duck Kicking Goofy coffee mug. Danielle Lang and Ruth Greenwood of the Campaign Legal Center are brilliant, tireless lawyers with an indomitable spirit who make this nation live up to its ideals every day.

Thank you, as well, to these fearless, generous democracy defenders: Norris Henderson, Matt Dunlap, Catherine Turcer, Sean Soendker Nicholson, Carol Kuniholm, John Kennedy, Kat Calvin, Kyle Bailey, Jeff Wice, Aylett Colston and Sarah Rawlings. Thank you, to Amanda Litman, Ross Morales Rocketto and Run for Something; Catherine Vaughan and everyone at Flippable; Vicky Hausman and Forward Majority; and Gaby Goldstein, Lala Wu, Lyzz Schwegler, Rita Bosworth and everyone at Sister District. Eric Holder and Patrick Rodenbush of the National Democratic Redistricting Commission kindly allowed me to tag along across three states. Doug Poland and Bill Whitford of the heroic and groundbreaking Wisconsin gerrymandering case have gone above and beyond, time and again. I'm indebted to you all.

The courage of Stephanie Hofeller transformed the battle against the citizenship question on the U.S. census and will go a long way toward the unrigging of North Carolina's congressional maps. I'm proud to call her a friend.

I'm deeply grateful to Arnold Schwarzenegger and Conyers Davis at USC's Schwarzenegger Institute; Kathay Feng and Dan Vicuna at Common Cause; Josh Silver and everyone at RepresentUs; the Reverend Jesse L. Jackson and Santita Jackson; the California Citizens Redistricting Commission; Lawrence Lessig and Equal Citizens; Brian Cannon and One

Virginia 2021; Sam Wang and the Princeton Gerrymandering Project; the Brennan Center; and Dean Obeidallah and Matt Tomasetti at Sirius XM.

Unrigged stands on a foundation of thinking about voting rights developed by many other writers and academics. My thanks and appreciation to my colleagues on the voting rights beat and all the writers and thinkers within the redistricting community whose work informs these pages and both inspired and helped me with my own: Ari Berman, Sam Levine, Jessica Huseman, Mark Joseph Stern, Carol Anderson, Stephen Wolf, Michael Wines, Emily Bazelon, Michael Tomasky, Lawrence Lessig, Larry Diamond, Astra Taylor, Kira Lerner, Tierney Sneed, Allegra Kirkland, Riley Beggin, Anne Helen Petersen, Eric McGhee, Nick Stephanopoulos, Michael McDonald, Jane Mayer, Carolyn Fiddler, Thomas Brunell, Nancy MacLean, Jeff Manza, Christopher Uggen, Daniel McCool, Daniel Nichanian, Justin Levitt and Richard Hazen.

Barak Goodman and Chris Dorrance did something magical with their documentary *Slay the Dragon*. They turned *Ratf**ked* and the anti-gerrymandering crusade in Michigan, Wisconsin and North Carolina into a film that's both rousing and deeply moving. Thank you for having me be part of it, and for bringing this story to such a wide audience.

I'm very appreciative of the support and friendship of Garvin Brown, Charles Cherington, Giulia Marchiori Ceresa and Kathleen Gasperine. The Glaser Progress Foundation provided a valuable research grant that made it possible to finish this book; my deep thanks to Rob Glaser, Martin Collier and Melessa Rogers.

Nothing energizes quite like a college campus. My thanks to Carlo Rotella and Heather Cox Richardson for welcoming me home to Boston College, and Anne Greene and Marc Eisner for their tremendous hospitality at Wesleyan University.

It's an honor to work alongside the great democracy champions at Fair-Vote. Ranked choice voting and multi-member districts—the key reforms in the gold-standard Fair Representation Act—provide the very best way to conquer not only partisan gerrymandering, but the existential crisis of deep partisan polarization. Rob Richie and Cynthia Terrell Richie are as kind and generous as they are visionary. Thank you, Sangita Sigdyal, Emily Risch, Drew Spencer Penrose and the entire dedicated, dynamic team who have turned this transformational change into reality.

I owe great thanks to the generous readers and good friends who gave their time to read this book in draft form, and tested and debated these ideas. My endless appreciation for Scott Timberg, who read the entire manuscript in draft form, and made every chapter better with his rigorous eye. Adam Eichen's passionate, persuasive optimism pulled the conclusion across the finish line. Seth Harwood, Mike O'Neil, Erin Keane, Brian Weinberg and Melissa Beck read early chapters and helped me focus and find the story I wanted to tell. Hannah Reale not only offered valuable advice on several chapters, but provided important research assistance.

Many good friends provided encouragement and enthusiasm, not to mention advice and distraction when the writing grew hard. Thank you, Bertis Downs, Tom Navin, Pam and Andrew Hannon, Mike and Sovina Mansfield, Matt Rattigan and Marilyce Hale, Krista Navin and Josh Schroeder, Molly Ringwald, Panio Gianopoulos, Elizabeth Riley, Sherri Long and Jack McFadden.

I'm glad that I can tell my mom, Toby Daley, the title of this book, and fortunate for a lifetime of her warmth and love. I'm just as lucky to have supportive and loving in-laws in George and Sarah Smedes, and sisters-in-law Kate Smedes and Kristen Murray.

What a privilege it is to call Liveright and W. W. Norton home. Bob Weil is that rare legend whose talent and thoughtfulness even exceed his grand reputation. He has published some of the most important and lasting books on this historical moment, and it's overwhelming to be among them. Marie Pantojan shaped this story with great energy and tremendous attention. Daniel Gerstle, Haley Bracken and Gina Iaquinta brought it across the finish line with great skill and care. My thanks to the entire team, especially Pete Miller, Cordelia Calvert , Allegra Huston, Nick Curley, Lauren Abbate, Amy Medeiros, Lynne Cannon Menges, Steve Attardo, Daniel Lagin, Joe Lops and Bill Rusin.

My extraordinary agent Alice Martell, ever cheerful and fierce, believed in this project from the very beginning. She not only shepherded this book into the world, but has been the most patient, reassuring ally and friend any writer could hope to have. I owe so much to her calm, her faith, and her enthusiasm. Onward!

My brilliant wife Jennifer Smedes redistricted my life in the very best ways. Her patience and support made the travel, reporting and writing possible, but most importantly, her love is home. And for our amazing, giant-hearted son, Wyatt: my greatest optimism for our future is you.

NOTES

Unrigged is a work of reportage. I spent much of 2018 watching these battles unfold in person, including trips across Utah, Idaho, Michigan, Florida, California, Arizona, Alabama, Maine, Ohio, Pennsylvania and multiple other states. Many follow-up interviews were conducted over the phone as major events unfolded. My own interviews are almost always noted as such in the text, except in cases like Idaho, for example, where it's clear from the storytelling. I've often added to these stories and interviews with details from trials, legal filings and court transcripts, for example, in Kansas and North Dakota, with the specific stories of plaintiffs who were not available to me, but are in the public record. I'm grateful to the brilliant reporters on the voting rights beat, particularly Jessica Huseman, Roey Hadar, Sam Levine, Kira Lerner, Ari Berman and others cited throughout the text. I also benefited tremendously from the work of the Brennan Center for Justice, the Sentencing Project, and historians of voting rights and the Reconstruction era, as well as the history of Native Americans and the vote. My thanks to everyone who spent time with me, and all whose work was such a help.

Introduction

1. "Voting Laws Roundup 2017," Brennan Center for Justice, May 10, 2017.
2. Ben Nadler, "Voting Rights Become a Flashpoint in Georgia Governor Race," *Associated Press*, October 9, 2018.
3. Karl Rove, "The GOP Targets State Legislatures," *Wall Street Journal*, March 4, 2010.
4. I watched Meade tell his story in Florida several times in addition to our conversations. He always tells it the same way, and it has also been masterfully captured by Emily Bazelon in the *New York Times Magazine* ("Will Florida's Ex-Felons Regain the Right to Vote?," September 26, 2018); Ari Berman in *Mother Jones* ("Inside the Unlikely Movement that Could Restore Voting

Rights to 1.4 Million Floridians," November/December 2018); and early on by Jessica Dickinson in the *Huffington Post* ("Florida Man's Journey from Inmate to Law School Graduate," May 30, 2014).

5. The Editorial Board, "Righting 150 Years of Wrong in Florida," *New York Times*, January 11, 2019.

6. For more on the radical grandmas, see Lorraine Woellert, "Badass Grannies, Activists Push to Clean Up Government," *Politico*, October 14, 2018.

7. For a fuller analysis of Ohio, see "Fraud Fiction Becomes Purge Reality" by the brilliant Dahlia Lithwick in *Slate*, June 11, 2018.

8. Lake Research Partners and WPA Intelligence, "Partisan Redistricting – New Bipartisan National Poll," memo, September 11, 2017, https://campaignlegal .org/sites/default/files/memo.CLCPartisanRedistricting.FINAL_.2 .09082017%20%28002%29.pdf.

9. *Gill v. Whitford,* 138 S. Ct. 1916 (2018).

10. Mark Joseph Stern, "You Can Now Hear Elena Kagan Read Her Searing Dissent in the Partisan Gerrymandering Case," *Slate*, October 25, 2019.

11. Christopher Ingraham, "Gerrymander Valentines Prove Nothing Says 'I Love You' Like Redistricting," *Washington Post*, February 14, 2018.

12. Tom Verducci, "Inside the Madness of Craig Consell's Brilliant Bullpen Management," *Sports Illustrated*, October 16, 2018.

13. Kelly Norris, "High School Student Invents Game on Evils of Gerrymandering. Arnold Schwarzenegger Plays," *NBC News*, August 11, 2018.

14. Transcript and video available at "House Democratic Agenda," C-SPAN, January 4, 2019, https://www.c-span.org/video/?456639-1/house-democrats -reporters-legislative-agenda.

15. Mitch McConnell, "Behold the Democrat Politician Protection Act," *Washington Post*, January 17, 2019.

Chapter 1: Second Chances and Rights Restored

1. "Alabama's 1901 Constitution: Instrument of Power," University of Alabama School of Law, Special Collections blog, December 9, 2016, https://www .law.ua.edu/specialcollections/2016/12/09/alabamas-1901-constitution -instrument-of-power/.

2. *Hunter v. Underwood*, US Supreme Court, 471 U.S. 222, 1985.

3. Mike Cason, "Former Alabama Speaker Mike Hubbard Sentenced to Four Years in Prison," *Birmingham News*, July 8, 2016.

4. Kira Lerner, "Alabama Restored Voting Rights to Thousands of Former Felons, but They May Never Know," *ThinkProgress*, August 1, 2017.

5. Sam Levine, "Suit Seeks to Force Alabama to Inform People about Restored Voting Rights," *Huffington Post*, July 1, 2017.

6. Jack Healy, "Arrested, Jailed and Charged with a Felony. For Voting," *New York Times*, August 2, 2018.

7. Andrew J. Yawn, "Alabama Sees Spike in Ex-Felon Voting Registrations, Advocates See Room for Improvement," *Montgomery Advertiser*, November 2, 2018.

8. Christopher Uggen, Ryan Larson, and Sarah Shannon, "Six Million Lost Voters: State Level Estimates of Felony Disenfranchisement, 2016," The Sentencing Project, 2016.

9. Volz tells his own story in an honest and humbling 2012 memoir, *Into the Sun*. It's also told by Berman in *Mother Jones*, Bazelon in the *New York Times Magazine*, and in a terrific video made by Ben and Jerry's on "The Power of Second Chances" and viewable at https://www.benjerry.com/whats-new/2018/10/neil-volz-story.

10. Ari Berman, "Inside the Unlikely Movement That Could Restore Voting Rights to 1.4 Million Floridians," *Mother Jones*, November/December 2018.

11. Ari Berman, "Inside the Unlikely Movement That Could Restore Voting Rights to 1.4 Million Floridians," *Mother Jones*, November/December 2018.

12. Important scholarship on this, from which many of these quotes are drawn, includes the work of Manza and Uggen, Pippa Holloway, Jarrell H. Shofner's "Political Reconstruction in Florida," James E. Bond's "No East Walk to Freedom," the Brennan Center report "Florida: An Outlier in Denying Voting Rights," and Thomas W. Long's "The Origin of Disenfranchisement: County-Level Resistance to African-American Voting in Post-Emancipation Florida."

13. Jerrell H. Shofner, "Custom, Law and History: The Enduring Influence of Florida's Black Code," *Florida Historical Quarterly*, January 1977.

14. Ari Berman, "Inside the Unlikely Movement That Could Restore Voting Rights to 1.4 Million Floridians," *Mother Jones*, November/December 2018.

15. Florida Historical Society, *The Florida Historical Quarterly* (Jacksonville, FL: Convention Press, 1963), 374.

16. Daryl Paulson, "How Florida Kept Blacks from Voting," *Tampa Bay Times*, October 17, 2013. This is part one of a terrific three-part series.

17. Mary Ellen Klas, "Florida Has a History of Making It Harder for Black Citizens to Vote," *Miami Herald*, August 12, 2016.

18. Mary Ellen Klas, "Florida Has a History of Making It Harder for Black Citizens to Vote," *Miami Herald*, August 12, 2016.

19. Christopher Uggen, Ryan Larson, and Sarah Shannon, "Six Million Lost Voters, State Level Estimates of Felony Disenfranchisment, 2016," The Sentencing Project, October 16, 2016.

20. Allegra Kirkland, "The Future of 1.4 Million Floridians with Felony Convictions Is on the Ballot in November," *Talking Points Memo*, September 26, 2018.

21. *The Miami Herald*'s Debbie Cenziper and Jason Grotto delivered an important and groundbreaking series on this topic at a time when few others paid attention. It included "Clemency Proving Elusive for Florida's Ex-Cons," October 31, 2004; "The Long Road to Clemency," November 7, 2004; "For Felons, Time in County Jails Carries Price: Life Without Rights," November 14, 2004; and "Violent Felons: Rights Restored While Lesser Offenders Waited," November 21, 2004.

22. "Florida Felons Losing Restoration Rights," WFTV-TV, https://www.wftv.com/news/9-investigates/9-investigates-florida-felons-losing-restoration-rights/188010127.

23. Greg Allen, "Felons in Florida Want Their Voting Rights Back without a Hassle," NPR, July 5, 2018.

24. The *Palm Beach Post* did an exhaustive study of whose rights were restored—and whose were not. Lulu Ramadan, Mike Stucks, and Wayne Washington, "Felon Voting Rights, Who Got Theirs Back under Scott," October 25, 2018. Other important and moving stories include Sam Levine, "24 Years Ago She Lost Her Voting Rights for Pushing a Cop. She Just Got Them Back," *Huffington Post*, June 23, 2018, as well as coverage by Allegra Kirkland in *Talking Points Memo*.

25. Lori Rozsa, "Voting Rights on the Line Tuesday for 1.6m Ex-Felons in Florida," *Washington Post*, November 3, 2018.

26. Lori Rozsa, "Voting Rights on the Line Tuesday for 1.6m Ex-Felons in Florida," *Washington Post*, November 3, 2018.

27. Sam Levine, "24 Years Ago She Lost Her Voting Rights for Pushing a Cop. She Just Got Them Back," *Huffington Post*, June 25, 2018.

28. Scott's fuzzy and inconsistent reasoning is on full display in the class-action complaint filed in *Hand v. Scott*, March 13, 2017, in US District Court and available at https://www.courthousenews.com/wp-content/uploads/2017/03/FLACONS.pdf.

29. Alex Pickett, "In Florida, Long Fight for Restored Vote Often Ends in Minutes," *Courthouse News*, May 31, 2018.

30. Lulu Ramadan, Mike Stucka, and Wayne Washington, "Florida Felon Voting Rights: Who Got Theirs Back under Scott?" *Palm Beach Post*, October 25, 2018.

31. Ramsden's entire harrowing story of addiction and recovery is told masterfully by Josh Salmon in the *Sarasota Herald-Tribune*'s "We Didn't Know What to Do," December 6, 2017.

32. Written testimony of the Alabama Voting Rights Project before the US House of Representatives' Committee on Administration, Subcommittee on Elections, May 13, 2019.

Chapter 2: Aboard Idaho's Medicaid Express

1. Marilynne Robinson, *Housekeeping* (New York: Picador, 2015), 91.

2. Betsy Z. Russell, "Redoubt Movement Helps Push North Idaho Politics to Extreme Right," *Spokane Spokesman Review*, May 15, 2016.

3. Mary Malone, "Woodward Outlines LPOSD Levy 'What Ifs,'" *Bonner County Daily Bee*, February 19, 2017.

4. Bill Manny, "60,000 Signatures and Counting: How Did the Upstart Medicaid Expansion Campaign Do It," *Idaho Statesman*, April 13, 2018.

5. That determined opposition continued even after Reclaim Idaho's victory. The IFF filed a campaign finance complaint against Reclaim Idaho in spring 2019; it was dismissed as groundless by the secretary of state's office two months later.

6. Nikki Torres, "Idaho's Prop 2 Passes with 62 Percent Voter Approval," KXLY.com, November 7, 2018.

Chapter 3: The Defeat of the Voter Fraud Myth

1. Jonathan Shorman, "Emails Show Kobach Crafting Changes to Federal Voting Law after Trump Win," *Wichita Eagle*, July 15, 2017.

2. Jonathan Shorman, "Kobach Took Plan for DHS into Trump Meeting," *Topeka Capital-Journal*, November 21, 2016.

3. Ari Berman, "The Man Behind Trump's Voter-Fraud Obsession," *New York Times*, June 13, 2017.

4. Jeannine Koranda, "Dead Folks Voting? At Least One's Still Alive," *Wichita Eagle*, October 29, 2019.

5. David M. Zimmer, "Trump in Bedminster: Here's Three Things to Know about His Golf Club," NorthJersey.com, July 28, 2018.

6. Adam Ganucheau, "Hosemann on Trump Voter ID Request: Go Jump in the Gulf," *Mississippi Today*, June 30, 2017.

7. Kris Kobach, "Exclusive: Kobach: It Appears that Out of State Voters Changed the Outcome of the New Hampshire Senate Race," *Breitbart News*, September 7, 2017.

8. John Wagner, "Trump Voter Fraud Commission Researcher Arrested on Child Pornography Charges," *Washington Post*, October 14, 2017.

9. *Dunlap v. Presidential Advisory Commission on Electoral Integrity*, US District Court for District of Columbia, complaint filed November 8, 2017.

10. Hunter Woodall, "Democrat on Trump's Voter Fraud Commission Sues Kobach, Pence and the Panel," *Kansas City Star*, November 9, 2017.

11. *Dunlap v. Presidential Advisory Commission*, US District Court for District of Columbia, memorandum opinion filed December 22, 2017.

12. "The Effects of *Shelby County v. Holder*," Brennan Center for Justice, August 6, 2018.

13. Bucci's story is detailed in her lawsuit against Kobach, *Fish, Ortiz, Bucci, Stricker, Boynton and Hutchinson v. Kobach*, a class-action complaint filed in the US District Court, Fourth District of Kansas, February 18, 2016.

14. *Fish et al. v. Kobach*, US District Court for the Fourth District of Kansas, findings of fact and conclusions of law, filed June 18, 2018.

15. Jessica Huseman chronicles Kobach and his experts' every embarrassment in her tour de force, "How the Case for Voter Fraud Was Tested—and Utterly Failed," *ProPublica*, June 19, 2018.

16. Jesse Richman and David Earnest, "Could Non-Citizens Decide the November Election?," *Washington Post*, October 24, 2016.

17. Richman's op-ed led to three rebuttals in the *Post*, as well as two peer-reviewed articles and comments, disputing his conclusions on non-citizen voting.

18. Jessica Huseman, "How the Case for Voter Fraud Was Tested—and Utterly Failed," *ProPublica*, June 19, 2018.

19. The ACLU has transcripts of the entire trial on its site.

20. Jessica Huseman, "How the Case for Voter Fraud Was Tested—and Utterly Failed," *ProPublica*, June 19, 2018.

21. Jessica Huseman, "How the Case for Voter Fraud Was Tested—and Utterly Failed," *ProPublica*, June 19, 2018.

22. *Fish et al. v. Kobach*.

23. All the emails can be read at https://www.americanoversight.org/investigation/dunlap-v-pacei-investigating-voter-fraud-commission.

Chapter 4: Native Americans Battle Back

1. Data available at https://www.pewtrusts.org/en/research-and-analysis/data-visualizations/2014/elections-performance-index#indicatorProfile.

2. Cheyenne Haslett and Roey Hadar, "North Dakota Native Americans Fight to Protect Right to Vote after Court Ruling," *ABC News*, October 21, 2018.

3. The "scared straight" detail and others can be found in the respondents' filing opposing an application to vacate the stay of preliminary injunction in *Brakebill v. Jaeger*, filed October 2, 2018.

4. Roey Hadar, "After Stunning Democratic Win, N.D. Republicans Suppressed the Native American Vote," *Nation*, May 2, 2018.

5. All the legal filings can be found at www.narf.org/cases/nd-voter-id.

6. Daniel McCool, Susan M. Olson and Jennifer L. Robinson, *Native Vote: American Indians, the Voting Rights Act and the Right to Vote* (Cambridge University Press, 2010) is essential reading.

7. These stories and others are chronicled brilliantly by Anne Helen Peterson and Graham Lee Brewer in "Why Is It So Hard for Native Americans to Vote in This Utah County," *BuzzFeed*, October 28, 2018; by Tim Murphy in "4000 Square Miles, One Post Office: Why It's So Hard to Vote in Arizona's Indian Country," *Mother Jones*, November/December 2018; by Kira Lerner in "Native Americans' Right to Vote Is under Attack," *ThinkProgress*, June 20, 2018; by Victoria Massie in "Voting from Native American Reservations Is Much Harder than It Should Be," *Vox*, October 28, 2018; and by the Brennan Center's March 2019 report "State of Native American Voting Rights."

8. For more details, see Jennifer Solis, "Tribes Get Their Own Polling Places, Some for the First Time," *Nevada Current*, October 31, 2018.

9. Native American Rights Fund, "Protecting Native American Voting Rights," YouTube video, December 14, 2016, https://youtu.be/xjT_2KyS9pw.

10. Anne Helen Petersen and Graham Lee Brewer, "Why Is It So Hard for Native Americans to Vote in This Utah County?" *BuzzFeed News*, October 28, 2018.

11. For more history, see Petersen and Brewer in *BuzzFeed*, and also Zak Podmore, "Here's How San Juan County Reached This Historic Point and Why

the Tension in SE Utah Won't End Anytime Soon," *Salt Lake Tribune*, July 7, 2019.

12. Matt Vasilogambros, "Native Americans Fight Back at the Ballot Box," *Stateline*, September 27, 2018.

13. *Navajo Nation v. San Juan County* (US District Court for the District of Utah, Central Division, 2016).

14. Robert Gehrke, "A County Clerk's Deceptive Attempt to Keep Grayeyes Out of the San Juan Commission Race Should Lead to Criminal Charges," *Salt Lake Tribune*, August 8, 2018.

15. Brian Maffly, "The San Juan County Clerk May Be Investigated After a Federal Judge Says He Crossed the Line in Illegally Dumping Navajo Willie Grayeyes from the Ballot," *Salt Lake Tribune*, August 10, 2018.

16. Robert Gehrke, "A County Clerk's Deceptive Attempt to Keep Grayeyes Out of the San Juan Commission Race Should Lead to Criminal Charges," *Salt Lake Tribune*, August 8, 2018.

17. Roey Hadar, "After stunning Democratic win, North Dakota Republicans suppressed the Native American vote," *The Nation*, May 2, 2018.

18. *Richard Brakebill, Deloris Baker, Dorothy Herman, Della Merrick, Elvis Norquay, Ray Norquay, and Lucille Vivier v. Alvin Jaeger* (US District Court for the District of North Dakota, 2016).

19. *Richard Brakebill, Deloris Baker, Dorothy Herman, Della Merrick, Elvis Norquay, Ray Norquay, and Lucille Vivier v. Alvin Jaeger* (US District Court for the District of North Dakota, 2016).

20. Detail included in the *Brakebill v. Jaeger* filing with the US Court of Appeals, Eighth Circuit, on June 1, 2018, online at https://turtletalk.files.wordpress.com/2018/06/appellee-response.pdf, and also noted by Hadar in the *Nation*.

21. *Richard Brakebill, Deloris Baker, Dorothy Herman, Della Merrick, Elvis Norquay, Ray Norquay, and Lucille Vivier v. Alvin Jaeger* (US District Court for the District of North Dakota, 2016).

22. Carrie Levine, "Backlash over North Dakota Voter ID Law Could Rally Native Americans," Center for Public Integrity and Public Radio International, October 30, 2018.

23. Jeremy Bynum, "Preserving Voter Rights with the Help of GIS," *Focus*, Summer 2019, on ESRI.com.

24. Erik Ortiz, "Native Americans Fighting Back against N.D. Voter ID Law," *NBC News*, October 31, 2018.

25. Carrie Levine, "Backlash over ND Voter ID Law Could Rally Native Americans," Public Radio International and the Center for Public Integrity, October 30, 2018.

26. Lang discussed her work in multiple interviews, but also went into more personal detail on a first-person piece on the Campaign Legal Center's website, "Fighting Disenfranchisement on Indian Reservations."

27. The legal filings that include these stories can be found online at https:// campaignlegal.org/story/north-dakota-native-americans-speak-out-protect -their-right-vote.

28. Turnout numbers noted by, among others, Carrie Levine in "ND Native Americans Surged to the Polls amid Disenfranchisement Fears," Center for Public Integrity, November 7, 2018.

29. Katie Reilly, "A New North Dakota Law Threatened Native American Votes. They Responded by Turning Out in Historic Numbers," *Time*, November 7, 2018.

30. Maggie Asher, "Meet the Native American Woman Who Beat the Sponsor of ND's ID Law," *New York Times*, November 13, 2018.

Chapter 5: Michigan's Redistricting Revolution

1. Details on the policy and how it came together can be found on the VNP site at https://votersnotpoliticians.nationbuilder.com/how_the_policy_was_drafted.

2. Erick Trickey, "A Grassroots Call to Ban Gerrymandering," *Atlantic*, September 23, 2018.

3. Quoted by the *Associated Press* in "Anti-Gerrymandering Ballot Drive Defies Odds," November 19, 2017.

4. Noted by, among others, Michael Crowe "Fight over MI Ballot Proposal Reveals Potential Conflict of Interest," *Click on Detroit*, July 6, 2018.

5. Jay Riestenberg, "Who Is Behind the Legal Challenge to Nonpartisan Redistricting in Michigan," *Common Cause*, May 7, 2018.

6. The emails were revealed through the discovery process in the League of Women Voters lawsuit against the state's gerrymandered congressional map; the *Detroit News* and the *Bridge* were first to report various batches.

7. Michael Wines, "Thomas Hofeller, Republican Master of Political Maps, Dies at 75," *New York Times*, August 21, 2018.

8. Hofeller's delightfully low-tech PowerPoint from 2011, "What I've

Learned about Redistricting—The Hard Way!" can be found online at https://www.ncsl.org/documents/legismgt/The_Hard_Way.pdf.

9. Watch video of the protest at https://act.represent.us/sign/michigandayof action.

10. Their inventive campaigns can be seen online at https://act.represent.us/sign/MI-dark-money-more-info.

11. Riley Beggin, "One woman's Facebook post leads to Michigan vote against gerrymandering," *The Bridge*, November 7, 2018.

12. Riley Beggin, "One Woman's Facebook Post Leads to Michigan Vote against Gerrymandering," *The Bridge*, November 7, 2018.

13. Riley Beggin, "One woman's Facebook post leads to Michigan vote against gerrymandering," *The Bridge*, November 7, 2018.

Chapter 6: Redistricting Goes National

1. Lois Beckett, "Colorado Redistricting Had Inside Help," *ProPublica*, February 9, 2012.

2. The best story of the plan's earliest days is covered by Jennifer Brown in "Will Two Redistricting Ballot Measures This Year Put an End to One of Colorado's Longest Running Political Feuds," *Colorado Sun*, September 22, 2018. Witwer and I also talked; his book *Blueprint: How the Democrats Won Colorado and Why Republicans Everywhere Should Care* is a fascinating story of the shenanigans that helped Democrats turn Colorado blue. See also Corey Hutchins, "A Star-Studded Campaign Launches to End Gerrymandering in Colorado. It Took a Grand Bargain to Get Here," *Colorado Independent*, August 28, 2018.

3. Corey Hutchins, "A Group Says It Wants to End Partisan Redistricting in Colorado. Would Its Plan Really Do That?" *Colorado Independent*, September 16, 2017.

4. Matt Canham and Thomas Burr, "The Hidden Room inside Mitt Romney's New Utah Home," *Salt Lake Tribune*, October 24, 2013.

5. Clean Missouri has more detail on the state's lobbying culture by the numbers at https://www.cleanmissouri.org/lobbyists.

6. Schaaf goes into great detail on this allegation in a St. Louis Public Radio interview that can be heard here: https://www.kcur.org/post/clean-missouri-proposition-puts-redistricting-front-and-center-limits-lobbyist-influence#stream/0.

Chapter 7: Donald Duck and Goofy No More

1. *League of Women Voters of Pennsylvania, Carmen Febo San Miguel, James Solomon, John Greiner, John Capowsky, Gretchen Brandt, Thomas Rentschler, Mary Elizabeth Lawn, Lisa Isaacs, Don Lancaster, Jordi Comas, Robert Smith, William Marx, Richard Mantell, Priscilla McNulty, Thomas Ulrich, Robert McKinstry, Mark Michty, Lorraine Petrosky v. The Commonwealth of Pennsylvania; the Pennsylvania General Assembly; Thomas W. Wolf; Michael J. Stack III; Michael C. Turzai; Joseph B. Scarnati III; Robert Torres; Jonathan M. Marks* (Pennsylvania, 2018).

2. L. Stuart Ditzen, "Judge's Outlandish Image Brings Fame and Infamy," *Philadelphia Inquirer*, February 18, 2001.

3. Marc Levy, "Retiring Pennsylvania Supreme Court Justice Seamus P. McCaffery Didn't Have the Typical Resume," Associated Press, October 28, 2014.

4. "What Was in Emails against Pennsylvania Supreme Court Justice?" Associated Press, December 11, 2015.

5. The emails all became public as part of the state investigation. For more detail, two of the best stories include "A Supreme Court Justice's Offensive, Racy Emails," *Above the Law*, by Joe Patrice, October 23, 2015, and "The Great PA Government Porn Caper," *Esquire*, by David Gambacorta, February 24, 2016.

6. *IN RE: J. Michael Eakin, Justice of the Supreme Court of Pennsylvania*, 13 JD 2015 (Pa. JD 2016).

7. Andrew Seidman, Holly Otterbein and Jeremy Roebuck, "Philly Labor Leader John 'Johnny Doc' Dougherty, under Federal Scrutiny, Raises More Campaign Money Than Ever," *Philadelphia Inquirer*, April 15, 2018.

8. *League of Women Voters of Pennsylvania, Carmen Febo San Miguel, James Solomon, John Greiner, John Capowsky, Gretchen Brandt, Thomas Rentschler, Mary Elizabeth Lawn, Lisa Isaacs, Don Lancaster, Jordi Comas, Robert Smith, William Marx, Richard Mantell, Priscilla McNulty, Thomas Ulrich, Robert McKinstry, Mark Michty, Lorraine Petrosky v. The Commonwealth of Pennsylvania; the Pennsylvania General Assembly; Thomas W. Wolf; Michael J. Stack III; Michael C. Turzai; Joseph B. Scarnati III; Robert Torres; Jonathan M. Marks* (Pennsylvania, 2018).

9. Katherine Reinhard and Carol Thompson, "Proven Right Before, Amanda Holt Weighs in with Her Own Map in Pennsylvania Gerrymandering Case," *Morning Call*, February 12, 2018.

10. Trial transcripts and other exhibits are available at https://www.brennan
center.org/our-work/court-cases/league-women-voters-pennsylvania-v-common
wealth-pennsylvania.

11. Jonathan Lai, "'This Is a Gerrymandered Map,' West Chester Professor Says
in Redistricting Trial," *Philadelphia Inquirer*, December 12, 2017.

12. *League of Women Voters of Pennsylvania, Carmen Febo San Miguel, James Solo-
mon, John Greiner, John Capowsky, Gretchen Brandt, Thomas Rentschler, Mary
Elizabeth Lawn, Lisa Isaacs, Don Lancaster, Jordi Comas, Robert Smith, William
Marx, Richard Mantell, Priscilla McNulty, Thomas Ulrich, Robert McKinstry,
Mark Michty, Lorraine Petrosky v. The Commonwealth of Pennsylvania; the
Pennsylvania General Assembly; Thomas W. Wolf; Michael J. Stack III; Michael
C. Turzai; Joseph B. Scarnati III; Robert Torres; Jonathan M. Marks* (Pennsylva-
nia, 2018).

Chapter 8: Mathematicians Enlist for Duty

1. Laura Vanderkam, "Blazing a Trail for Women in Math: Moon Duchin," *Scien-
tific American*, June 23, 2008.

2. Moon Duchin, *Outlier Analysis for Pennsylvania Congressional Redistricting*,
Pennsylvania Governor's Office, February 15, 2018, https://www.governor
.pa.gov/wp-content/uploads/2018/02/md-report.pdf.

3. Jessica Jones, "Duke Mathematicians Investigate 2012 Election Results in
North Carolina," WUNC (North Carolina public radio), November 25, 2014.

4. Laura Vozzella and Ted Mellnik, "Va. Election Officials Assigned 26 Voters to
the Wrong District. It Might've Cost Democrats a Pivotal Race," *Washington
Post*, May 13, 2018.

5. Ralph Hise and David Lewis, "We Drew Congressional Maps for Partisan
Advantage. That Was the Point," *Atlantic*, March 25, 2019.

6. *Common Cause, et al. v. Robert A. Rucho* (United States District Court for the
Middle District of North Carolina, 2018).

7. *Common Cause, et al. v. Robert A. Rucho* (United States District Court for the
Middle District of North Carolina, 2018).

8. *Common Cause, et al. v. Robert A. Rucho* (United States District Court for the
Middle District of North Carolina, 2018).

9. Tribune News Service, "Herpes, Nickelback Are More Popular Than Congress, Schwarzenegger Says in Call for Redistricting Reform," *San Francisco
Examiner*, February 14, 2017.

Chapter 9: People Power

1. Patricia Sullivan, "Voter Access: 'Bringing in People Who Haven't Had a Voice,'" *Washington Post*, October 14, 2018.
2. Numbers from the Brennan Center, cited, among other places, in Patrick Marion Bradley, "The Invisibles: The Cruel Catch-22 of Being Poor with No ID," *Washington Post*, June 15, 2017.
3. Mark Niesse, "Long Lines and Equipment Problems Plague Election Day in Georgia," *Atlanta Journal-Constitution*, November 6, 2018.
4. "Broken Machines to Threats of Violence among Voting Problems," Associated Press, November 7, 2018.

Chapter 10: Punching Up Down-Ballot

1. Cameron Joseph, "NC GOP Looks to Ram Through Anti-Abortion Law," *Talking Points Memo*, May 23, 2019.

Chapter 11: Maine's Ranked Choice

1. Joe Lawlor, "Group Promotes Voting Change for Maine with Ranked-Choice Beer Tastings," *Portland Press Herald* (Maine), August 24, 2016.
2. Video available at "Gubernatorial Candidate Profile, Paul LePage, Republican," *Bangor Daily News*, by Kevin Miller, September 20, 2010.
3. WGME, "Gov. LePage's Comments about Blacks, Hispanics, Ignite New Controversy," WGME-13, August 24, 2016.
4. Camila Domonoske, "Listen: Maine's Governor Unleashes Obscenities on Lawmakers Who Criticized Him," NPR, August 26, 2016.
5. Jessie Scanlon, "Could Maine's New Ranked-Choice Voting Change American Elections?" *Boston Globe Magazine*, October 17, 2018.
6. Michael Shepherd, "How an 1880 Maine Insurrection Could Sink Ranked-Choice Voting," *Bangor Daily News*, January 21, 2016.

Chapter 12: Youth Saves the Day

1. "Expand Early Voting," Brennan Center, February 4, 2016.
2. Megan Newsome, "Give College Students Equal Access to Early Voting," *Gainesville Sun*, November 21, 2017.

3. *League of Women Voters of Florida v. Detzner*, US District Court, Northern District of Florida, order granting plaintiffs motion for preliminary injunction, July 24, 2018.

4. Hannah Beatty, "First Two Days of Early Voting at Reitz Draws in More Than 1,000 People," *Independent Florida Alligator*, October 22, 2018.

5. Julie Beck and Caroline Kitchener, "Early Signs of a Youth Wave," *Atlantic*, November 6, 2018.

6. Danny Hakim and Michael Wines, "'They Don't Really Want Us to Vote': How Republicans Made It Harder," *New York Times*, November 3, 2018.

7. *LULAC of Iowa and Blair v. Paul Pate*, Iowa District Court, complaint filed May 30, 2018 and available online at https://www.courthousenews.com/wp-content/uploads/2018/05/IowaLULAC.pdf.

8. Stephen Gruber-Miller, "Judge Tells State to Undo Some Early Voting Restrictions," *Des Moines Register*, July 25, 2018.

9. Expert report by Stanford professor Jonathan Rodden in *College Democrats of Michigan v. Ruth Johnson*, filed September 8, 2018. The report was covered impressively in Kalen Hall and RJ Wolcott, "Young People in Michigan Vote a Lot Less Than Everywhere Else. This Might Be Why," *Battle Creek Enquirer*, November 1, 2018.

10. Expert report by Stanford professor Jonathan Rodden in *College Democrats of Michigan v. Ruth Johnson*, filed September 8, 2018.

Conclusion

1. "What We Do," The Ballot Initiative Strategy Center, https://ballot.org/what-we-do.

2. Associated Press, "Florida One of Many States Where GOP Lawmakers Seek to Limit Voter Initiatives," *Tampa Bay Times*, June 22, 2019.

3. Patrik Jonsson, "Florida Voters Gave Ex-Felons Right to Vote. Then Lawmakers Stepped In," *Christian Science Monitor*, May 17, 2019.

4. Lawrence Mower, "Amendment 4 Creators Want to Help Felons Pay Off Court Fees and Fines," *Tampa Bay Times*, July 2, 2019.

5. Daniel Rivero, "Miami-Dade State Attorney Preparing Plan to Restore Voting Rights, Even If Money Is Owed," WLRN (South Florida public media), July 17, 2019.

6. Rob Griffin, Paul Gronke, Tova Wang, and Liz Kennedy, "Who Votes with Automatic Voter Registration?" Center for American Progress, June 7, 2017.

7. Liam Stack, "Texas Secretary of State Questions Citizenship of 95,000 Registered Voters," *New York Times*, January 25, 2019.

8. Niraj Chokski, "Federal Judge Halts 'Ham-Handed' Texas Voter Purge," *New York Times*, February 28, 2018.

9. The specifics of the intense Hofeller family dispute can be found in the wonderful profile by Charles Bethea, "A Father, a Daughter and an Attempt to Change the Census," *New Yorker*, July 12, 2019.

10. *North Carolina v. David Lewis*, 18 CVS 014001, Stephanie Hofeller, recorded deposition (May 17, 2019), https://www.documentcloud.org/documents/6142288-Common-Cause-v-Lewis-6-6-19-PLDG-Plaintiffs.html#document/p18/a505965.

11. "The Hofeller Files," Common Cause, June 17, 2019, https://www.common cause.org/resource/the-hofeller-files/.

INDEX